Southern Literary Studies

FRED HOBSON, EDITOR

Wild Blessings

THE POETRY OF LUCILLE CLIFTON

Hilary Holladay

 LOUISIANA STATE UNIVERSITY PRESS

BATON ROUGE

Copyright © 2004 by Louisiana State University Press
All rights reserved
Manufactured in the United States of America
FIRST PRINTING

DESIGNER: Barbara Neely Bourgoyne
TYPEFACE: Whitman
TYPESETTER: Coghill Composition Co., Inc.
PRINTER AND BINDER: Thomson-Shore, Inc.

Library of Congress Cataloging-in-Publication Data
    Holladay, Hilary.
    Wild blessings : the poetry of Lucille Clifton / Hilary Holladay.
    p.   cm.— (Southern literary studies)
    Includes bibliographical references and index.
    ISBN 0-8071-2987-9 (alk. paper)
    1. Clifton, Lucille, 1936– —Criticism and interpretation.   2. Women and
    literature—Southern States—History—20th century.   I. Title.   II. Series.

    PS3553.L45Z68   2004
    811'.54—dc22

                                                    2004005642

Portions of this work appeared previously in slightly different form in the following essays and
are reprinted here with permission of the publishers: "No Ordinary Woman: An Interview with
Lucille Clifton," *Poets & Writers Magazine* special issue, "Poetry in America" (April 1999); "'Our
Lives Are Our Line and We Go On': Concentric Circles of History in Lucille Clifton's *Generations*,"
Xavier Review 19, no. 2 (1999); "'I Am Not Grown Away from You': Lucille Clifton's Elegies for
Her Mother," *CLA Journal* 42, no. 4 (June 1999); "Song of Herself: Lucille Clifton's Poems about
Womanhood," in *The Furious Flowering of African American Poetry,* ed. Joanne V. Gabbin (Univer-
sity Press of Virginia, 1999); and "'Splendid in Your Red Dress': Menstrual Imagery in Lucille
Clifton's Poetry," *Abafazi: The Simmons College Journal of Women of African Descent* (2000).

Poems by Lucille Clifton that first appeared in *Two-Headed Woman* (University of Massachusetts
Press, 1980) and subsequently appeared in *Good Woman: Poems and a Memoir, 1969–1980* (BOA
Editions, Ltd.) © 1980, 1987 by Lucille Clifton are reprinted by permission of Curtis Brown, Ltd.
Poems that appeared in *Next* (BOA Editions, © 1987 by Lucille Clifton), *Quilting* (BOA Editions,
© 1991 by Lucille Clifton), *The Book of Light* (Copper Canyon, © 1993 by Lucille Clifton), *The
Terrible Stories* (BOA Editions, © 1996 by Lucille Clifton), and *Blessing the Boats* (BOA Editions,
© 2000 by Lucille Clifton) are reprinted by permission of the respective publishers.

The paper in this book meets the guidelines for permanence and durability of the Committee
on Production Guidelines for Book Longevity of the Council on Library Resources.⊗

For my father

GEORGE RICHMOND HOLLADAY

and in memory of my mother

CATHARINE MITCHELL HOLLADAY

Contents

Acknowledgments

MY COLLEAGUES AND STUDENTS AT the University of Massachusetts Lowell helped bring this book to life through their interest in my work; I thank them all. I would especially like to thank William H. Roberts, chair of the English Department, for his encouragement and enthusiasm for this project.

My thanks also go to the Virginia Foundation for the Humanities in Charlottesville for granting me a fellowship during the early stages of my research. Joanne V. Gabbin of James Madison University, chair of the VFH board of directors, was particularly encouraging; as editor of *The Furious Flowering of African American Poetry*, she published my first essay on Lucille Clifton.

For reading and responding to chapters in draft form, I am deeply indebted to my friends Anthony Szczesiul and Keith Clark. I am also grateful to Candis LaPrade for her insights into Lucille Clifton's poetry and Erik Shaw for his moral support and unflagging kindness throughout the writing of this book.

Finally, I thank my parents and my sisters, Julia Holladay Mann and Cary C. Holladay, for their faith in me.

Chronology

1936   On 27 June, Thelma Lucille Sayles is born in Depew, New York, to Samuel Louis Sayles Sr., a steelworker, and Thelma Moore Sayles, a laborer and homemaker.

1937   Half sister, Elaine Sayles, is born.

1938   Brother, Samuel Sayles Jr., is born.

1941   Moves with family to Buffalo.

1949   Graduates from School #17 in Buffalo.

        Becomes acquainted with Ishmael Reed, who also lives in Buffalo.

1953   Graduates from Fosdick-Masten High School in Buffalo.

1953–54   Attends Howard University on a full academic scholarship. Majors in drama.

        At Howard, meets professors Sterling Brown and Owen Dodson and fellow students Roberta Flack, LeRoi Jones (Amiri Baraka), and Toni Morrison, her future editor at Random House.

        Performs at Howard in the premiere of James Baldwin's *The Amen Corner*. Owen Dodson directs, with Baldwin's assistance.

1955   Briefly attends Fredonia State Teachers College (now the State University of New York at Fredonia) on an academic scholarship.

1958   On 10 May, marries Fred James Clifton, a Dunham, Kentucky, native and student at the University of Buffalo, whom she meets through Ishmael Reed. The couple lives in Buffalo.

1958–60   Works for New York State Division of Employment, Buffalo, as claims clerk.

1959   Clifton's mother, suffering from epilepsy, dies at age forty-four. Daughter Sidney is born.

1961   Daughter Fredrica is born.

1962   Son Channing is born.

1963   Daughter Gillian is born.

1964   Son Graham is born.

1965   Daughter Alexia is born.

1967   The Cliftons move to Baltimore, where Fred Clifton is education coordinator for Baltimore's Model Cities Program, which seeks to improve educational opportunities for minority students living in the city.

1969   Corresponds with Langston Hughes.

Robert Hayden shows Clifton's poetry to poet Carolyn Kizer. Kizer enters the poems in the YW-YMCA Poetry Center Discovery Award competition, which Clifton wins.

Good Times published (Random House).

Some of the Days of Everett Anderson (Holt), a picture book for children, published, the first of many books for children by Clifton, eight of which make up the Everett Anderson series concerning a young black boy's family life.

Good Times named one of the best books of 1969 by the *New York Times*.

Samuel Sayles Sr. dies of a heart attack at age sixty-seven.

1969–71   Works for U.S. Office of Education, Washington, D.C., as literature assistant for CAREL (Central Atlantic Regional Educational Laboratory).

1970   Clifton's poetry is included in *Poetry of the Negro, 1746–1970*, edited by Langston Hughes and Arna Bontemps (New York: Doubleday, 1970).

1972   *Good News about the Earth* published (Random House).

1974   *An Ordinary Woman* published (Random House).

1974–79   Poet in residence, Coppin State College.

1975   Experiences supernatural contact, via Ouija board and automatic writing, with her deceased mother. Later transcribes observations of "The Ones Who Talk," spirits who advise Clifton on what she identifies as "the fate and danger of the world of the Americas."

1975–85   Poet laureate of Maryland.

1976   *Generations: A Memoir* published (Random House).

Receives an Emmy award from the American Academy of Television Arts and Sciences for cowriting the screenplay for *Free to Be You and Me,* a children's program hosted by Marlo Thomas.

1980   *Two-Headed Woman* published (University of Massachusetts Press). Wins Juniper Prize sponsored by the University of Massachusetts Press. Nominated for Pulitzer Prize.

Jenny Moore Fellow, George Washington University.

1984   Fred Clifton dies of cancer at age forty-nine.

Everett Anderson's Goodbye, children's book about a little boy's five stages of grief after the death of his father, wins the American Library Association's Coretta Scott King Award.

1985–89   Teaches at University of California, Santa Cruz.

1987   *Next* and *Good Woman: Poems and a Memoir, 1969–1980* simultaneously published by BOA Editions. Finalist for Pulitzer Prize.

1988   *Ten Oxherding Pictures,* limited-edition chapbook, published (Moving Parts Press).

1989   Featured on *The Power of the Word,* PBS documentary hosted by Bill Moyers.

Named "Literary Lion" by the New York Public Library.

1989–91   Visiting Distinguished Professor of Literature, St. Mary's College of Maryland.

1991   Appointed Distinguished Professor of Humanities, St. Mary's College of Maryland.

Quilting published (BOA Editions). Nominated for Pulitzer Prize.

1992   Awarded Shelley Memorial Prize by the Poetry Society of America.

1993 *The Book of Light* published (Copper Canyon Press).

   Awarded Andrew White Medal by Loyola College of Baltimore.

   Named a Maryland Living Treasure.

1993–94 Teaches at Columbia University.

1994 Diagnosed with breast cancer; undergoes lumpectomy.

1995 Appears on *The Language of Life,* PBS documentary narrated by Bill Moyers.

1996 *The Terrible Stories* published (BOA Editions). Finalist for National Book Award, the Lenore Marshall Prize, and the Los Angeles Times Book Award.

   Receives Lifetime Achievement Award for Excellence from the Lannan Foundation.

1997 Kidney transplant from daughter Alexia.

1998 *The Terrible Stories* published in England (Slow Dancer Press).

   Receives Lila Wallace *Reader's Digest* Writers' Award.

   Inducted into Phi Beta Kappa.

1998–99 William Blackburn Distinguished Visiting Professor in creative writing at Duke University.

1999 Elected to Board of Chancellors of the Academy of American Poets.

   Named a fellow of the American Academy of Arts and Sciences.

   Appointed to Hilda C. Landers Chair in the Liberal Arts, St. Mary's College of Maryland.

2000 *Blessing the Boats: New and Selected Poems, 1988–2000* published (BOA Editions).

   Daughter Fredrica dies of a brain tumor.

   Blessing the Boats wins the 2000 National Book Award for poetry.

2001 Wins Anisfield-Wolf Lifetime Achievement Award from the Cleveland Foundation.

2004 Son Channing dies of heart failure.

Abbreviations

GW   *Good Woman: Poems and a Memoir, 1969–1980* (1987). This volume contains *Good Times; Good News about the Earth; An Ordinary Woman; Two-Headed Woman;* and *Generations: A Memoir.*

N   *Next: New Poems* (1987)

Q   *Quilting: Poems, 1987–1990* (1991)

BL   *The Book of Light* (1993)

TS   *The Terrible Stories* (1996)

BB   *Blessing the Boats: New and Selected Poems, 1988–2000* (2000)

Wild Blessings

Introduction

I FIRST HEARD LUCILLE CLIFTON read her poetry in January 1992 when I was a graduate student at the University of North Carolina at Chapel Hill. When Clifton took the stage in Greenlaw Hall, she gripped the unsteady lectern and said, "I suppose it wouldn't be the end of the world if this fell over." After a pause, she added, "And if it *was* the end of the world, nobody would know."

Everybody laughed. We were relaxed, receptive, and ready to listen to this poet, a stout African American woman wearing large glasses and smiling at us. For the next hour, she read new poems that would be published in *The Book of Light* as well as signature works such as "homage to my hips" and "wishes for sons."

For all of her good humor and smiles, however, she struck me as someone who was very careful with other people and with herself. It was obvious from her poems that she was an intensely emotional person whose wit and charm belied a meditative, serious spirit. She had evidently given a lot of thought to the fall of a lectern, the end of the world. Either event could happen; consequences had to be considered. On that January evening in Chapel Hill, there were no crashes, no cataclysmic endings. She put on a good show even as her poems made the performance a high-stakes juggling act—"my eyes bright, my mouth smiling, / my singed hands burning" (*N* 71).

Among her new poems was "dear jesse helms," aimed at North Carolina's senior senator, the self-proclaimed opponent of all things obscene. Helms had once quipped that North Carolina could establish a state zoo just by putting a fence around Chapel Hill. Clifton had correctly guessed that this liberal zoo's inhabitants would share her dislike of the military euphemisms used during the Gulf War. The poem concludes:

the smart bombs do not recognize
the babies. something

is happening obscene.

they are shrouding words so that
families cannot find them.

civilian deaths have become
collateral damage, bullets

are anti-personnel. jesse,
the fear is anti-personnel.

jesse, the hate is anti-personnel.
jesse, the war is anti-personnel,

and something awful is happening.
something obscene.

(BL 39–40)

Although I admired the poem then, I can better appreciate its symmetry and precision now that its occasion has receded. Clifton has a way of tapping into the zeitgeist and writing poems that a lot of people enjoy and intuitively understand. But the real test comes years later. Do the poems still move us? Do they still feel like they're beamed from a secret, extraperceptive corner of our own brains? For me, Clifton's poems have made a deeper, more profound sense over time. I have never tired of her work.

Six years after I first heard Clifton read, I sat in her townhouse living room in Columbia, Maryland, testing my tape recorder and inhaling the scent of burning incense. I was excited and nervous about interviewing the author of the poems I'd been poring over for the past year. It was the day before Easter—a fortuitous time to meet with a poet who drew so much inspiration from the Bible.

Seated on a sofa diagonally across from me, Clifton was smiling a little but not much. Rather than talking to me on this beautiful spring day, she could have been resting, reading the newspaper, or writing a poem. But there I was, with my new tape recorder and note pad, and she was going to let me do my job.

A lot had happened to Lucille Clifton since I had last seen her. She had endured a lumpectomy, dialysis, and a kidney transplant; her brother had died. *The Book of Light* was in print, as was *The Terrible Stories* (1996).

She had continued to write books for young children and give numerous poetry readings, and she was working on the new poems that would be in *Blessing the Boats: New and Selected Poems, 1988–2000* (2000), the volume that would earn her the National Book Award for poetry. She was holding a visiting professorship at Duke University that spring semester. When I met with her, she was home for the weekend with two of her daughters in the house that they shared.

The interview began. In keeping with my first impressions of her, she was even-tempered and playful, fun to talk to. But I noticed that she would sometimes repeat remarks that I recognized from other interviews—or she would preface a comment by saying that it was something she had recently told someone else. Whenever possible, she was going to quote herself, it seemed, rather than give me a truly spontaneous answer. There was a reticence just below the surface of her candor.

It was only when her daughter Gillian walked into the house that she truly relaxed. She suddenly seemed softer, more comfortable, safer in her own house. We had been discussing her shyness—a revelation about her personality that most people, she said, did not believe. I said I believed her, and for a moment, she seemed genuinely delighted with me. Her voice sounded downright southern when she called out to Gillian, "*She believes I'm shy!*" Gillian confirmed it: her mother was very shy, the shyest person she knew.

What the truly extroverted don't often realize is that shyness does not stand in the way of an eventful life, a career in the public eye, or even an outgoing personality. Shyness is a strange sort of protective covering that reveals the very things that it tries to hide: a fear of being hurt, a horror of messing up, an existential question mark hovering over one's own head. Shy people put a lot of effort into self-discipline and self-control. Cautious and reined-in, they often cannot resist the stage. There, in carefully measured quantities, they release some of the energy that threatens to explode into life—their own lives—all around them. These representations of exuberance are often one and the same with art.

So it is with Lucille Clifton, who has frequently described herself as a typical Cancer: maternal, sensitive, perilously vulnerable. But her fervent belief in her own message keeps her in the public arena.

The interview was winding down. After I shut off the tape recorder, she showed me books and pictures, and I took several photos of her. We began saying our good-byes. To my abundant pleasure, she asked me to call her Lucille and gave me a hug.

Then she showed me to the door. Our visit was almost over, and both of us were glad. She said cheerfully, "Well, that wasn't too painless."

All the way back home, I rewrote that line in my head. "Well, that wasn't too *painful*," I imagined her saying. Or maybe she had called out, "Well, *that* was painless!"

I kept hoping I had misheard her, but I hadn't. Her last comment— was it a Freudian slip?—had revealed an essential truth that our long, thoroughly amiable conversation had only touched on. Offstage, Lucille Clifton was shy, and she did not find it easy talking about her life. That's why she wrote the poems: to do the talking for her.

In late June 2000, I returned to Maryland to attend a reading Clifton was giving as part of the city of Columbia's annual arts festival. Waiting for another poet to finish, she looked serious and ever so slightly impatient. When it was her turn, she read with her usual vigor and aplomb. The emotional firepower of her poetry was very much in evidence. The audience gasped when she read "moonchild," a poem about being sexually abused by her father when she was a little girl, and tears were shed at the end when she revised "come celebrate with me" to make it a collective praise song honoring all the brave persons who survive daily assaults on their existence.

The resounding pain of "moonchild," one of the new poems in *Blessing the Boats,* builds on earlier poems about her mother and her husband, both of whom died young, and her poems about social injustice. Those who attend closely to her know that Clifton has suffered a great deal; even her poems of joy and triumph often have an elegiac edge to them. To celebrate survival with Clifton is to acknowledge not only the beauty of a resilient spirit but also the excruciating losses that inevitably accompany a long life.

Clifton is a strong presence in her poems, just as she is a strong presence in person. But her poems, even the ones containing intimate details of her life, make room for everyone's sorrows, every survivor's noble plight. She invites us into her art form in such a way that we quickly realize this is *our* world, these are our times, and Clifton is one of our own, no matter who *we* are.

Gillian showed up during the reading and stayed for a panel discussion in which her mother took part. Clifton told me later that her children rarely attend her readings, so it had startled her to see her daughter in the audience. She was, however, clearly delighted to have her there. The two of them walked across the auditorium with arms around each other's waists after the afternoon's final event.

Clifton had spent a long day among her hometown fans, but she gladly answered the questions that I shouted over the hubbub in the lobby. Her daughter listened attentively as Clifton reminisced about her own mother and father. The two posed for a picture before heading out the door. Glancing back just long enough to catch my eye, Clifton asked me to send her a copy of the photo.

I'm looking at it now. Lucille is at the center of the frame, her lips compressed into a smile, her hoop earrings glinting. Gillian is close by her side, her face radiant. I can feel their presence and their love for each other as I look at the photo and remember chatting with them on that warm summer afternoon.

Wild Blessings: The Poetry of Lucille Clifton is a comprehensive introduction to her full-length volumes of verse and her memoir, which I view as an extended prose poem. Although Clifton is a pleasure to read, her poetry is neither as deceptively simple nor as blithely celebratory as casual readers sometimes assume. Clifton is not trying to deceive anyone with her stylistic clarity, nor is she rallying around any group or social cause just for the sake of a rally. She is both clear and deep. The bursts of joy that we find in her polished, elegant body of work are set against a backdrop of regret and sorrow. Her elegiac poems are pleasing to the ear, but in their use of white space and enjambment, they are written for the eye. They are alternately consoling, stimulating, and wrenching to read. They do not leave us alone.

In this book, I explore the thematic concerns that unify her poetry and her memoir. To do this, I make use of the small but excellent body of criticism on Clifton and draw on other relevant secondary works as well. I rely primarily, however, on a series of my own close readings while remaining aware of her multiple contexts—personal, political, and poetic. The first two chapters provide a survey of her full-length volumes of verse published between 1969 and 2000. The next six chapters consist of thematic discussions, alternating between overviews and analyses of specific works. The third chapter deals with her poems about womanhood, a central concern in her poetry; this provides the context for Chapter 4's comparison of her fertility poems with Sylvia Plath's. Chapter 5's survey of her biblical poems leads into the following chapter's close reading of "brothers," her 1993 sequence about Lucifer. Chapter 7 addresses her use of the elegy, primarily in poems about her mother. Chapter 8 analyzes her elegiac family memoir, *Generations*. The final chapter is my 1998 interview with Clifton.

In "wild blessings," Clifton wryly admits that of the many blessings in her life, she is not necessarily grateful for "the gift of understanding, / the wild one" that has exposed her to so much human suffering (Q 47). Yet one senses from her poems that she would not have it any other way. With this book, I hope to enhance the critical understanding of a poet whose contributions to American literature are just beginning to be recognized.

CHAPTER 1

Light Years

LUCILLE CLIFTON IS AMONG THOSE time-traveling souls who Walt Whitman believed would "look back on me because I look'd forward to them."[1] In her sweeping, elegiac vision of the world, she is the Good Gray Poet's descendant, his sister, his dark reflection in the waves. Her earnest voice bears witness to what she calls "the bond of live things everywhere" (*GW* 149). Combining Christian tenets with pantheistic African lore, the philosophy evident in her poetry holds that all life is sacred and all lives are interdependent. But because she was born "both nonwhite and woman" (*BL* 25), some fifty years after the elder poet's death, her world is quite different from Whitman's. As an African American woman, whose great-great-grandmother was captured as a young child in Dahomey, Africa, and brought to the United States as a slave, Clifton is especially sensitive to the injustices that blacks, women, and poor people have suffered in the United States. Her poetry is in large part a response and antidote to these injustices as well as a tribute to the human spirit's will to endure, and even soar, in the face of pain and loss.

Although she is not a strictly autobiographical poet, her identity is integral to everything she writes: "A person can, I hope, enjoy the poetry without knowing that I am black or female. But it adds to their understanding if they do know it—that is, that I am black and female. To me, that I am what I am is *all* of it; all of what I am is relevant."[2] Upon reading Clifton, one finds that her poems often manage to be deeply personal while also speaking directly to universal emotions as well as social and political realities.

The poem "1994," for instance, was inspired by the poet's breast cancer diagnosis: "i was leaving my fifty-eighth year / when a thumb of ice / stamped itself hard near my heart" (*TS* 24). In addition to recounting a

---

1. Walt Whitman, "Crossing Brooklyn Ferry," in *Leaves of Grass*, ed. Sculley Bradley and Harold W. Blodgett (New York: Norton, 1973), 162.

2. Charles H. Rowell, "An Interview with Lucille Clifton," *Callaloo* 22, no. 1 (1999): 58.

personal ordeal, the poem acknowledges the looming threat of breast cancer to women as well as the risks that women and blacks assume every day: "you know how dangerous it is / to be born with breasts / you know how dangerous it is / to wear dark skin." History is, in large part, the story of a continuous assault on vulnerable groups, and Clifton assumes that her readers know that story, regardless of their role in it. The poem's sorrowful reproach—"have we not been good children / did we not inherit the earth"—suddenly gives way to an unnervingly direct appeal: "but you must know all about this / from your own shivering life." One would be hard pressed to read this poem without experiencing a spine-tingling shock of recognition. Such is often the case in Clifton's poems, which time and again illuminate the universal within the individual, the black, and the female.

Born with twelve fingers, like her mother and her firstborn daughter, Clifton often uses her hands to symbolize a spiritual connection with others, a deep and abiding empathy flowing involuntarily from her body and soul. Her extra digits were removed when she was an infant, but their seeming magic (growing out of the old superstition that witches had twelve fingers) is still with her: "I've always had a kind [of] sixth sense— especially when somebody talks about hands. Yes, a sixth sense—if you want to call it that—that deals with spirituality and the sacred."[3] In the mid-1970s, Clifton was in contact, through a Ouija board and automatic writing, with her deceased mother, Thelma Sayles; poems in *An Ordinary Woman* and *Two-Headed Woman* draw on that moving but profoundly unsettling experience. Around the same time, she also wrote a series of poems based on the words of "The Ones Who Talk," disembodied spirits commenting on "the fate and danger of the world of the Americas."[4] In a variation on the traditional reading of palms, she said that she could sometimes sense important things about people just by touching their hands.[5] This phenomenon is the subject of "wild blessings" (Q 47). The poem begins with the fragmented revelation "licked in the palm of my hand / by

3. Rowell, 68.

4. Clifton quoted in Akasha (Gloria) Hull, *Soul Talk: The New Spirituality of African American Women* (Rochester, Vt.: Inner Traditions, 2001), 244. *Soul Talk* includes brief excerpts from Clifton's unpublished sequence based on "The Ones Who Talk."

5. See Chapter 9 of the present volume, 198.

an uninvited woman," which is possibly a reference to Thelma Sayles's posthumous visitations. The poem goes on to list some of the hands Clifton has held, including "the hand / of a girl who threw herself / from a tenement window, the trembling / junkie hand of a priest." Given this history, the distraught poet declares:

> do not ask me to thank the tongue
> that circled my fingers
> or pride myself on the attentions
> of the holy lost.
> i am grateful for many blessings
> but the gift of understanding,
> the wild one, maybe not.
>
> (Q 47)

No matter its attendant difficulties, the gift of understanding has served Clifton and her readers exceptionally well. Reading her elegantly arranged volumes, in which hope just barely outweighs despair, we begin to see the mythic sweep of our own lives, the connections across generations and cultures, and we begin to feel that Clifton, in speaking for herself, is inviting us to listen, very carefully, to ourselves.

Like many of her poems, the story of Clifton's youth is more complex than it initially seems. Born in 1936 to a steel worker and a homemaker in Depew, New York, she grew up in Depew and later in Buffalo, a child of the Great Migration of southern blacks to the industrial North:

> Depew is where I was born. Depew New York, in 1936. Roosevelt time. It was a small town, mostly Polish, all its life turned like a machine around the steel mill. We lived in a house on Muskingum Street, and my Mama's family lived on Laverack. My grandparents lived in this big frame house on Laverack Street with one toilet. And in that house were my Mama's family, the Moores, and a lot of other people, lines of people, old and young. (GW 265)

Though her southern-born African American parents had very little formal education, they both loved to read books and newspapers and tell family stories. Their daughter looked on with interest as Thelma Moore Sayles wrote poetry in iambic pentameter and Samuel Sayles read the

Bible—the text that would become central to so many of Clifton's later poems.

The Sayles family appeared happy on the outside, but Clifton has exposed the painful troubles beneath the placid surface. Her father had two daughters in addition to Lucille: one by his first wife, who predeceased him, and another by a neighbor woman, around the same time that Lucille was born. Samuel Sayles Sr. stopped sharing a bed with Thelma Sayles after the birth of their son, Lucille's younger brother. These circumstances would have been difficult in themselves, but the trouble was greatly compounded by Samuel Sayles's abuse of Lucille, who has written about the molestation in several of her poems and spoken of it in interviews. Clifton insists that this was not the whole story of her relationship with her father. In *Generations*, she writes forgivingly that "He hurt us all a lot and we hurt him a lot, the way people who love each other do" (*GW* 273). But the abuse was clearly a defining component of her youth and has been a continuing source of melancholy.

Despite her early private suffering, Lucille Sayles's intelligence and academic achievement boded well for her future. She was not only the first in her family to graduate from high school but also the first to attend college, thanks to an academic scholarship, one of a small number that Howard University awarded to incoming students in 1953. A drama major with a keen interest in literature and writing, she met professors (and distinguished poets) Sterling Brown and Owen Dodson as well as fellow students Toni Morrison and LeRoi Jones (Amiri Baraka). The example of her professors and her gifted peers was an inspiration to the young poet from Buffalo.

That inspiration did not extend to studying, however, and Clifton's low grades cost her the coveted scholarship. She returned to Buffalo, deeply embarrassed, and enrolled in Fredonia State Teachers College. That experience lasted only a couple of months, however. Although she would eventually become a professor of creative writing, Clifton herself was not cut out for college life. She preferred, instead, to fashion her own approach to education, an approach that stood her in good stead as a poet and role model for her students. Noting that "there's a way of being that tends to be necessary for poets," she explained that, for her, that meant an active pursuit of knowledge and understanding: "You know, a way of not just accepting the taught, passed-on information, but trying to get more than that. That comes from being a little black girl in Buffalo, New York, and understanding that what people were going to teach me might not be all that I needed to know, and so choosing at some point to learn, not just be taught."[6]

In 1958 she married Fred Clifton, who was completing his senior year at the University of Buffalo. She had met her future husband through Ishmael Reed, an up-and-coming black writer who was part of her circle of friends in Buffalo. The newly married couple lived in Buffalo for about a decade while Fred, a yogi with wide-ranging philosophical interests, pursued a Ph.D. in philosophy at the University of Buffalo. Lucille, who worked for the first several years of her marriage as a claims clerk for the New York state employment office, had six children between 1961 and 1967. All the while, she was writing poems.

During those busy years, the subject of race relations often dominated the national news. While Clifton was at Howard, the Supreme Court had ruled in *Brown v. Board of Education* that segregated schools were unconstitutional, and the following year Rosa Parks refused to give up her front seat on a bus in Montgomery, Alabama. After the Cliftons had married, the upheaval continued. The assassinations of President Kennedy, Malcolm X, and Martin Luther King Jr. shocked the country. Race riots and campus turmoil added to the trauma. Still, there was the pervasive sense that black people were finally beginning to come into their own politically and artistically in the United States. The Black Arts Movement was proof of this phenomenon. Gwendolyn Brooks, the movement's elder stateswoman, issued a passionate call for nationalism among black authors: "The prevailing understanding: black literature is literature BY blacks, ABOUT blacks, directed TO blacks. ESSENTIAL black literature is the distillation of black life. Black life is different from white life. Different in nuance, different in 'nitty gritty.' Different from birth. Different at death."[7]

Little did Clifton know that her own life was about to become quite different from what it had been, thanks to the (black) poet Robert Hayden and the (white) poet Carolyn Kizer. After Clifton had read about Hayden in the magazine *Negro Digest* and written to him in hopes that he would

---

6. Rowell, 64.

7. Gwendolyn Brooks, *A Capsule Course in Black Poetry Writing* (Detroit: Broadside, 1975), 3.

help her publish her work, Hayden showed a selection of her poems to Kizer, who in turn entered the poems in the YW-YMCA Poetry Center Discovery Award competition. By this time Fred and Lucille Clifton were living in Baltimore, where Fred was educational coordinator for the Model Cities Program and Lucille worked for the U.S. Office of Education. Clifton did not know that Kizer had entered her poems in the contest, so her selection as the winner came as a happy surprise. The Discovery Award drew the attention of Random House, where her first three books of poetry and her memoir would be published, with Toni Morrison as her editor.

Given all of the political and social tumult that accompanied her youth, it seems fitting that Clifton published the provocatively titled *Good Times* in 1969—a decidedly dramatic, news-filled year. Amid the nation's impassioned debates about war, black power, and women's rights, Clifton learned that the *New York Times* had named her debut volume one of ten notable books of the year: now she had a nascent national reputation. Her career as an author of children's picture books was taking off at the same time, with the publication of *Some of the Days of Everett Anderson* also occurring in 1969. It was a bittersweet time for her, however, since 1969 was also the year that her father died. Still, she was a black woman succeeding as a writer—a living paradox—and thus fulfilling her father's abundant hopes for her. In 1972, she followed up her debut success with *Good News about the Earth*, a book that is more explicitly political than her first.

As the women's movement gathered momentum in the 1970s, an increasingly self-confident and self-aware female persona began to appear in Clifton's poems and in her memoir, *Generations* (1976). In *An Ordinary Woman* (1974) and *Two-Headed Woman* (1980) we see a feminist spirituality infusing her poems. Her private spiritual experiences—notably her supernatural communications with her deceased mother—became central to her vision of the world. After the publication of *Two-Headed Woman*, however, Clifton did not publish another poetry book until *Good Woman: Poems and a Memoir, 1969–1980* (1987), the retrospective of her first decade as a published writer, and *Next* (1987). Important changes in her life—the death of her husband at age forty-nine in 1984 and her new teaching position at the University of California, Santa Cruz—were no doubt partly responsible for this relatively quiet period in her writing career.[8] Her subsequent books reveal that her spirituality and mortality had become the definitive core around which her poetry revolved. Between 1991 and 2000, despite bouts with breast cancer and kidney failure, she published four volumes of poetry: *Quilting* (1991), *The Book of Light* (1993), *The Terrible Stories* (1996), and *Blessing the Boats: New and Selected Poems, 1988–2000* (2000). Social justice, African American history, and the innate strength of womanhood remain important themes, but her own life cycle and her quest for self-understanding give her later poetry its primary force and direction. This development confirms her candid admission that "I don't write because I have a mission to heal the world. My mission is to heal Lucille if I can, as much as I can."[9]

Though her books earned her a steady stream of national honors, including her 1999 appointment to the previously all-white Board of Chancellors of the Academy of American Poets, and her university teaching positions also bespeak mainstream status, Clifton is a voice speaking from, and for, the racial and social margins of American society. Her writing reveals her strong social conscience and broad awareness of human suffering. The concept of a "double consciousness"—W. E. B. Du Bois' term for the pained recognition and tacit acceptance of a mainstream white vision at odds with blacks' own perceptions—takes on new meaning in Clifton's poetry, which simultaneously asserts a minority world view and a universal one. Blackness and femaleness are at one with her art's humanity. Clifton asks us to see individual experience, race, and gender not as qualifiers limiting one's ability to relate to others but as revelations of selfhood that open up new possibilities of communication, communion, and collective action.

Clifton's concerted exploration of the self and American society gives her volumes a distinct feeling of wholeness. Each book seems to grow naturally out of its predecessor. As Jean Anaporte-Easton has written of Clifton's 1987 compilation, *Good Woman: Poems and a Memoir, 1969–1980*,

---

8. During this decade, Clifton also published a limited-edition chapbook, *Ten Oxherding Pictures* (Santa Monica, Calif.: Moving Parts, 1988). The sequence, based on a twelfth-century Buddhist meditation aid, is reprinted in *Callaloo* 22, no. 1 (1999): 47–50.

9. Michael S. Glaser, "'I'd Like Not to Be a Stranger in the World': A Conversation/Interview with Lucille Clifton," *Antioch Review* 58, no. 3 (Summer 2000): 312.

"Like layers of transparencies, each contributing another detail or strengthening a line, her poems and the vignettes of *Generations* offer nuance by nuance and detail by detail a whole more complex than its parts."[10] The same is true of Clifton's entire oeuvre. As the first two chapters of this study will demonstrate, a consecutive reading of her books reveals Clifton's increasing confidence in her ability to articulate the fears and self-doubts that plague us all. The resulting tension between her questionings and the certainty of her expression is a hallmark of her mature work.

Clifton's first volume of verse, *Good Times,* responds to the Civil Rights movement and the black-centered poetics of the Black Arts Movement, which saw Gwendolyn Brooks, Haki R. Madhubuti (Don L. Lee), Larry Neal, and Amiri Baraka, among others, arguing for a newly politicized form of black literature. In 1968, Larry Neal declared, "The Black Arts Movement is radically opposed to any concept of the artist that alienates him from his community. Black Art is the aesthetic and spiritual sister of the Black Power concept. As such, it envisions an art that speaks directly to the needs and aspirations of Black America."[11] *Good Times* fulfills these criteria but resists pigeonholing as a polemical text. Though only a foretaste of her poetic range and vision, the volume introduces much of the subject matter found in her subsequent volumes of poetry. Oscillating between family and neighborhood portraits, the book occasionally ventures into more abstract considerations of race, humanity, and spirituality. Its organization implies that the local and familial flow naturally into and out of the larger currents of society and history. *Good Times* sets the course for a thematically unified body of work in which such patterns can be explored from many different vantage points.

This volume also illustrates Clifton's unique ability to assert a truth and an irony simultaneously. In these poems the most innocent-sounding phrase can take on a complex meaning. The volume's title poem, "good times," is a case in point. This poem is about a household's struggle to pay

10. Jean Anaporte-Easton, "'She Has Made Herself Again': The Maternal Impulse as Poetry," *13th Moon* 9, nos. 1–2 (1991): 124.

11. Larry Neal, "The Black Arts Movement," in *The Norton Anthology of African American Literature,* ed. Henry Louis Gates Jr. and Nellie Y. McKay (New York: Norton, 1996), 1960.

the bills and play by mainstream rules, but it is also about family unity and spontaneous joy. The insistent repetition of "good times" begins as an incantation staving off financial hardship and ends as an echoing sigh entreating young people to savor the pleasure in their lives:

my daddy has paid the rent
and the insurance man is gone
and the lights is back on
and my uncle brud has hit
for one dollar straight
and they is good times
good times
good times

my mama has made bread
and grampaw has come
and everybody is drunk
and dancing in the kitchen
and singing in the kitchen
oh these is good times
good times
good times

oh children think about the
good times

(GW 24)

The kitchen setting puts the members of this extended family in close quarters, and they are obviously happy with one another. They have reason to be happy, as Joyce Johnson explains in her gloss of Uncle Brud's gambling success: "Hitting the numbers is the dream many in the [black] community hold, for it spells the end of struggle, the answer to prayers, the beginning of a new life, or so they think. . . . Uncle Brud's one dollar hit assured a $500–600 return, and calls for a party."[12] Having made it through tough times, the members of this family will celebrate the windfall un-self-consciously and unrestrainedly. Their communal life has its

12. Joyce Johnson, "The Theme of Celebration in Lucille Clifton's Poetry," *Pacific Coast Philology* 18, nos. 1–2 (November 1983): 72.

own internal order and logic; the poem does not concern itself with mainstream expectations of what a black family should do or feel.

Similarly, "in the inner city" undercuts stereotypical notions of the black neighborhood as a dreary, dangerous place:

> in the inner city
> or
> like we call it
> home
> we think a lot about uptown
> and the silent nights
> and the houses straight as
> dead men
> and the pastel lights
> and we hang on to our no place
> happy to be alive
> and in the inner city
> or
> like we call it
> home.
>
> (GW 15)

Here, the generalized, subtly demonized "inner city" gives way to the warmth of "home." The latter word functions as a mascon—to borrow Stephen Henderson's term for "a massive concentration of Black experiential energy"[13]—connoting safety, warmth, and a refuge from social ills. The white neighborhoods, rather than the black ones, appear desolate and forbidding—a view that might surprise many white suburbanites determined to avoid the "inner city" at all costs. For them, the "inner city" functions as a corrupted mascon telegraphing poverty, danger, and despair to outsiders who avoid the all-too-energetic epicenter of black life. Black residents, though they may not like everything about their urban neighborhoods, would nevertheless recognize the imposed label of "inner city" as a distancing device that has little to do with their own identity and a great deal to do with segregation.

13. Stephen Henderson, *Understanding the New Black Poetry: Black Speech and Black Music as Poetic References* (New York: Morrow, 1973), 44.

As the first poem in her first book, "in the inner city" makes an important point that Clifton will make many times, in many different ways, throughout all of her volumes of poetry: language itself often holds the key to the way we perceive people and their circumstances. Clifton herself immediately realized that "in the inner city" was an important breakthrough that would provide a model for her future work. The diction she used was *her* diction; the subject matter and viewpoint were hers as well. She recalls thinking, "'Now that's what I want to say in the way I would say it. That's what I'm going to do. I don't know if it's going to be a poem or not. I don't know if others will call it that. But I know that's what I'm supposed to do.'"[14] Understated yet precise, the poem subtly supports Maulana Karenga's bold proclamation: "Black art must expose the enemy, praise the people and support the revolution."[15] For Clifton, that revolution began in working-class black people's own homes and neighborhoods, the so-called "inner city" decried by those who knew little of it beyond what they glimpsed through car windows or on TV.

There is a depth, a seriousness of purpose, evident in *Good Times* that belies its seemingly modest exterior. Clifton's early poems are filled with multiple meanings and the unsettling emotions that accompany ambiguity. But the book never loses sight of the comfort found in family solidarity (implicitly a model for black solidarity) or the power that blacks can access once they speak up and describe the world as they see it. *Good Times* contains poems about the aftermath of Martin Luther King's assassination ("after the savior gone"), disaffected black youths playing at the battles adults fight in earnest (the "buffalo war" series), and the threat of apocalypse ("if something should happen"). But it is ultimately a hopeful book. We see this in "admonitions," the concluding poem. Addressing the poet's children, "admonitions" is a poem about a black family's closing of the ranks in the face of racial and sexual oppression:

> girls
> first time a white man
> opens his fly

14. Rowell, 70.

15. Maulana Karenga, "Black Art: Mute Matter Given Force and Function," in Gates and McKay, *Norton Anthology of African American Literature*, 1974.

like a good thing
we'll just laugh
laugh real loud my
black women
                    (*GW* 51)

One can imagine the black women's derisive laughter easily vanquishing the great white phallus. In the poem's closing lines, Clifton affirms herself as a poet while acknowledging the eccentricity often associated with that role. Regardless of what other people may think, the poem implies, you can take charge of your own identity:

children
when they ask you
why is your mama so funny
say
she is a poet
she don't have no sense
                    (*GW* 51)

Unlike Countee Cullen—whose 1925 sonnet laments, "Yet do I marvel at this curious thing: / To make a poet black, and bid him sing!"[16]—Clifton is much more at ease with her potentially problematic artistic identity. On this topic, Clifton comments in a 1995 interview: "[I]n this culture females have not even had permission to be poets until fairly recently. As an African American person I'm fortunate in being outside those boundaries of definition, so I could be whatever. I mean, no one thought I was going to be a poet anyway. As a rule in this culture those boundaries about what one is supposed to be as a visible human being didn't include people of African descent, so I ignored them."[17] As "admonitions" makes perfectly clear, Clifton will not deny who she is, nor will she try to control what other people think of her. The double negative in the last line of "admonitions" captures black vernacular speech but also asserts that the

16. Countee Cullen, "Yet Do I Marvel," in Gates and McKay, *Norton Anthology of African American Literature*, 1305.

17. Bill Moyers, "Lucille Clifton," interview in *Language of Life: A Festival of Poets* (New York: Doubleday, 1995), 84.

speaker does in fact have "sense"—the intuitive sense of a poet who knows how to use language to suit her own ends.

She was a step ahead of the reviewer of *Good Times* who praised Clifton's "sense of humanity, an instinct for consolation that overrides a cynicism," but advised that the newly published poet "needs now only to grasp other forms and subjects that do not smack of self-consciousness."[18] It is hard to imagine a white poet, especially a white male poet, receiving the same criticism. Clifton's unapologetic preoccupation in *Good Times* with her life as an African American woman is what makes her poetry new and newsworthy.

Clifton stayed true to her natural subject matter and her sparsely punctuated free-verse style in which few words merit capitalization. Hers was a carefully distilled version of a style that many black poets of the era were using, a style that R. Roderick Palmer argues is intrinsically political: "The use of the four-letter word and other obscenities, the abbreviated word, the slashed word, the fused word, the small letter 'i,' and the omission of capital letters and certain punctuation marks are—in themselves— experimentally revolutionary, and befit the poetic utterances of revolutionary writers."[19] Like the Beat poets, black activist poets were reacting against the political and literary establishment, and one way to do that was to reject the conventions of standard English. E. e. cummings provided an important model for that rejection. With varying degrees of success, many poets coming after him, including Clifton, have emulated his use of lowercase where capital letters would normally appear.

But it is the rare poet who can use unconventional punctuation in such a way that it appears revolutionary rather than merely reactionary. The contemporary section of Stephen Henderson's landmark anthology, *Understanding the New Black Poetry* (1973), contains a number of poems with the characteristics that Palmer describes. Baraka, Sonia Sanchez, Bob Kaufman, Nikki Giovanni, Ted Joans, Mari Evans, Don L. Lee, and

18. Ramona Weeks, "A Gathering of Poets," *Western Humanities Review* 24, no. 3 (1970): 295.

19. R. Roderick Palmer, "The Poetry of Three Revolutionists: Don L. Lee, Sonia Sanchez, and Nikki Giovanni," in *Modern Black Poets: A Collection of Critical Essays,* ed. Donald B. Gibson (Englewood Cliffs, N.J.: Prentice-Hall, 1973), 146.

Carolyn Rodgers are among the poets experimenting with punctuation and typography. Their work is passionate, inventive, rebellious. One imagines that much of it was written to be performed. Like Beat poetry and the spoken-word poetry of today, it has the feverish quality of verse that needs to be shouted from a stage. If not truly revolutionary, it is still stirring to read.

As "good times" and "in the inner city" reveal, Clifton's early poetry does use some of the stylistic elements associated with the Black Arts Movement. Throughout her body of work, in fact, we see the first-person singular pronoun deprived of its standard capitalization (and implicit entitlement), the strategic omission of other capital letters and punctuation, and the occasional cleaving of compound words into their original components. Though rare in her verse, profanity does make a few memorable appearances—in, for instance, "pork chops" (*GW* 48), "leda 1" (*BL* 559), and "leaving fox" (*TS* 16). But what distinguishes her poems from much of the work of her contemporaries in *Understanding the New Black Poetry* (which, surprisingly, does not include Clifton) is the seamless unity of style and subject matter. Her stylistic variations are not done randomly or just for the sake of being different, and the brevity of her lyrics forestalls the tedium that hampers long works using unconventional punctuation. Clifton's own comments on her creative process reveal the amount of forethought going into her poems:

> I'm really trying to listen to the poem, hear it, try[ing] to help the poem become what it wants to be, not what I want it to be. . . . [B]y the time I get to where I'm sitting down to print out on a word processor, I've edited in my head. I work in my head a lot. I can't work with a pen and paper either. I need to see the look of the thing as close to print as I can. I learned to work in my head a lot because of the kids. . . . A poem is the sum of everything we are. It's a balance between intellect and intuition, between sound and sight. You should be able to physically feel a poem.[20]

Although Clifton's political concerns during the 1960s and 1970s were much the same as those of other young black women poets of her era, she was not an activist in the same sense that Sonia Sanchez, Nikki Giovanni,

---

20. Susan B. A. Somers-Willet, "'A Music in Language': A Conversation with Lucille Clifton," *American Voice* 49 (Summer 1999): 81.

and Audre Lorde were. As Clifton says, "Well, during the 1960s, I was pretty much pregnant."[21] Even if she hadn't had six children, Clifton would probably still have chosen the poem over the manifesto, the poetry reading over the march on Washington. Mild mannered and pragmatic, she was not predisposed to write a violent prose poem like Giovanni's thunderous "Reflections on April 4, 1968": "What can I, a poor Black woman, do to destroy america? This is a question, with appropriate variations, being asked in every Black heart. There is one answer—I can kill. There is one compromise—I can protect those who kill. There is one cop-out—I can encourage others to kill. There are no other ways."[22] Clifton knew that there were other ways. In her own poem about King's assassination, she writes, "what we decided is / you save your own self. / everybody so quiet. / not so much sorry as / resigned" ("the meeting after the savior gone," GW 31).

Clifton, furthermore, was not going to engage in the intraracial verbal combat that would characterize Sanchez's criticism of black men, as seen in Sanchez's play Uh Huh: But How Do It Free Us? (1975). Clifton was devoted to black subject matter and passionate about civil rights, but, in contrast to outspoken men like Baraka and Neal and equally outspoken women like Sanchez, Giovanni, and Lorde—who was to become an important voice for feminists, both black and white, gay and straight—she was not a self-styled revolutionary. Unlike her peers, she did not publish essays outlining her beliefs. If people wanted to know what her politics were, they could read her poems.

Asked to comment on the Black Arts Movement thirty years after its inception, Clifton voiced ambivalence. She allowed that "it brought to American literature a long missing part of itself. I think it made a gateway for younger non-white people to come into American poetry, into American literature."[23] But, in her view, much of the race-related rhetoric of the 1960s was an elitist construction that ignored history at its own peril. Clifton recoiled from the idea of a protest that seemed oblivious to past struggles and gains. Her own family had suffered too many hardships for her to feel that her generation had sole proprietorship of moral outrage. One

21. Rowell, 66.
22. Nikki Giovanni, "Reflections on April 4, 1968," in Henderson, 279.
23. Rowell, 67.

can imagine her shaking her head in bemusement at Stephen Henderson's rallying cry in *Understanding the New Black Poetry*. While allowing that "a Black Aesthetic, a Black value system, [and] a Black Nation" were not exactly new, he declared: "What is new, however, is the widespread sophistication regarding means as well as ends. What is new is the large numbers of people who have become aware of the international dimensions of the Black Struggle."[24]

Henderson had a better ally in Sonia Sanchez, who enthusiastically embraced the concept of activist art. Her stance is clear in her description of her first public poetry reading, which took place at a Harlem bar. Along with Amiri Baraka, Askia Muhammad Touré, "and a bunch of other poets from the Black Arts Movement,"[25] Sanchez convinced the skeptical owner that a poetry reading would not interfere with his business:

> It was a neighborhood bar, nothing fancy, with people drinking at the bar on stools and at little tables. And so we came back that night to read. Someone—I don't know who—pulled the plug on the jukebox, and that got everybody's attention. We said, "We want to read some poems," and before the people in the bar could moan because the music's gone, we started to go "pshm t-t-t-t," staccato-style, "d-d-d-d"—you know, like machine guns. And of course we used a couple of curse words because we knew that would gather them. People stopped when they heard the curse words. After we got them, we didn't use any more curse words, but they were listening now. It must have taken all of 15 minutes, and when we finished, they clapped and said, "Good, good, good." But we weren't going to overstay our time.
>
> I remember walking down Lenox a couple days later, and some guy across the street says, "Hey, ain't you the lady that came into—" And I said, "Uh-huh." He said, "That was good! I went home and told my lady. And she cursed me out because I didn't have her there. You gonna come back?" And I said, "Yep, we gonna come back."
>
> We didn't go back to that particular bar that I remember, but afterwards a lot of us went out to San Francisco and Oakland, where on Sun-

24. Henderson, 183.

25. David Reich, "'As Poets, As Activists': An Interview with Sonia Sanchez," *World: The Magazine of the Unitarian Universalist Association* (May/June 1999), http://www.uua.org/world/0599feat1.html (accessed 16 July 2002).

day mornings we'd go out with musicians and dancers and gather the people into the square to listen to poetry.[26]

Sanchez's recollection illuminates the Black Arts Movement's motives and methods. What might seem to some (perhaps including Clifton) like guerrilla tactics were, for Sanchez and her fellow activist-poets, the best way to get people's attention at that time.

Though reluctant to identify herself with the Black Arts Movement's politics, to which Sanchez, Giovanni, and Brooks so fervently subscribed, Clifton nevertheless epitomizes several of the ideals that the movement symbolized. For Clifton, as for her activist peers, race is a given that cannot be extricated from one's identity, one's experiences in the world, or one's self-expression. Her writing never tries *not* to be black. Although it is not an overt concern in each poem—and, as later chapters in this study will illustrate, need not be the sole lens through which we view her poetry—her race is always part of the larger context, and her experience as a black woman knowledgeable about black history is an enormously important influence on her writing. Furthermore, the poems in which her race plays a part often concern social justice, a focus of the Black Arts Movement. And finally, like much of the poetry performed and published during the Black Arts Movement, her work is accessible and often contains a topical element. The clarity of her vocabulary, symbolism, and themes appeals to audiences of widely divergent ages and backgrounds, but those same elements of her writing can accommodate multiple readings and careful analysis.

Her second book, *Good News about the Earth,* illustrates her affinity with the Black Arts Movement while showcasing her unique strengths. The volume's first two sections, "about the earth" and "heroes," contain race-centered poems, whereas the last part, "some jesus," is a series of biblical portraits. This progression places topical poems such as "after kent state," "malcolm," and "apology (to the panthers)" in a continuum with "adam and eve," "the calling of the disciples," and "good friday." The juxtaposition enables Clifton to create her own typology, in which contemporary matters and biblical stories inform and illuminate one another. In doing so, she states in poetic form Larry Neal's belief that "In a context

---

26. Ibid.

of world upheaval, ethics and aesthetics must interact positively and be consistent with the demands for a more spiritual world."[27]

The poems in *Good News* remain understated in their brevity and scant punctuation, but they are nevertheless sharp indictments of atrocities Clifton associates with white men. Here is "after kent state," the volume's opening poem:

only to keep
his little fear
he kills his cities
and his trees
even his children   oh
people
white ways are
the way of death
come into the
black
and live

(*GW* 57)

In a few short lines, the poem captures three pressing concerns of the 1970s: the deterioration of America's major cities, the debilitating effects of development and pollution on the environment, and the death toll of the Vietnam War. The withering allusion to the white man's "little fear" immediately conjures up cowardice and willful ignorance, a self-destructive combination. After the fourth line's visual pause, the "oh" functions as an ironically uninflected expression of surprise as well as an invocation to readers, whose race is left undetermined. The poem entreats the reader to reject the white patriarchy's oppressive influences and embrace the affirming dimensions of black culture. The poem blames the white patriarchy—the American government, the leaders of industry—for the horror of the Kent State shootings and indeed all of the country's social ills. For Clifton, coming "into the black" way of life meant embracing a socially marginalized but nevertheless self-affirming—and life-affirming— identity. It did not mean killing white people, in the name of justice or equality or anything else.

27. Neal, 1962.

As an admirer of Langston Hughes's poetry who corresponded with him late in his life, Clifton was familiar with his important essay "The Negro Artist and the Racial Mountain" (1926), in which Hughes decries "this urge within the race toward whiteness, the desire to pour racial individuality into the mold of American standardization, and to be as little Negro and as much American as possible."[28] To many of the black writers coming of age in the 1960s, Hughes was headed in the right direction but not going far enough. They opted for an angrier, more strident form of self-expression and disavowed any latent urge "toward whiteness." But in "apology (to the panthers)," Clifton admits that she, too, had stood in the shadow of the oppressive racial mountain that Hughes described. The poem recalls her "obedient" girlhood "among the ones who wore / bleaching cream to bed" (GW 62). It is only now, in "these mannish days," that she remembers "the wise one / old and telling of suicides / refusing to be slaves." The poem ends on a note of gratitude:

> i had forgotten and
> brothers i thank you
> i praise you
> i grieve my whiteful ways
> (GW 62)

"Whiteful" contains a hint of "awful," and even "white fool." The expression "whiteful ways," furthermore, contrasts with the "mannish days" at the end of the second stanza. The narrator passed through a phase of embracing prejudiced white values, but now, under the influence of radical black male activists—the Black Panthers—she embraces her racial identity and recalls, belatedly, her early lessons in African American history. She does not condone antiwhite political tactics (doing so would have allied her more closely with Giovanni and Sanchez), but she does openly admire the Panthers' bold, black-centered self-image. In a poem such as this, we see Clifton bridging the gap between past and present generations. She tacitly admits to having had an urge "toward whiteness" that

28. Langston Hughes, "The Negro Artist and the Racial Mountain," in Gates and McKay, *Norton Anthology of African American Literature*, 1267.

has now been reversed. Her newfound racial pride results not just from the Panthers' example but also from her recollection of the wise elder's tales. Though the poem honors and thanks the Black Panthers for their public stance, it also serves as a reminder to them that they are not the first generation of activists.

Clifton's lyric meditations on identity, regardless of what they say about her life, typically enable her to contemplate humanity at large. Even in works that are not obviously autobiographical, she is staking out metaphorical terrain crucial to her understanding of herself and her world. We see this in the poems employing biblical personas in the "some jesus" section. A little like jazz improvisations, these poems bring an African American perspective to familiar biblical stories and characters. Consider "moses":

> i walk on bones
> snakes twisting
> in my hand
> locusts breaking my mouth
> an old man
> leaving slavery
> home is burning in me
> like a bush
> God got his eye on
>
> (GW 93)

The poem takes Old Testament travails—Moses's encounter with a snake miraculously turned to a rod, the threat of pestilence always hanging over God's chosen people, the famously burning bush—and makes them part of Moses's physical experience. In keeping with the nationalist emphasis elsewhere in *Good News*, Clifton's Moses clearly provides a model for twentieth-century black leaders. He is at one with his people's history, and he carries that history with him everywhere. Like Moses and the nineteenth-century slaves who found inspiration in him, modern-day black leaders have faced significant obstacles in their pursuit of a collective spiritual freedom.

Other poems in the "some jesus" section also draw typological parallels between biblical history and African American life. Just as the Bible's parables are inherently ambiguous, so, too, are the "some jesus" poems. These highly compressed poems depend on our skills in interpolation as well as interpretation. Moving back and forth between the topical poems and the biblical ones, we see the complexity and, ultimately, the humanity of Clifton's enterprise. As a writer for the *Saturday Review* noted in his review of *Good News about the Earth*, Clifton's "urban world is a mini-Vietnam—a landscape of inner desolation. [But] beneath her anger and the recounting of history is the saving (and soothing) grace of tenderness."[29]

In *An Ordinary Woman* and *Two-Headed Woman*, Clifton's poetry swells to fill the growing vessel of her consciousness. The poems of these volumes are more deeply rooted in her own experience, her own self-understanding. Whereas *Good News about the Earth* focuses mainly on race, an often autobiographical black female sensibility pervades *An Ordinary Woman* and *Two-Headed Woman*. Issues related to gender, family, and spirituality, introduced in her first two books, now become integral dimensions of her poetic identity.

An Ordinary Woman consists of two parts, "sisters" and "i agree with the leaves." Containing many poems dedicated to female family members and friends, the book is about being a questing woman, just as *Good News about the Earth* is implicitly about race, racial difference, and being black. Once again, Clifton illustrates—and personalizes—a cultural paradigm shift. Poems like "sisters," "leanna's poem," and "harriet" recognize not only the affection but also the mutual identification that like-minded women feel, whether blood sisters or not. Female bonding seems to presage self-affirmation, as Clifton's increasingly confident voice makes clear. In the second half of "sisters," she writes:

>me and you
>got babies
>got thirty-five
>got black
>let our hair go back
>be loving ourselves
>be loving ourselves

29. Norman Rosten, "SR Reviews Books," *Saturday Review* (August 12, 1972): 58.

be sisters.
only where you sing
i poet.
                    (GW 112)

These siblings are strong, self-confident black women; the repetition of
"be loving ourselves" describes their unabashed enthusiasm for who and
what they are. The last two lines have a surprising, staccato sound to them
after the poem's otherwise steady waterfall of words. They signal a recog-
nition of individuality within the sisterhood. Significantly, the singer and
the poet have an artistic and professional kinship; they complement
rather than oppose one another. The words "i poet" can be read as a ver-
nacular elision of "i am a poet" or, more provocatively, as if "poet" were
a verb comparable to "sing." In either case, the emphasis is on the creative
individuality that flourishes in the spirit of sisterhood.

Confirmation likewise merges with affirmation in "leanna's poem"
and "harriet." In the former, the poet quotes her friend's comment over
lunch that "one / is never enough for me" (GW 113). Her own ruminations
"about meals / and mealmates and hunger" lead her to declare that her
friend is correct,

and so this poem is for us,
leanna, two hungry ladies,
and i wish for you
what i wish for myself—
more than one
more than one
more than one.
                    (GW 113)

The repeated line's indeterminacy allows us to fill in the blank however
we want—more than one tasty treat, more than one lover, more than one
great poem, perhaps? That is left up to each "hungry lady" to decide.
Maybe the point is simply that it is better not to be all alone. The poet's
love for her friend is the logical extension, maybe even manifestation, of
her love for herself.

Similarly, in "harriet" Clifton identifies with other women even as
she decides what her own course in life will be. In contrast to "leanna's

poem" and "sisters," however, here she identifies with her foremothers, both historical and genealogical, rather than with women of her own time. Looking to Harriet Tubman, Sojourner Truth, and her own grandmother for inspiration, she addresses each one with the line "if i be you" (*GW* 119). She alternately envisions herself as an activist, pursuing social change in behalf of black people, and a matriarch, stoically providing for future generations: "let me not forget to / work hard / trust the Gods / love my children and / wait." The poem implies that one persona does not necessarily exclude the other. Each role requires patience and courage, attributes the poet seeks to instill within herself. The poet's keen awareness of history, furthermore, confirms Susan Willis's comments about black women writers:

> In their hope for their children's future, black women have learned to be attentive to moments of historical transition and many have struggled for social change. In their role as producers, black women have known the present; then, in relation to the economics of reproduction, they have envisioned and strived for the future. As workers, they have sustained their families; as mothers, they have borne the oral histories from their grandmothers to their children. For all these reasons, today's black women writers understand history both as period and as process.[30]

Although Willis is writing about novelists rather than poets, her observations aptly describe the portrait in "harriet" as well as Clifton's overall approach to history, an approach also seen in *Generations,* the story of her paternal ancestry and her own childhood.

The poems in the "sisters" section are not all as upbeat as the ones discussed so far. The section's first poem, "in salem," vilifies white women, as does "to ms. ann." In these works white women are hostile sisters, refusing to acknowledge their sororal bond with black women. In its title and initial imagery, "in salem" alludes to the women persecuted for witchcraft during the Salem witch trials, perhaps especially to Tituba, the West Indian slave woman memorialized in works by Arthur Miller, Ann Petry, and Marise Condé. Clifton quickly establishes a kinship between a black female speaker and a black female audience:

30. Susan Willis, *Specifying: Black Women Writing the American Experience* (London: Routledge, 1990), 7.

weird sister
the black witches know that
the terror is not in the moon
choreographing the dance of wereladies
and the terror is not in the broom
swinging around to the hum of cat music
nor the wild clock face grinning from the wall

(*GW* 111)

The compound images of "wereladies" and "cat music" playfully tease the brain, while the abundant internal rhymes create an aural cohesion that might well be cat music. If all this is supernatural, then it is surely more pleasing than the allegedly natural world where

the terror is in the plain pink
at the window
and the hedges moral as fire
and the plain face of the white woman watching us
as she beats her ordinary bread, . . .

(*GW* 111)

The word "plain" hangs in the air heavily, without any magic, as the self-righteous white woman expresses her rage against black women through her beating of the bread. Reminiscent of the stultifying white neighborhoods of "in the inner city," this woman's "moral" hedges symbolize a self-imposed isolation as well as a tendency to circumvent, or hedge, incendiary conflict. The poem brings to mind Toni Morrison's insistence on the need for studying "the impact of racism on those who perpetuate it. It seems both poignant and striking how avoided and unanalyzed is the effect of racist inflection on the subject."[31] Racial tensions among American women continue to exist, though often in sublimated form. Clifton places this particular social ill in a historical context by connecting the Puritans' persecution of "weird" women with nineteenth-century slavery and twentieth-century racial friction. The poem's smirking "clock face" acknowledges how little times have changed.

31. Toni Morrison, "Black Matters," in *Playing in the Dark: Whiteness and the Literary Imagination* (Cambridge: Harvard University Press, 1992), 11.

The white title character in "ms. ann" is another flat, baleful presence who seems incapable of hearing a black woman's declamations. With "ms. ann" representing the generic white mistress, the first three stanzas move from the antebellum era to the present:

> i will have to forget
> your face
> when you watched me breaking
> in the fields,
> missing my children.
>
> i will have to forget
> your face
> when you watched me carry
> your husband's
> stagnant water.
>
> i will have to forget
> your face when you handed me
> your house
> to make a home, . . .
>
> (GW 122)

The black female speaker grimly recalls chores she performed for a white woman unwilling to acknowledge any commonality of experience. The repeated line suggests that the speaker will not, in fact, forget the white woman or her obtuse behavior:

> and you never called me sister
> then, you never called me sister
> and it has only been forever and
> i will have to forget your face.
>
> (GW 122)

As an emblem of white women's reluctance to befriend black women, "ms. ann" is a maddeningly eternal verity. No matter how many times the speaker says "i will have to forget your face," the dispassionate white woman cannot be entirely erased. Her transgression is not the drudgery she has imposed on the narrator but her refusal to recognize kinship. The repeated line "you never called me sister" is both reproach and accusation.

The narrator's pain and anger stem as much from what might have been as from what was.

The second part of *An Ordinary Woman,* "i agree with the leaves," has a contemplative, mystical feel to it. The section contains a series of poems about Kali, the terrifying black Hindu goddess whom the poet regards as a dangerously powerful but not exactly evil spirit occupying her own body and soul. In "the coming of Kali," "she insists on me," and "calming Kali," among other poems, Clifton tries to come to terms with an inner demoness who is just as compelling as she is demanding. It is a feminized dimension of herself that the poet castigates even as she acknowledges it as integral to her identity: "gently gently now / awful woman, / i know i am your sister" (*GW* 140). In a volume largely dedicated to sisters in blood and spirit, Clifton's Kali is a female essence craving the nurturing that black woman have historically given to others. Through the figure of Kali, the all-powerful Great Mother of Hindu mythology, the poet recognizes her own intrinsic need for nurturing—a mindful tending of the female self. If there is evil within her, it is an evil growing out of unfulfilled needs, unmet desires. For Clifton, Kali appears to be a dimension of the female self demanding the love and recognition that the poet-mother gladly gives to others.

The highlight of the "i agree with the leaves" section, and of the whole volume, is "the thirty eighth year," one of Clifton's best known poems as well as the source for the book's understated yet evocative title, "an ordinary woman." At sixty lines, "the thirty eighth year" is one of the longest poems, excluding the multipart sequences, that Clifton has published. The words "an ordinary woman" occur four times (*GW* 158–59), with each reiteration containing more power and poignance. She has lived through and for her mother for many years: "i have dreamed dreams / for you mama / more than once. / i have wrapped me / in your skin / and made you live again / more than once," but she now hopes to become fully herself, a woman secure in her identity even in the face of inevitable disappointments and losses. The poem is a watershed in Clifton's journey into her own interior; it acknowledges her deep and continuing bond with her mother while admitting a fervent desire to be independent and whole, free of the sadness she associates with her mother's lost life.

Clifton's increasingly open self-representations seem closely connected to her willingness to write about her mother. Whereas Clifton's mother makes only cameo appearances in *Good Times* and *Good News about the Earth,* Thelma Sayles is a presiding spirit in *An Ordinary Woman.* It appears that Clifton's spiritual fulfillment will be linked to an exploration of the female life that called her own life into being. Such an endeavor, it turns out, does not have to be uniformly poignant or solemn. In "if mama," for example, the first stanza imagines what it would be like "if mama / could see" (*GW* 146), and the second stanza continues the conceit:

> if mama
> could hear
> she would hear
> lucysong rolled in the
> corners like lint
> exotic webs of lucysighs
> long lucy spiders explaining
> to obscure gods.
>
> (*GW* 146)

These indulgent, whimsical images suggest that "lucy" now fills up the space her mother has left behind; the daughter is nothing if not a pervasive presence. But the poem ends on a humorous, deprecating note:

> if mama
> could talk
> she would talk
> good girl
> good girl
> good girl
> clean up your room.
>
> (*GW* 146)

Here, the mother's voice takes over, drowning out the "lucysighs" and gently criticizing the lazy daughter-housekeeper's spiders and lint. Thelma Sayles clearly lives on in her daughter's newly awakened love for herself, a self-love tempered by an imaginative sense of humor.

The poem "light" further explores identity through the poet's relation to her mother, while introducing Clifton's fascination with her name's origin in *lux,* the Latin root for *light.* In what will be the first of many poems placing her name—and her representation of herself—in a biblical context, "light" begins: "light / on my mother's tongue / breaks through her soft / extravagant hip / into life. / lucille / she calls the light" (*GW* 148). If the poem's beginning is reminiscent of the early chapters of Genesis, then the rest of the first stanza, tracing the name "Lucille" to the foremother who "shot the whiteman off his horse, / killing the killer of sons," evokes the biblical genealogy found in the latter chapters of Genesis.

The allusions help Clifton mythologize her own experience, increasingly the focus of her poetry, while also suggesting that every birth effectively reenacts the Creation story and initiates a new chapter of an ever-expanding Bible. But the maternal lineage recorded here, combined with the first Lucille's bold shooting of a "whiteman," hints at the possibility of an alternative sacred text in which black women manifest their own destinies in both word and deed. The poem also foreshadows the family history that will be shared in Clifton's prose memoir, *Generations,* in which we learn just how important names, family origins, and matrilineage are to this poet. It is as if she is responding to the call to action in Adrienne Rich's "Diving into the Wreck"; in the 1970s, Clifton was among the women gradually realizing that they didn't have to settle for what Rich called "a book of myths / in which / our names do not appear."[32]

In *Generations: A Memoir,* Clifton records her family's own names and myths. The immediate impetus for this prose work seems to have been twofold. Clifton's father, Samuel Sayles, had died, and she had talked to a white woman named Sale who had compiled a history of the Bedford, Virginia, family that did not mention the family slaves—Clifton's ancestors. Intent on correcting this oversight as well as paying tribute to her late father, Clifton writes in *Generations* of Caroline Donald, her paternal great-great-grandmother who was captured in Dahomey, Africa, and brought to the United States as a slave in 1830. Speaking through her father's persona, Clifton writes, "[Caroline] was born among the Dahomey people in 1822, Lue. Among the Dahomey people, and she used to always say 'Get what you want, you from Dahomey women.' And she used to tell

32. Adrienne Rich, "Diving into the Wreck," in *The Fact of a Doorframe: Poems Selected and New, 1950–1984* (New York: Norton, 1984), 164.

us about how they had a whole army of nothing but women back there and how they was the best soldiers in the world" (*GW* 232). Caroline's later life as a slave is portrayed as difficult but not without dignity. She is at the beginning of "a line / of black and going on women" that Clifton proudly claims as her own in "for deLawd" (*GW* 32), a poem in *Good Times*.

Made to walk from New Orleans to Virginia as an eight-year-old child, Caroline grows up to be a well-respected midwife and the matriarch of a large family. The example of Caroline inspires and motivates both Samuel Sayles and his daughter. Samuel attributes much of his own self-confidence to his African ancestry, and he frequently reminds his daughter of the Dahomey women's powerful legacy. In the Sayles family, this ancient legacy counts for much more than the relatively brief period during which Clifton's ancestors were enslaved. Though she endured thirty-five years in slavery, Caroline was "born free among the Dahomey people" and "died free in Bedford Virginia in 1910" (*GW* 260); this is the triumph of the indomitable Dahomey spirit. As Samuel tells his daughter, "'We fooled em, Lue, slavery was terrible but we fooled them old people. We come out of it better than they did'" (*GW* 260). Clifton reports that her mother seconded this opinion in her own quiet, less confrontational way: "[M]y mama told me that slavery was a temporary thing, mostly we was free and she was right" (*GW* 275).

The elegiac *Generations* gives us the biographical context for Clifton's poems that draw inspiration from her African heritage and family life. Though "ca'line's prayer" in *Good Times* makes sense even if we don't know Caroline Donald's story, it is more moving if we have read about the family matriarch in *Generations*. The persona who says "remember me from wydah / remember the child / running across dahomey / black as ripe papaya / juicy as sweet berries" is Clifton's vivid rendering of a foremother of profound importance to her (*GW* 33). To remember Caroline's childhood is to remember a land that Clifton has not seen but nevertheless feels in her bones; to contemplate Africa is to contemplate the enigmatic Caroline, a definitively African American woman whose blood courses through the poet's veins.

Generations shows us that Caroline has been on Clifton's mind for much of her life—and has been partly responsible for her career as a poet.

After dropping out of college, Clifton faced her father's anger and disappointment:

> Daddy, I argued with him, I don't need that stuff, I'm going to write poems. I can do what I want to do! I'm from Dahomey women!
> You don't even know where that is, he frowned at me. You don't even know what it means.
> And I ran to my room and cried all night and waited for the day. Because he was right. I cried and cried and listened. (*GW* 250)

Her poems invoking Africa, meditating on slavery, and memorializing slaves are proof, along with the memoir *Generations,* that Clifton listened well. What she didn't yet know as a teenager about her heritage, she was willing to learn.

Two-Headed Woman is a seemingly inevitable extension of both *Generations* and *An Ordinary Woman.* The volume continues to work with the autobiographical material presented in the memoir, as Clifton finds art in the raw symbolism of her own life and her mother's. Though Thelma's story provides a sort of coda to the stories of Samuel Sayles's side of the family in *Generations,* she now assumes an awe-inspiring importance. Together, she and Clifton may be the two heads of the new volume's two-headed woman, the hoodoo figure with magical powers. The two-headed woman thus takes her place alongside the ordinary one in Clifton's oeuvre, as the strange and the usual begin to seem like sister strengths rather than oppositions. As *Two-Headed Woman* unfolds, we see that though Clifton may not have sought out the "wild blessings" of her life, they remain blessings all the same.

Nominated for the Pulitzer Prize and winner of the University of Massachusetts Press's Juniper Prize, the book consists of three sections, "homage to mine," "two-headed woman," and "the light that came to lucille clifton." The first part continues to explore the poet's identity in body and spirit. Poems such as "homage to my hair," "homage to my hips," "what the mirror said," and "there is a girl inside" are upbeat and witty, whereas "i was born with twelve fingers," another poem about the poet's body, has a more mysterious yet self-affirming feeling. Picking up on the witchcraft theme that "in salem" introduces in *An Ordinary Woman,* "i was born with twelve fingers" alludes to the long-ago belief that persons born with extra fingers were witches. Clifton writes that she and her mother and oldest daughter were "born wearing strange black gloves / extra baby fingers hanging over the sides of our cribs and / dipped into the milk" (GW 166). Though their "wonders were cut off," the three women have not lost the magical powers that those fingers bestowed on them. Here are the concluding lines:

> we take what we want
> with invisible fingers
> and we connect
> my dead mother   my live daughter   and me
> through our terrible shadowy hands.
>
> (GW 166)

Clifton is proud of the sorcery embodied in the "invisible fingers" and eager to claim this legacy linking her to her mother and her daughter. Just as she had previously incorporated racial politics into her poetry, now Clifton begins to embrace feminist spirituality, a loosely organized body of beliefs emphasizing self-nurturing female powers that transcend the limits most religious denominations place on women.

The women in "i was born with twelve fingers" will not be held back by their "shadowy" skin color or even by death. As Andrea Musher points out, "In the spaces we see the invisible connection; we see the interpenetration of the living and the dead, of the past and the present."[33] The surgical removal of the extra fingers is proof, according to Clifton, that "somebody was afraid we would learn to cast spells," but that has not stopped the three women from doing just that. Musher observes, "The knives in Clifton's poem were not used by mothers and daughters against each other, but were wielded by 'somebody' who feared black, female power and what was perceived as a deviation from the norm."[34] The poem is itself an example of spell-casting,[35] as is "speaking of loss," another poem

---

33. Andrea Susan Musher, "Vital Connections: The Poetics of Maternal Affiliation in Sylvia Plath, Anne Sexton, Adrienne Rich, Lucille Clifton, and Judy Grahn" (Ph.D. diss., University of Wisconsin–Madison, 1989), 479.

34. Ibid., 478–79.

35. Ibid., 479.

dealing with the absent fingers: "my extra fingers are cut away. / i am left with plain hands and / nothing to give you but poems" (*GW* 174). Though the lines are plaintive, they imply that the poems are the manifestation of magic as well as a means of remembering and reclaiming what is lost.

The introspection deepens in the "two-headed woman" section of the book, which begins with "in this garden." Here we meet "the sensational / two-headed woman / one face turned outward / one face / swiveling slowly in" (*GW* 185). The two-headed woman with supernatural powers can also be seen as a female Janus, the Roman god of beginnings and endings. Somewhat reminiscent of Plath's Lady Lazarus, another feminized icon, the arrival of the two-headed woman signals a new turn in Clifton's mythologizing of the self. But whereas Plath's persona snappishly proclaims that "dying is an art,"[36] the as-yet voiceless two-headed woman takes up the art of introspection. Even as she continues looking out at the world, she begins to turn inward, to examine the woman within. For Clifton, introspection as we typically think of it is nothing new. She has always brooded, in the manner of Emily Dickinson, over the concentric circles of soul, self, and society. What is new, as the poems in the "two-headed woman" and "the light that came to lucille clifton" sections reveal, is a willingness to entertain a whole new set of questions revolving around the possibility that the known, visible self is only a small portion of the whole person.

In a series of highly mystical, often biblically inspired poems, we see that Clifton's search for self-enlightenment has barely begun. Like Mary awaiting the birth of Jesus, she knows that she contains wonders that are as yet obscure to her. Imagining, and hence believing in, her own depths is world-changing, scary. She seems to be becoming part of the Bible that has been so important to her life and her poetry. This is evident in the untitled concluding poem of "two-headed woman," a revealing poem of transition: "the light that came to lucille clifton / came in a shift of knowing / when even her fondest sureties / faded away" (*GW* 209). The poem responds to, and builds on, the brief description of the two-headed woman at the section's beginning. The now-named self—"lucille clifton"—has some personal dimension but remains at a third-person dis-

---

36. Sylvia Plath, "Lady Lazarus," in *The Collected Poems*, ed. Ted Hughes (New York: Harper and Row, 1981), 245.

tance, an indication that this particular self is still more of an object than a fully integrated component of the poet's identity:

> she closed her eyes, afraid to look for her
> authenticity
> but the light insists on itself in the world;
> a voice from the nondead past started talking,
> she closed her ears and it spelled out in her hand
> "you might as well answer the door, my child,
> the truth is furiously knocking."
>
> (*GW* 209)

This self-knowledge will be all-pervasive, engaging all of the poet's senses. Clifton, the listener, knows that this new truth, "knocking" at the door of her life, is also a form of opportunity knocking: answering the door will leave her transformed, newly challenged, perhaps unfamiliar to herself.

The book's last section bravely takes up this challenge, as Clifton gradually grows more comfortable with the possibility that the vast spiritual realm figured in the Bible has an equally vast analogue in her own soul. The living generations, the dead ones, her as yet unborn descendants—all are vital, often querulous voices insisting on an audience. Though at times she feels she must admit "mother, i am mad"—the title of a poem in the final section—at other times she can say, definitively, of the voices she hears: "they are present as air. / they are there" ("friends come," *GW* 218). Supernatural cacophony gives way to a natural symphony, and a quiet certainty begins to creep into Clifton's long meditation on the self. When she turns to Joan of Arc in "for joan," it is to a sister in spirit who literally fought for what she believed:

> did you never wonder
> oh fantastical joan,
> did you never cry in the sun's face
> unreal   unreal? did you never run
> villageward
> hands pushed out toward your apron?
>
> (*GW* 219)

These lines envision a fallible Joan who may have doubted her sanity even as she insisted on the sanctity of her mission. But the poem goes on to imply that her inner voices were finally a comfort rather an affliction. Even when death was certain, Joan would have heard the angels and claimed them as her own:

> sister   sister
> did you not then sigh
> my voices   my voices   of course?
>
> (*GW* 219)

Given Clifton's own spiritual questings, her identification with Joan of Arc is understandably strong. They are both soldiers of inner fortune. The young female mystic, who must masquerade as a male soldier in order to accomplish her aims, provides an objective correlative for the middle-aged black female poet trying on multiple personas in pursuit of spiritual wholeness. For either one, to acknowledge inner voices is to accept a multiplicity of selves. Are these selves friends or foes? Angels of enlightenment or demons of dementia?

In *Two-Headed Woman* Clifton lets the voices into her life and begins to write increasingly intimate, spiritually charged poems. "As the past and future exist simultaneously in the present, so Clifton comes to see herself as a totality of all that was, is, and will be," Deborah Plant observed in her review of *Good Woman: Poems and a Memoir, 1969–1980*. "Her sense of herself underscores and reinforces all her connections—to her environment, herself, her children, her mothers."[37] As Clifton's conception of herself grew, her art had to change as well.

37. Deborah Plant, review of *Good Woman: Poems and a Memoir,* in *Prairie Schooner* 63, no. 1 (1989): 116.

CHAPTER 2

Dark Blessings

AFTER FRED CLIFTON DIED OF CANCER in 1984, Lucille Clifton left Baltimore for a teaching position at the University of California, Santa Cruz, a position she had secured before her husband's illness struck. She did not publish another book of verse until 1987, when BOA Editions simultaneously released *Good Woman: Poems and a Memoir, 1969–1980* and *Next: New Poems.* Both were finalists for the Pulitzer Prize in poetry, a singular achievement in the history of that award. Representing her first decade as a published poet, *Good Woman* feels unified and complete, and the inclusion of *Generations* creates a context that is mythic as well as autobiographical. *Good Woman* showcases Clifton's racial and gender politics, her belief in social justice, her evolving religious faith, and her yearning for human connection.

As Liz Rosenberg wrote in a *New York Times* review of *Good Woman,* Clifton's "concerns are both earthbound and mystical, and what may appear stylistically simple, is upon close examination, an effort to free the true voice clear and plain."[1] Upon finishing *Good Woman,* one feels the sort of satisfaction that accompanies the reading of an engaging novel. Such richness and wholeness would almost seem to preclude a followup—unless that volume could significantly develop the poet's main themes and concerns. That is precisely what happens, however, in *Next* and Clifton's subsequent volumes.

Published when Clifton was fifty-one years old, *Next* retains the mysticism of *Two-Headed Woman,* but the new book sounds older, more deliberate, and more self-consciously artful than the poetry collections marking the first decade of her career. Even before the poems begin, *Next* insists on an imaginative juxtaposition of hope and grief. The wry dedication to Fred Clifton reads, "to fred / see you later alligator" (*N* 5). This casual tag line takes on a greater significance when we realize that it antic-

---

1. Liz Rosenberg, "Simply American and Mostly Free," *New York Times Book Review,* 19 February 1989, 24.

ipates a posthumous reunion between Clifton and her husband. The epi-
graph, providing a metaphysical dimension to the book's title, is drawn
from a poem in Galway Kinnell's *The Past* (1985) titled "December Day in
Honolulu": "This one or that one dies but never the singer . . . [O]ne
singer falls but the next steps into the empty place and sings. . . ." (*N* 11).
Concerned with both the dying and the singing, *Next* shows how closely
the two are allied. In the section titles—"we are all next," "or next," and
"singing"—we sense both the nearness of death and the necessity of art
as a sustaining life force. Instead of dwelling on the poet's personal pain,
Next historicizes and contextualizes the elegiac drama of loss and shows
Clifton turning to friends for solace in her time of need.

In many of the poems in this new volume, Clifton aspires to interna-
tional concerns and expands her awareness of cultural diversity. Before,
she had primarily concerned herself with the political and social relations
among African Americans, whites, and Native Americans, but poems in
Next touch down in South Africa, China, and Lebanon, among other
places. Her poems about women and womanhood are also broader based:
we see her longing for a global community of women working together to
end warfare. Interestingly, the Bible is not a significant presence here;
only two poems even allude to it. Though there are moments of hope and
humor, the volume's pervasive mood is mournful and elegiac. It is the
work of a poet whose stylistic confidence belies her uncertainty about the
future.

The innate strength of women commemorated in *An Ordinary Woman*
and *Two-Headed Woman* remains an important preoccupation, but in *Next*
Clifton yearns for a solidarity among women that is often hard to find.
The opening poem, "album," illustrates the grace of female communion:

> we have dropped daughters,
> afrikan and chinese.
> we think
> they will be beautiful.
> we think
> they will become themselves.
>   (*N* 15)

When a friendship between two women flourishes, perhaps especially a
cross-cultural friendship, it is an act of affirmation that bodes well for the

daughters of those women. Such a pure bond is difficult to achieve, however. In an interview published six years after *Next,* Clifton observed that friendship between women of different races can be self-serving and subtly racist: "A lot of [white] people like to have a black friend. It's nice. [*Laughs*] It's true. And they can then have you in front of the others. It gives them a good feeling about themselves."[2] In light of this view, the focus on the "afrikan and chinese" in "album" circumvents the problems arising in a relationship between a white woman, representing mainstream society, and a black woman. The black woman and her Chinese friend may be seen as unifying against stereotypes imposed on them by whites.

In "the lost women," Clifton further explores the complexities and shortcomings of female friendship: "what would we have called each other laughing / joking into our beer? where are my gangs, / my teams, my mislaid sisters?" (*N* 29). This absence of casual friendship is another loss in the female speaker's life. If she and a group of female friends had the easy camaraderie of men sharing an interest in sports, maybe that would assuage some of her loneliness—and theirs.

On the home front, the poet also experiences feelings of alienation, even in her daughter's presence. In "grown daughter," the gaps within lines represent an emotional chasm. The poet sits with her daughter,

watching her   learning to love her but
who is she   who is she   who

(*N* 31)

The daughter's evolving maturity makes her new and interesting to behold but also mysterious and a little intimidating. As in "the lost women," the poem acknowledges a loss—in this case, the loss of the known child, supplanted forever by the grown woman. The daughter's transformation means that the mother, too, must adapt and change. She must begin to accept her daughter as an independent adult rather than as a beloved extension of herself. Such acceptance will alter, if not necessarily diminish, the speaker's maternal role even as it represents her own growing matur-

2. Shirley M. Jordan, "Lucille Clifton," *Broken Silences: Interviews with Black and White Women Writers* (New Brunswick, N.J.: Rutgers University Press, 1993), 41.

ity and autonomy. The poem wonders not just about the grown daughter but also about the grown mother: Who is she? Who will love her? Poems such as these two imply that a woman's self-affirmation depends at least in part on a gathering of female souls. Unfortunately, the women friends and relatives who could offer validation and companionship do not necessarily appear on command, nor do they always fulfill one's expectations of them. The absence of communion occasions the poet's bafflement and grief.

This juxtaposition of a beautiful ideal and a series of painful, all-too-familiar realities has thematic importance in *Next*. In the series of poems titled "l. at creation," "l. at gettysburg," "l. at nagasaki," and "l. at jonestown," Clifton imagines three defining moments in history and concludes with a catastrophe that took place during her own lifetime. The "l." in each title seems to stand for "lucille," as Clifton places herself in each scene. Not so much recalling past lives as synthesizing her present life with the past, she begins with "the long / slide out of paradise" (*N* 22), moves through the Civil War and World War II, and ends with the 1978 mass suicide of religious cult members in Guyana. The first poem emphasizes the harmony of all living things, the mainstay of paradise: "all life is life. / all clay is kin and kin" (*N* 22). The second poem, referring to the Battle of Gettysburg, departs sharply from the idealized communion of "creation." Here, the speaker has heard that "this is somehow about myself, / this clash of kin across good farmland" (*N* 23), and the Civil War's aftermath seems to stretch forever. The speaker decries "the ghosts of the brothers and cousins" who are "wailing toward me in their bloody voices, / who are you, nigger woman, who are you?" Both defined and derided according to her gender and race, she faces the sad truth that many white men still have little understanding of the people whose enslavement precipitated the Civil War. The rhetorical question recalls the querulous ending of "grown daughter," but here the focus is on the speaker's identity, which has been alternately ignored and maligned. The kinship of Creation has given way to division and destruction, and "l." is left to ponder a question that her interrogators do not necessarily want her to answer.

The speaker's feelings of alienation and nullity are amplified in "l. at nagasaki." In the wake of the bombing of Nagasaki, "the things of my world / glisten into ash" (*N* 24). The bomber planes, "the silver birds," have reduced her and her surroundings to "nothing," though she has "done nothing / to deserve this." The destruction has been dehumanizing for all involved. This sequence is thus becoming a searing indictment of men, especially white American men, who have not thought through the murderous actions that have devastating ramifications for so many.

The final poem, "l. at jonestown," confirms that judgment, though the speaker does admit to some complicity. The poem alludes to the mass suicide of 913 followers of Jim Jones, founder of the People's Temple. This religious and activist organization, which gradually devolved into a cult, started out in the Midwest, relocated to California, and finally came to rest in the South American jungle, in the Guyanan settlement called Jonestown. Jones, a white American, said he was the savior incarnate and espoused liberal ideals, including racial tolerance, that attracted many African Americans to his flock. Charismatic and manipulative, Jones commanded his followers to drink poisoned punch in a supposedly revolutionary act; in order to ensure complete obliteration, he had the poison sprayed into the mouths of babies. Jones himself was also found dead, of gunshot wounds to the head. The carnage took place shortly after California congressman Leo Ryan and several others in his party were murdered during their investigation of People's Temple followers held in Jonestown against their will. The suicide seemed to be Jones's way of retaining final control of a lost cause.

In her poem, Clifton imagines the thoughts of a Jones disciple about to drink the deadly punch:

> on a day when i would have believed
> anything, i believed that this white man,
> stern as my father, neutral in his coupling
> as adam, was possibly who he insisted he was.
> now he has brought me to the middle of the
> jungle of my life. if i have been wrong, again,
> father may even this cup in my hand turn against me.
>
> (N 25)

The opening makes it clear that anyone believing Jones would have to be extraordinarily suggestible. But that is not to say that he was not a riveting presence fully capable of winning converts—as an African American, herself convinced of the benefits of communion, Clifton was potentially vulnerable to his allure. It is not a great leap for her to conjure the thoughts of a Jones follower. Drawing on the image of the South American jungle where the catastrophe took place, the "jungle of my life" succinctly describes the speaker's feelings of spiritual disorientation. Before drinking from the poisoned cup, she anticipates divine judgment and decides to accept it, no matter what it is. Although all of the poem's figures of oppressive and judgmental power are male, including the "father" in the closing line, the speaker is making her own decision. Out of innocence, ignorance, or a fatally misguided desire to connect with the very person intent on her destruction, she submits to her own death. Thus "l. at jonestown" illustrates the fallibility of individuals, female as well as male, in the midst of moral and mortal crisis. Unable to determine whether she is victor or victim, she does the best she can with the limited information she has.

Many of the poems in *Next* have a similar urgency about them, as if their messages, no matter how deeply wrenched, must be shared with others. This is true of the middle section's elegiac sequences, which will be discussed in greater detail in Chapter 7. The subjects of these sequences— Clifton's mother, her husband, a family friend, and, in a departure from the otherwise personal nature of the series, the Indian warrior Crazy Horse—are all people who died young. The unexpectedness of their deaths gives a terrible gravity to the section title, "or next," since we never know who will be the next to die. The juxtaposing of the Crazy Horse sequence with the personal sequences suggests a kinship between the Indian warrior's family and Clifton's own. As in "album," in which the poet commemorates her friendship with a Chinese woman, these poems forge a cross-cultural identification and imply that American minority groups are integral to the nation's mythopoetic history.

In that they are written from the perspective of the deceased, these elegies build on the mystical poems in *Two-Headed Woman*. The "messages" of these individuals, as the poems' titles designate them, are artful representations of supernatural communications. By speaking through her subjects—in effect, channeling their messages—Clifton seems to be reconciling herself to profound loss as well as insisting on a continuing connection with persons of great importance to her. Though gone from the living world, they are not gone from her life.

In the book's final section, "singing," Clifton shares some of her private thoughts about her public life as a poet. The six-part sequence titled "in white america," the section's strongest, explores Clifton's identity as an African American woman traveling around the country giving poetry readings. In "i come to read them poems," she describes the poetry reading as "a fancy trick i do / like juggling with balls of light" (N 70). The image is especially appropriate, since Clifton so often identifies herself (via the name Lucille) with light and divine illumination. Yet she is a black woman, "a dark spinner," who has entertained audiences in decidedly modest places, "in the grange hall, / in the library, in the / smaller conference room." Her blackness contributes, it seems, to the feverish intensity of her performance, "my eyes bright, my mouth smiling, / my singed hands burning."

The poem implies that the black poet, like the minstrel performers of old, is trying to charm and win over a resistant white audience. Clifton wonders about this compromising situation in *Generations* when she recounts her conversation with the white woman named Sale: "And I rush to reassure her. Why? Is it in my blood to reassure this thin-voiced white lady?" (*GW* 228). The poet does not provide an answer to this in either her memoir or this poem, but clearly, winning over an audience does require charm and a certain amount of artifice. The poet's "singed hands" indicate, however, that this performer is actually in pain. The poems burning in her hands express her powerful feelings about her life in "white america." Because audiences often see only what they want to see, they may overlook the complexity of such a performance as well as the poet's emotional stake in her art form.

Clifton's poem recalls Paul Laurence Dunbar's "We Wear the Mask" (1895), in which Dunbar writes, "We sing, but oh the clay is vile / Beneath our feet, and long the mile; / But let the world dream otherwise, / We wear the mask!"[3] The poet, who is in the business of masks or personas, is especially attuned to artifice in one's self-presentation, but Dunbar is writing about African Americans in general, not just poets. His poem anticipates the notion of the double consciousness expressed by W. E. B. Du Bois in *The Souls of Black Folk* (1903). Clifton, for her part, does not

3. Paul Laurence Dunbar, "We Wear the Mask," in Gates and McKay, *Norton Anthology of African American Literature*, 896.

represent herself as being tragically torn in two, though in "i come to read them poems" she does recognize that her reality is very different from that of her white audience. Like Dunbar, she knows that she has constructed the very mask that prevents white people from fully understanding her. Neither poet seems certain whether the mask protects the performer or the audience or both; the mask is perhaps an a priori condition, as Du Bois implies, for black people.

Despite the difficulties involved, Clifton ultimately portrays the sharing of poems as beneficial for both her and her white listeners. Her performances open up a dialogue between races. In "the reading," she assesses the situation with guarded optimism: "i look into none of my faces / and do the best i can" (N 75). She looks for what they all have in common: "the human hair between us / stretches but does not break. / i slide myself along it and / love them, love them all." Intimate and sensual, a hair symbolizes the human bond between the poet and a room full of strangers. The poems that she reads are like strands of hair, simultaneously delicate and strong, conveying a common humanity.

The importance of communing is also evident in *Quilting,* the volume that reestablishes Clifton's pattern of publishing a new poetry collection every few years. Happier and more hopeful than its immediate predecessor, *Quilting* seems determined to find models for positive interaction in women's friendships and folk art, especially that of black women. The book's title and organization allude to the author's African ancestry and the sources of her ethos and aesthetic. Folklorists have found that quilts made by nineteenth-century enslaved women draw on African design techniques and spiritual beliefs as well as European and Native American traditions.[4] Since Clifton's work reflects multiple influences while remaining loyal to her African and African American heritage, the quilt is a poetic conceit of unusual resonance. Traditional quilt designs provide the names for section titles—"log cabin," "catalpa flower," "eight-pointed star," and "tree of life." Through these titles, Clifton implies that the social elements associated with quilting—goodwill and friendly cooperation—are embed-

4. Harryette Mullen, "African Signs and Spirit Writing," in *African American Literary Theory: A Reader,* ed. Winston Napier (New York: New York University Press, 2000), 629–30.

ded in the book and her life. As one reviewer of the book noted, the titles "supply a visual metaphor for the vibrant wholeness of vision the book achieves through its many patterns of speech and points of focus."[5] Yet Clifton is still working toward that state of communion that is so elusive yet wonderful when found. It is true that Clifton "is a passionate, mercurial writer, by turns angry, prophetic, compassionate, shrewd, sensuous, vulnerable and funny,"[6] and those many moods infuse her poetry with both versatility and vitality.

As in her earlier volumes, Clifton makes sure that we recognize the importance of race to individual and social identity. In "at the cemetery, walnut grove plantation, south carolina, 1989" and "slave cabin, sotterly plantation, maryland, 1989," she once again links slave history with present-day race relations. Addressing the plantation's long-dead—and long-unacknowledged—slaves in "at the cemetery," she writes:

> tell me your names
> foremothers, brothers,
> tell me your dishonored names.
> here lies
> here lies
> here lies
> here lies
> hear
>
> (Q 11–12)

During her tour of Walnut Grove plantation, she noticed some graves near the plantation's family burial ground. Although her guide did not comment on them, Clifton surmised that they belonged to slaves. After the tour, she asked a plantation staff member why the tour guide had said nothing about slavery:

> The first answer was "Maybe the guide didn't want to embarrass you." "Well," I said, "I'm not a slave. I don't know why he would think I'd be embarrassed." Then I asked again, and the answer was, "Maybe they

5. Leslie Ullman, "Book Reviews," *Kenyon Review* 14 no. 3, new series (1992): 178.

6. Bruce Bennett, "Preservation Poets," *New York Times Book Review*, 1 March 1992, 22.

didn't have any." Well, they had two thousand acres in South Carolina in the early part of the nineteenth century. Be serious!

When I suggested that the guide check the inventory—because slaves were considered property and were often inventoried—they discovered that the plantation had an inventory of ten slaves, but they might have had more because women weren't counted. Now, well, I had to find out about that! I mean, some things say, hey, like "No!" Then when I learned that the women were not considered valuable enough to inventory, I definitely wanted to write about that.[7]

Having explained the inspiration for the poem, Clifton goes on to explicate the last few lines in which "here lies" gives way to "hear": "I want [readers] to recognized that only half the truth was being told. At that time [1989] schoolchildren were taken there on field trips to Walnut Grove, and half the children in the town were denied the knowledge that their ancestors had helped to build that plantation. That is unjust, and I'm into justice big-time."[8]

Justice is also the subject of "slave cabin, sotterly plantation, maryland, 1989." In this companion to "at the cemetery," Clifton continues to contrast the complex, frustratingly elusive identities that slaves formed for themselves with the superficial ones their oppressors imposed on them. The label "aunt nanny's bench" in a restored slave cabin does more to obscure the long-dead woman's identity than to reveal it (Q 13). The poem ends with the poet envisioning the slave woman sitting on the bench, "feet dead against the dirty floor / humming for herself humming / her own sweet human name." The humming is a kind of spontaneous poetry, an expression of the woman's selfhood that no master can take away. No matter how long and hard she works in the service of others, she is still a sentient human being who knows her identity better than anyone else does. As Clifton herself noted, "It is important for us to know what people call themselves and not to mistake what *we* call them for what they call themselves. We have the right as living creatures to name ourselves. Then when people call us something else, we can allow it or not. But 'aunt nanny's bench'? Even at their most wonderful, the people who gave her that name perhaps didn't know who she was."[9]

7. Moyers, 86–87.
8. Ibid., 87.
9. Ibid., 88.

The chasm separating one's self from the historical record of one's life is further explored in "somewhere." In this poem, Clifton envisions her earlier self writing her first book of poems. The woman who "lays out tomorrow's school clothes, / sets the table for breakfast early," is the same one who "sits down and writes the words / Good Times" (Q 48). Clifton cannot entirely reconcile how she got from the "this" of her past to the "that" of her present life: "i think of her as i begin to teach / the lives of the poets, / about her space at the table / and my own inexplicable life." The lines beg the question of whether Clifton does in fact have a space at the poets' table, long dominated by white men. The image of the table also ironically recalls that breakfast table where she fed her family and wrote her poems. In Clifton's life, the familial and the literary cannot be separated.

Although in recent years much good work has been done in women's biography, it is worth noting that the famous compendiums that Clifton alludes to—Theophilus Cibber's *The Lives of the Poets of Great Britain and Ireland* (1753) and Samuel Johnson's *Lives of the English Poets* (1779)—concern themselves, inevitably, with British white men. Louis Untermeyer's twentieth-century survey, *Lives of the Poets: The Story of One Thousand Years of English and American Poetry* (1959), contains a handful of women but no blacks, male or female. Even with all of the attention now being paid to African American literature and women's literature, Clifton's place at the canonical table is far from assured, and this uncertainty is due at least in part to an outmoded, male-centered approach to the writing of biography. In contrast to the "relatively uncomplicated presentation of the persona" in a biography of a successful man, Linda Wagner-Martin writes, "Telling a woman's life . . . is less formulaic. For one thing, most women's lives are a tightly woven mesh of public and private events. The primary definition of a woman's selfhood is likely to be this combined public-private identity."[10] A certain amount of mystery and happenstance obscures the full meaning of a woman's life, a life that cannot be summed up in a curriculum vitae. One thinks, for instance, of Emily Dickinson, whose secluded life in Amherst has long vexed scholars. In retrospect, her few trips away from home have the drama of a lunar launch. Wagner-

10. Linda Wagner-Martin, *Telling Women's Lives: The New Biography* (New Brunswick, N.J.: Rutgers University Press, 1994), 6.

Martin goes on to explain the dilemmas that biographers face: "While writing biography of men means concentrating on the subject's accomplishments, one of the main questions in writing women's biography is, What *are* the accomplishments in a woman's life? What motivation has driven the subject's choices? What led the subject to do more than lead a traditional woman's life? Historically, most women lived within family households; even in this century, women who have gained public recognition have also run homes."[11] Should she decide to share her story with the world, the so-called ordinary woman poet knows that the depth and complexity of her life will fall outside the traditional, male-oriented narratives of achievement and adventure. Her poems may be the only tangible record of her life, and their permanency will depend on the willingness of future readers to believe that her outlook on life had value.

In *The Book of Light* (1993), we see the guarded hopefulness of *Quilting* flowering into metaphysical wonder. This transcendent volume begins with "LIGHT," an artfully constructed list of synonyms for the most symbolic word in Clifton's body of work. Among the thirty-nine terms, attributed to *Roget's Thesaurus* at the end of the poem, are "reflection," "lightning bolt," and "splendor," which are the titles of the book's three sections.

In "reflection," most of the poems are about family members and the poet's identity as an aging woman, a survivor of many hardships. In "lightning bolt" we find a mix of political poems, family poems, and poems to "clark kent," a comic book character who seems to represent a love interest for Clifton. The final section, "splendor," contains biblical poems—notably "brothers," the culminating sequence written from Lucifer's perspective—and a series of poems responding to Yeats's "Leda and the Swan." While Clifton is addressing many of the themes significant to her throughout her career, she is now doing so with a cool clarity. Her speakers seem to be at peace with their own revelations.

Since Clifton's desire for self-knowledge typically involves an assessment of her family origins, it is not surprising to see her once again recalling her female ancestors in "daughters." A tribute to her maternal greatgrandmother, the poem begins, "woman who shines at the head / of my

11. Ibid.

grandmother's bed, / brilliant woman, i like to think / you whispered into her ear / instructions" (*BL* 13). These lines immediately establish the unnamed "woman" as a source of profound strength. The poem goes on to imagine the ancestor as "the oddness in us," "the arrow / that pierced our skin / and made us fancy women," yet this important figure is shrouded in mystery: "you became the name / we were cautioned to forget." The silence regarding her name becomes a source of strength in itself, however. It is as if the silence is a secret name that only the poet and the other women in her family can penetrate. Her own name grows triumphantly out of this silence, via her mother's, grandmother's, and great-grandmother's identities: "woman, i am / lucille, which stands for light, / daughter of thelma, daughter / of georgia, daughter of / dazzling you." This light-filled matrilineage suggests the power of naming but also the power of names not mentioned. In keeping with Caroline's silence on the subject of her African name in *Generations,* "daughters" subtly argues for a meaning attached to names that is beyond ordinary measure. We don't need to know the name of "dazzling you" to know that she has had a huge impact on her descendants.

Just as the section titled "reflection" aptly deals with contemplations of self, "lightning bolt" concerns electrifying connections with others. Clifton has said that this section's poems to "clark kent" grew out of her relationship with a man who considered himself the model for Superman.[12] In these poems, we see her reaching beyond the mournful, ethereal considerations of her late husband to other men, other relationships. In "final note to clark," for instance, she writes,

> they had it wrong,
> the old comics.
> you are only clark kent
> after all. oh,
> mild mannered mister,
> why did i think you could fix it?
>
> (*BL* 47)

The humor mingles with a feeling of disappointment and loss, a mingling that continues throughout the poem. But in the end, the mood is concilia-

---

12. Conversation with the author, 11 April 1998.

tory: "we are who we are, / two faithful readers, / not wonder woman and not superman." The female speaker realizes that she, too, is subject to misinterpretation. Rather than superheroes, she and her friend are mortal beings constantly reading and interpreting the world around them.

The companion poem, "note, passed to superman," develops the humorous aspects of the conceit Clifton has chosen for this relationship:

> maybe that choirboy clark
> can stand around
> listening to stories
> but not you, not with
> metropolis to save
> and every crook in town
> filthy with kryptonite.
> > (BL 48)

Imagining the man in his public persona, she gently mocks his inflated estimation of himself. In the conclusion, the narrator continues to profess her understanding at the same time that she reenvisions the man's heroic image as a defense mechanism:

> lord, man of steel,
> i understand the cape,
> the leggings, the whole
> ball of wax.
> you can trust me,
> there is no planet stranger
> than the one i'm from.
> > (BL 48)

Superman's fantastic attire is rendered bluntly, in all of its foolishness, as the speaker vigorously asserts her understanding and acceptance of his idiosyncrasies. These two are both in the business of personas, and the speaker's extreme awareness of her own planet's strangeness suggests that she, too, needs disguises (or poetic guises) in order to cope with life. Superman emerges as a surprisingly vulnerable outsider who cannot trust anyone or anything in the very environment he strives to protect. The woman who renders him in a few brisk images is herself stronger than kryptonite: she knows that he is a mere projection of the humble Clark, an ordinary man who shares her own yearnings for superpowers.

The section closes with an alternative reconciliation of the problems of human relationships that the Clark Kent poems touch on obliquely. With an epigraph from Gary Snyder—"love the human"—serving as its de facto title, this poem is both somber and earthy:

> the rough weight of it
> scarring its own back
> the dirt under the fingernails
> the bloody cock   love
> the thin line secting the belly
> the small gatherings
> gathered in sorrow or joy
>
> (BL 49)

Without identifying the lovers or even distinguishing one from the other, the poem sketches a sex act, labels it love, and commemorates the beauty and the poignancy of this primal coupling. The poem's subsequent directives—"love the silences / love the terrible noise / love the stink of it"— seem to celebrate not just sexual love but all human connection and communion. But as is so often the case in Clifton's poems, the ending rearranges the meaning of all that came before: "love it all love / even the improbable foot even / the surprised and ungrateful eye" (BL 49). In its final phrase, the poem seems to turn on itself. It is as if the speaker, feverishly asking others to love the human, suddenly remembers the risk and danger of the very thing being recommended. Loving the revelations of those risks and dangers—the feelings that do not reinforce the beauty of physical love—is the most difficult act of all.

The mood of high seriousness continues in "splendor." Most of the poems here articulate the perspectives of biblical and mythological characters such as Sisyphus, Atlas, Cain, Sarah, and Naomi. In keeping with Clifton's interest in feminist spirituality, the enigmatic "far memory," a seven-poem sequence, imagines the poet's past life as a nun, whereas the militant "leda" poems give a voice to the violated girl in Yeats's "Leda and the Swan": "at night my dreams are full / of the cursing of me / fucking god fucking me" ("leda 1," BL 59). By speaking for and through these characters, Clifton revises the way we view them as they appear in other texts. This is in keeping with T. S. Eliot's idea of tradition and the individual talent. The poems of our era change our reading of poems of the past, and vice versa; the long continuum of poetry is ever vital, thanks to the endless communication among poems, poets, and readers of all generations.

In "brothers," the book's final sequence, Clifton returns to the Creation story that has preoccupied her in past volumes. Like Milton, she is intent on reimagining Creation and its immediate aftermath. But unlike the venerable, wondrously long-winded author of *Paradise Lost,* she allows Lucifer to speak for the entire poem, which Chapter 6 will take up in detail. The parenthetical note below the poem's title identifies the sequence as "a conversation in eight poems between an aged Lucifer and God, though only Lucifer is heard. The time is long after" (*BL* 69). Since we hear only Lucifer, God's side must be inferred. But for that we have the Bible itself as well as *Paradise Lost* and innumerable other Christian theological texts. Clifton is speaking for and through a character with whom she strongly identifies: "I know there's Lucifer in Lucille, because I know me—I can be so petty, it's amazing! And there is therefore a possibility of Lucille in Lucifer. Lucifer was doing what he was supposed to do, too, you know? It's too easy to see Lucifer as all bad. Suppose he were merely being human."[13] For Clifton, the human is divine; there is only language separating the one from the other. The humanized Lucifer, who still wears a sort of divine badge, mediates between the two realms. From Clifton's perspective, he is not so much God's evil opposite as a talkative, earthbound twin who yearns for reconciliation with the silent brother gazing down from the sky.

Three years after *The Book of Light,* Clifton returns in *The Terrible Stories* (1996) to the complexities of her own mortal landscape. The mood of this volume is very different from that of *The Book of Light.* Lee Phenner aptly observes that the new book "embodies a world-weary ambivalence: clarity about right action obfuscated by the doubt that goodness can prevail. Charged with potent lyric verse, this collection examines the moral, spiritual and emotional conflicts experienced by a pure heart in a hostile land."[14] The book exudes a loneliness and a rawness of feeling connected

13. See Chapter 9, 188.

14. Lee Phenner, "clifton notes," review of *The Terrible Stories,* in *George Jr. Internet Monthly* (June 1997), http://www.georgejr.com/jun97/phenner.html (accessed 8 August 1999).

to Clifton's experience with breast cancer. This is especially true of the first two sections, "A Dream of Foxes" and "From the Cadaver," meditations on loneliness and physical decline that poignantly supplant the ebullient "homage to my hips" and "homage to my hair" of earlier years. The rest of the book, though it contains moments of humor, never fully rebounds from the somber mood established at the outset. "A Term in Memphis," which draws on Clifton's experience as a visiting professor at Memphis State University (now the University of Memphis), deals with race relations and the legacy of slavery in the contemporary South. Implicitly alluding to *Generations,* "In the Meantime" contains poems about Clifton's immediate family as well as her ancestors. The final section, "From the Book of David," returns to biblical themes—in this case, the life of King David, a character of great interest to Clifton. Phenner describes this last series as "a moving assemblage that upholds the theme Clifton proposes yet cannot wholeheartedly endorse: the triumph of a noble spirit over tribulation—particularly adversity thrust upon a peaceful soul."[15]

A poem titled "telling our stories" opens the volume. Setting the mood for the rest of the book, it establishes the presence of a fox that visits the poet's home night after night. Clifton fears the fox because it seems to be an emblem of her own life drama. The poem ends, "child, i tell you now it was not / the animal blood i was hiding from, / it was the poet in her, the poet and / the terrible stories she could tell" (*TS* 9). This brings to mind Ted Hughes's "The Thought Fox," in which the creature symbolizes a wellspring of poetic inspiration. But Clifton's fox represents a more malevolent force than Hughes's, a feral version of her poetic self. Given the poem's second stanza, "at dawn we would, each of us, / rise from our haunches, look through the glass / then walk away," it seems obvious the poet imagines that her life and the fox's are running a parallel course. But as this poem and the others in the section indicate, the fox also symbolizes a state of abject unfulfillment. Clifton herself explained it this way: "[F]or me the fox began to stand for desire, and to stand for desire coming looking for me and my not answering it."[16]

In "leaving fox," we see exactly what she means: "so many fuckless days and nights. / only the solitary fox / watching my window light / barks

15. Ibid.
16. Rowell, 60.

her compassion" (*TS* 16). Significant for being so rare, Clifton's use of pro-
fane language commands our attention. Here, the "fuckless days and
nights" graphically conjure up the poet's loneliness, her feelings of disaf-
fection and disconnection. The fox's rough cry is hardly consoling, so she
finally decides to make her home elsewhere. In that new place, she is re-
lieved to find that "so far / i am the only animal. / i will keep the door
unlocked / until something human comes." She has not yet resigned her-
self to the isolation that the fox symbolizes. Yet by identifying herself as
"the only animal" as she waits for "something human," she implies that
she has effectively taken over the fox's role. Like the fox that waited out-
side her old home, now the poet waits inside her new abode for meaning-
ful companionship. There is passivity here, but also a glimmer of hope
and faith in the future.

The last two poems in the sequence offer divergent endings to Clif-
ton's meditation on foxes. The first, "one year later," asks what would
have happened if the poet had "reared up baying, / and followed her off /
into vixen country?" (*TS* 17). These lines invite multiple interpretations.
The poet may be imagining herself finally telling the "terrible stories" that
have been building up inside her; she may be expressing curiosity about
unexplored terrain, sexual or otherwise; or the lines may even be a subli-
mated death wish. What is certain is that she is imagining a life for herself
beyond her familiar landscape: "what then of the moon, / the room, the
bed, the poetry / of regret?" Implicit in this last question is the belief that
the poet's home and her art somehow need her as much as she needs
them; the humanity of the familiar house and the elegiac poems depends
on a human presence—her own. To leave home and poems behind would
be a sort of domestic suicide, an act that by its nature seems to defy the
poet's understanding even as it piques her curiosity.

Much preferable is the alternative envisioned in "a dream of foxes,"
in which the word fox subtly takes on the colloquial connotation of an
attractive, sensual woman. The poem imagines an idealized world without
violence: "only a lovely line / of honest women stepping / without fear or
guilt or shame / safe through the generous fields." Women, like foxes, are
hunted, and they long for the safety and peace of a society that lets them
live their lives without constant fear of assault. In this poem, then, Clifton
shifts the terms of the conceit she has been using. She identifies with the
fox in a new way and allows the creature, in all of its beauty and vulnera-

bility, to identify with her in a new way, too. The fox and Lucille now freely define each other, their "terrible stories" yielding to the sweetest of dreams. Like "album" and "l. at creation," two idealistic poems in *Next,* "a dream of foxes" is a snapshot of a perfect world, a moment of grace that provides some solace during the bleakest of times.

In the nineteen new poems collected in *Blessing the Boats: New and Selected Poems, 1988–2000* (2000), Clifton mourns the cruelties that humans inflict on one another and worries about the violent legacy that children inherit from their elders. In "jasper texas 1998" she writes in the voice of James Byrd Jr., the black man deliberately dragged to his death: "why and why and why / should i call a white man brother? / who is the human in this place, / the thing that is dragged or the dragger? / what does my daughter say?" (*BB* 20). In the poem on the facing page, "alabama 9/15/63," she continues to ask plaintive, unanswerable questions, this time in relation to the bombing of the Birmingham church where four young black girls were killed. As if recalling jokes, she ironically poses questions beginning with "Have you heard the one about . . . ?" The poem quickly becomes metaphysical, as she asks, "Have you heard the one about / the four little birds / shattered into skylarks in the white / light of Birmingham?" (*BB* 21). Both "jasper texas 1998" and "alabama 9/15/63" are pointed indictments of the American society that permitted such atrocities to happen. Clifton is thus returning to the social concerns that filled *Good News about the Earth,* but her new poems are less hopeful, less idealistic, than those in the 1972 volume. The bombing of the Birmingham church was one in a disgracefully long line of atrocities committed in the name of virulent racism. The murder of James Byrd Jr. in 1998 reveals that African Americans are still at great risk in their own country.

The volume's opening poem, "the times," calls to mind *Good Times,* the title of Clifton's first book of poetry. Here, however, the modifier "good" is noticeably absent. This poem shows how entwined race and violence have become in the United States and in the poet's own mind: "another child has killed a child / and i catch myself relieved that they are / white and i might understand except / that i am tired of understanding" (*BB* 13). This admission is startling, the more so because it carries so much latent, ambiguous meaning. The news story in question—which the poem leaves unspecified—does not involve the sacrifice of another black life;

thus it cannot implicate black people in any way, and Clifton is spared the sorrow and humiliation she feels when confronted with news stories blaming crime on black people, even when they are the victims. The poet could perhaps understand the contorted thinking that leads to such stories; she could understand her own alarmingly essentialist thinking on the subject; she could even understand why a child killed another child. But her powers of empathy have weakened in the face of repeated assault. She is tired of the way the world so often tilts toward self-destruction. Having imagined a series of signs indicating the end of the world, she concludes with an image of sand grains spelling out a message on the street: "these too are your children this too is your child." The psychological pain she is in, the pain the whole country is in, does not totally negate the feelings of love and responsibility that make humans protect and care for their own.

There are also personal poems among the new works, and these, too, are aggrieved, sorrowful poems. She writes in "moonchild," for instance, of the humiliation she suffered as a child molested by her father, a topic also explored in earlier volumes, notably the "shapeshifter poems" in *Next* and "to my friend, jerina" in *Quilting* ("when i found there was no safety / in my father's house / i knew there was none anywhere" [Q 55]). What is different here is that "moonchild" leaves no doubt about the assault or the perpetrator. Clifton writes,

> we girls were ten years old and giggling
> in our hand-me-downs. we wanted breasts,
> pretended that we had them, tissued
> our undershirts. jay johnson is teaching
> me to french kiss, ella bragged, who
> is teaching you? how do you say; my father?
>
> (BB 15)

The playful innocence of the stanza's opening images makes the revelation at the end all the more horrifying. The violation, though Clifton has downplayed it in interviews, still causes pain. Having established herself as a "moonchild" born in late June, she concludes: "the moon is queen of everything. / she rules the oceans, rivers, rain. / when I am asked whose tears these are / I always blame the moon." The lines project Clifton's sorrows onto both the natural world and the mythological realm where the moon has special powers, notably over a woman's menstrual cycle. The poem's poignancy comes from the speaker's reluctance to talk about the long-ago violation and her lonely suffering. Her childhood shame lives on in her reticence and her unexplained tears.

Clifton writes about violation from a different perspective in the searingly honest "donor." The poem acknowledges that she tried to abort the daughter who would survive, grow up, and eventually donate a kidney to her. Here is the first stanza:

> when they tell me that my body
> might reject
> i think of thirty years ago
> and the hangers i shoved inside
> hard trying to not have you.
>
> (BB 17)

In the end, her daughter's enduring spirit shores up the poet's own: "again, again i feel you / buckled in despite me, lex, / fastened to life like the frown / on an angel's brow." The poem articulates the self-doubt, fear, and guilt that accompany a ferocious will to survive, both her own and her daughter's. Clifton herself takes the part of a frowning angel, displeased with her circumstances but determined to hold on to the life granted to her.

The new poems of *Blessing the Boats* provide a sort of cover letter for the other poems excerpted from previous volumes. Just as the four books collected in *Good Woman* have a wholeness to them, so do the four represented in *Blessing the Boats.* Together, *Next, Quilting, The Book of Light,* and *The Terrible Stories* chronicle Clifton's later life as a courageous African American woman with a heightened social conscience. Often lonely, angered by arrogance and injustice, and all too aware of her own mortality, she is nevertheless inexorably drawn to the infinite possibilities that life holds for each person, each generation.

The title poem of *Blessing the Boats,* which originally appeared in *Quilting,* is an ecumenical blessing bestowed on all people: "may you in your innocence / sail through this to that" (*BB* 82). In her new poems, however, as much as she may yearn for a safe passage for herself and others, a cold wind seems to have swept across her soul. The bleak new poems do not negate the complex yet ultimately affirming message of the preceding four books or, indeed, of her whole body of work, but they do complicate it and demand our careful attention. If Clifton is sounding a clarion call, if she is serving as a moral witness at the turn of the millennium, her longtime readers who have read her work through the years are in a unique position to take heed.

Prophet as well as poet, Clifton demands that we acknowledge the profound and palpable dangers of life on Earth, especially the dangers that children face. These dangers, in society and in our own families, must be named and examined before they can be vanquished. Though Clifton admits in "the times" that she is tired of empathizing, she knows that attempting to understand is still the best thing, the right thing, to do in a difficult situation. As the new poems in *Blessing the Boats* make clear, understanding the dangers of the world involves a probing of one's own secret corners of pain and despair. These feelings are as old as the world, and Clifton knows it. In "grief" (*BB* 30–31), she looks back on the Garden of Eden ("imagine / the original bleeding, / adam moaning / and the lamentation of the grass") and then hovers momentarily over her own life ("pause for the girl / with twelve fingers /who never learned to cry enough / for anything that mattered") before calling her readers home to the broken paradise that she has loved for so long:

> then end in the garden of regret
> with time's bell tolling grief
> and pain,
> grief for the grass
> that is older than adam,
> grief for what is human,
> grief for what is not.
>
> (*BB* 31)

CHAPTER 3

Song of Herself

TO READ ONE OF LUCILLE CLIFTON'S poems is to experience an epiphany, a swift flowering of personal observation into social insight. To read all of them is to apprehend a far-reaching, essentially hopeful vision of humanity. Clifton has dedicated her work and her life to "the celebration of the spirit and flesh of what is a whole human."[1] Starting with *Good Times,* her free-verse lyrics consistently speak to the spirit and the flesh, not only because she writes mainly about human connections and relationships, but also because a Clifton poem has the effervescence of unbidden thought. If, as Helen Vendler has argued, "the purpose of lyric, as a genre, is to represent an inner life in such a manner that it is assumable by others,"[2] then Clifton is a definitive lyric poet, for that purpose is repeatedly fulfilled in her verse. Her mastery of the lyric recalls the stylistic pleasures of imagism and the visceral emotion of confessional poetry. Like William Carlos Williams, Ezra Pound, H.D., and Wallace Stevens, she is capable of the stunning miniature. She shares Williams's interest in vernacular speech and Stevens's penchant for word play. But whereas the imagists went on to longer, more complicated verse forms to accommodate their increasingly meditative verse, Clifton did not; even her sequence poems are made up of brief lyrics. "I am interested in trying to render big ideas in a simple way," she maintains.[3] Her goal is in keeping with the "complex simplicity" that Richard Wright believed best conveyed the realities of African American life.[4]

Much of Clifton's complex simplicity stems from her use of a thor-

1. Lucille Clifton, quoted in *Confirmation: An Anthology of African American Women,* ed. Amiri Baraka and Amina Baraka (New York: Quill, 1983), 403.

2. Helen Vendler, *The Given and the Made: Strategies of Poetic Redefinition* (Cambridge: Harvard University Press, 1995), xi.

3. Lucille Clifton, "A Simple Language," in *Black Women Writers (1950–1980): A Critical Evaluation,* ed. Mari Evans (Garden City, N.Y.: Anchor Books, 1984), 137.

4. Richard Wright, "Blueprint for Negro Writing," in Napier, *African American Literary Theory,* 50.

oughly developed female persona. Throughout her career as a poet, the nature of womanhood has been her consuming subject. Some poems emphasize her identity as a woman; others, her identity as a black woman; still others, her individual identity as Lucille Sayles Clifton. The changing emphasis helps create the social context integral to Clifton's work and suggests that, even though there are distinct points to be made about different dimensions of one's identity, those dimensions do not have fixed boundaries. That is, poems about womanhood can overlap with those about being black, and those that appear quite personal inevitably address the poet's race and gender. These poems do not ask us to extrapolate or to generalize but rather to see identity as a work in progress that resists easy categorization. By turns joyfully resilient and perilously vulnerable, Clifton writes about both the strengths and frailties of the female body and bravely chronicles every hill and shadow in the landscape of her spirit.

Her poems often challenge pervasive societal attitudes that cast women, especially black women, in the role of victim, adversary, or nonentity. As far as she is concerned, being female is hardly cause for self-castigation or self-pity. A look at one of her frequently anthologized poems is instructive here: In "there is a girl inside," the focus is on an older woman's abundant vitality: "she is a green tree / in a forest of kindling"—that is, the only one in the crowd who still has life in her (*GW* 170). If we read the poem autobiographically, then Clifton's third-person description of herself as "a green girl / in a used poet" is a witty play on racial identity as well as a proclamation of her own youthful spirit. But even if there *is* a girl inside Clifton, the poem is not solely about her, as the expansive imagery makes clear. This woman's body may look old, but like "a nun," she is waiting for the sexually suggestive "second coming, / when she can break through gray hairs / into blossom." Effectively combining images of nature, sex, and spiritual renewal, the poem concludes with an orgy of all the senses: "and her lovers will harvest / honey and thyme / and the woods will be wild / with the damn wonder of it." More than one lover is anticipated for this energetic woman, and the word "damn" suggests a gleeful abandonment of her chaste, nunlike existence. The harvest is also significant: sweet, sensual honey stays fresh for a very long time. There is a parallel, then, with the sweet, sensuous woman, who only needs time (or "thyme") to share herself with others. Given the opportunity, she will inspire delight and gratification in those around her and, indeed, her whole environment. The poem thus proposes that women, no matter what their age, are a wondrous resource waiting to be tapped both creatively and sexually.

Her poems consistently argue for the special properties of the female spirit and body, and that places Clifton in the long tradition of poets mythologizing womanhood. Hers is a uniquely female vision, however; the romanticism that infuses her poetry has a feminist twist. In the spirit of "there is a girl inside," for instance, "female" and "nude photograph" put womanhood front and center. The seven-line "female" in *Next* (1987) begins, "there is an amazon in us. / she is the secret we do not / have to learn" (*N* 33), thereby implying that women, especially black women, possess an internal fortitude of mythic proportions. Rather than suggesting a pathologically divided female self (as Anne Sexton does in "Her Kind"), Clifton creates the illusion of objectivity in order to develop her notion of a multilayered, inherently female identity. If, as Wordsworth claims, "The Child is father of the Man,"[5] then Clifton would have it that the "girl inside" every woman is not only sexy but amazingly strong. Wordsworth may have yearned for the innocent, seemingly pure vision of youth, but Clifton implies that real insight comes from a mature recognition of one's role at the vanguard of history.

While "female" mythologizes and romanticizes the spirit, "nude photograph" accomplishes the same for the female body. Here, Clifton relishes "the woman's / soft and vulnerable body, / every where on her turning / round into another / where" (*Q* 31). Like Wallace Stevens's "Study of Two Pears," this poem both represents and provides an alternative to the physical object being described. It is hard to say whether Stevens's "Study" depicts a painting of pears, an idea about pears, or the pears themselves; nor can we be sure whether Clifton's "nude photograph" describes a photographic image, an imagined rendering of the female body, or a real woman's body, perhaps the speaker's own. But whereas Stevens, bemused by his own paradox, pulls back from his material and views it abstractly, Clifton moves closer, finally identifying with the body she describes:

5. William Wordsworth, "Ode: Intimations of Immortality," in *English Romantic Writers*, ed. David Perkins (New York: Harcourt Brace Jovanovich, 1967), 280.

who could rest one hand here or here
and not feel, whatever the shape
of the great hump longed for
in the night, a certain joy, a certain,
yes, satisfaction, yes.

(Q 31)

Her rhetorical question swiftly becomes a rhythmic, even orgasmic, af-
firmation of female beauty and potency. This climax effectively removes
the distance between observer and object that Stevens takes such pains to
preserve. Clifton's imagery is much less specific than Stevens's, yet "nude
photograph" definitely has an erotic momentum. That momentum comes
partly from the suggestive-sounding off-rhymes ("where" and "here") and
partly from an absence of detail that requires one to imagine the woman's
body as one wants it—or, as Stevens would say, as one wills it—to be.

The evocative "nude photograph" is one of an impressive concentra-
tion of poems concerning the female body in Clifton's sixth book, *Quilting*.
Elsewhere in the volume, "poem in praise of menstruation," "poem to my
uterus," "to my last period," and "wishes for sons"—which will be dis-
cussed in Chapter 4—take on the still-delicate topics of menstruation and
female fertility in ways that are by turns joyous, poignant, sorrowful, and
comical. Clifton does not yield to the ambiguous signals American society
sends women about their bodies. For her, the female body's ability to re-
produce deserves reverence, while its loss of that ability due to disease or
aging is to be mourned. Even so, she stresses that there is much more life
awaiting the woman who outlives her ability to bear children, and the loss
of reproductive powers may be accompanied by a new understanding of
one's self.

Also in *Quilting*, we find "water sign woman" and "moonchild,"[6]
seemingly personal poems (alluding to Clifton's birth sign, Cancer) that
nevertheless speak to the experience of many women. In "water sign
woman," "the woman who feels everything" is set against an amorphous
group that dismisses her yearnings: "they say to the feel things woman /
that little she dreams is possible, that there is only so much / joy to go

---

6. This is the first time Clifton uses the title "moonchild." The second instance occurs
in *Blessing the Boats*.

around, only so much / water" (Q 50). But the woman rejects these im-
posed limits, preferring instead to believe that "water will come again / if
you can wait for it." In the context of the poem, the title takes on new
meaning: The "water sign woman" is waiting for a sign of water—that
is, of renewed possibility in her life, and she prefers to believe that her
watchfulness and her patience will eventually pay off. The long-suffering
woman in "moonchild" is likewise hopeful about the future. For her, the
moon is a "small light" assuring her that she will "rise again and rise again
to dance" (Q 68). The repetition of "rise again" is itself evidence of rejuve-
nation and continuity.

In Clifton's poetry, a woman's physical activity is often a metaphor
for taking hold of life instead of passively yielding to all the troubles in
the world. This metaphor appears in the first poem in *The Book of Light,*
"climbing," which seems to take up where "water sign woman" and
"moonchild" leave off. No longer waiting for a sign or promising herself
that things will get better, the female persona now seems much more ac-
tively engaged in her own life, but she is nevertheless plagued by self-
doubt. Perhaps alluding to Langston Hughes's "Mother to Son," which
also employs the metaphor of climbing, "climbing" begins,

> a woman precedes me up the long rope,
> her dangling braids the color of rain.
> maybe i should have had braids.
> maybe i should have kept the body i started,
> slim and possible as a boy's bone.
> maybe i should have wanted less.
>
>   (BL 11)

We don't know the identity of the woman on the rope; she could be a
friend, an ancestor, or an emblem of a life that the poet chose not to lead.
Calvin Bedient has called this figure a "mysterious, barely specified other
Clifton, the elementally ageless one (part child, part cyclically renewable
rain) who nonetheless precedes the poet up the rope of her life."[7] Just as
important as the other woman's identity, however, is the narrator's anx-
ious, self-referential response to her. The poet's doubts concentrate on her

7. Calvin Bedient, "Short Reviews," *Poetry* 163, no. 6 (March 1994): 345.

body and the life she might have led if she hadn't had sex or children. But thoughts of what might have been only remind her of the life that was and is her own:

> maybe i should have ignored the bowl in me
> burning to be filled.
> maybe i should have wanted less.
> the woman passes the notch in the rope
> marked Sixty. i rise toward it, struggling,
> hand over hungry hand.
>
> (*BL* 11)

A questing soul, the poet knows she cannot dwell in limbo forever. Although she is not rising to dance as she had imagined she would in "moon-child," at least she is rising and climbing, and, in her climb, there is the same burning desire for fulfillment that motivated her earlier decisions in life. The figure ahead of her on the rope is an archetypal role model, a woman growing old but not giving up. If the woman with braids can climb bravely and stubbornly into old age and the unknown, so can the poet; so can all women who share her profound hunger for life.

When race enters into Clifton's poems about womanhood, they take on additional complexity. In her own words: "I've always enjoyed being female and not felt myself put upon because of it. If I were put upon, I always believed it was for race."[8] In keeping with this sentiment, some of her poems about black women define themselves in sharp opposition to white people, especially white men. In "if i stand in my window," for instance, a black woman refuses to yield to the expectations of a white male establishment. This poem in *Good Times* begins with the woman literally and figuratively taking a stand:

> if i stand in my window
> naked in my own house
> and press my breasts
> against my windowpane
> like black birds pushing against glass

8. Jordan, 48.

because i am somebody
in a New Thing

        (GW 25)

In its subject matter and conditional syntax, this poem resembles William Carlos Williams's "Danse Russe," in which a man delights in his nude body while his family sleeps. But unlike Williams's insouciant persona, who asks rhetorically, "Who shall say I am not / the happy genius of my household?"[9] Clifton's persona seems braced for a real battle. The unnerving, racialized image of the "black birds," combined with the woman's nudity, ironically plays off the stereotype of the black woman as a sexual primitive who simultaneously threatens and titillates. In this poem, the woman is chafing against social and cultural confines even as she holds her ground.

The poem argues that black people deserve to be, and in fact are, part of the so-called mainstream: people working, buying property, and rearing children in the United States. In the second stanza, the poet imagines "the man" who would object to her, "saying i have offended him / i have offended his / Gods." One suspects that these "Gods"—which Clifton pointedly capitalizes and pluralizes—have more to do with power and money than with spirituality. In any case, they will not frighten off the "New Thing" whose singular (and defiantly capitalized) self presides over the poem. It is the white man who is in for a shock:

let him watch my black body
push against my own glass
let him discover self
let him run naked through the streets
crying
praying in tongues

        (GW 25)

The poem rails against the disenfranchisement of black women and effectively turns the tables on the white men whose self-image partly depends on the oppression of others.

9. *The Collected Poems of William Carlos Williams*, vol. 1, *1909–1939*, ed. Walton Litz and Christopher MacGowan (New York: New Directions, 1986), 86.

Here, the black woman embodies self-determinacy and self-posses-
sion. In imagining her enemy, the white man, undergoing an identity cri-
sis of biblical proportions, she transforms herself into an apocalyptic vi-
sion. During the socially turbulent 1960s, a vision of a distinctly black,
female self really was a whole New Thing, not just in a colloquial sense
but also in a political one. The black woman angrily demanding her rights
represented a tangible new social force, which had to be accepted because
its constituency would no longer be locked out, beaten down, or ignored.

Race contributes to the meaning of many of Clifton's other poems
about womanhood. This is true of "the lost baby poem," in *Good News
about the Earth,* which is addressed to a baby lost through abortion. The
poem is elegiac, but it concerns the female speaker's ability to be responsi-
ble to her living children as much as it does the loss of the aborted child.
Clifton has said that this poem "would not have been possible" without
Gwendolyn Brooks's "the mother," an abortion poem that Brooks pub-
lished in her 1945 collection, *A Street in Bronzeville.*[10] Like Clifton's later
poem, "the mother" takes the form of an apology spoken by the mother
to the aborted. Brooks's title ironically names the woman who chose not
to carry her children to term, while the text reveals the woman's un-
quenched maternal longing for her lost children: "I have heard in the
voices of the wind the voices of my dim killed children. / I have con-
tracted. I have eased / My dim dears at the breasts they could never
suck."[11] This mother does not explain what led her to have her abortions;
she says only, "Believe that even in my deliberateness I was not deliber-
ate." In the next several lines, however, she qualifies this vague defense:

> Though why should I whine,
> Whine that the crime was other than mine?—
> Since anyhow you are dead.
> Or rather, or instead,
> You were never made.

This, too, requires correction: "But that, too, I am afraid, / Is faulty: oh,
what shall I say, how is the truth to be said?" The poem concludes with a

---

10. Conversation with the author, 24 June 2000.

11. Gwendolyn Brooks, "the mother," in *Selected Poems* (New York: HarperPerennial,
1999), 4–5.

pathetic proclamation: "Believe me, I knew you, though faintly, and I loved, I loved you / All."

By contrast, Clifton's narrator in "the lost baby poem" explains why she chose not to have the aborted child. She admits that her family was very poor at the time of the pregnancy and her only alternative to abortion would have been giving up the baby for adoption: "we would have made the thin / walk over genesee hill into the canada wind / to watch you slip like ice into strangers' hands" (GW 60). If there is regret in this poem, it is regret tinged by a weary recognition that the child, had it lived, would have had a difficult start in life: "you would have been born into winter / in the year of the disconnected gas / and no car," the mother says, adding that "you would have fallen naked as snow into winter." In the conclusion, she vows that

> if i am ever less than a mountain
> for your definite brothers and sisters
> let the rivers pour over my head
> let the sea take me for a spiller
> of seas   let black men call me stranger
> always   for your never named sake
>
> (GW 60)

As Erica Jong pointed out in a 1972 review, citing "the lost baby poem" in particular, "The spaces in [Clifton's] poems are not just typographical blanks."[12] The gaps in this poem's closing lines function as a small memorial to the aborted child, who contributes just as much to the narrator's identity as her living children do. As an intractable mountain of strength, moreover, the mother in this poem feels a special obligation to black men, the poem's one indication of her own race—an indication notably absent from Brooks's "the mother." To fail her children in any way, Clifton's poem implies, would be to fail as a black woman, a partner in the shaping of the race. In her desire to fulfill her maternal and racial duties, she threatens herself with Old Testament–style punishments worthy of a terrible sinner. For those who fail in their moral and social duties to others,

12. Erica Jong, "Three Sisters," review of Good News about the Earth, in Parnassus: Poetry in Review 1, no. 1 (1972): 85.

Clifton insists, apocalypse is imminent. In contrast to the not entirely sympathetic speaker in "the mother," Clifton's mournful persona invites our admiration. She seems intent on learning from her past and making things right. Her apology becomes the basis for a strong resolve.

The emotional complexity of "the lost baby poem" gives way to Clifton's plain good cheer in other poems about black womanhood. For her, a healthy black woman's body represents strength, joy, and liberation. We see this in the exuberant "homage to my hair" and "homage to my hips," both published in *Two-Headed Woman*. Although "homage to my hips" does not refer to race directly, the hips in question evidently belong to a black woman: "these hips have never been enslaved, / they go where they want to go / they do what they want to do" (*GW* 168). The poem recognizes not only exuberance but also sexual allure: "these hips are magic hips. / i have known them / to put a spell on a man and / spin him like a top!" In "homage to my hair," the hair takes on a (female) life of its own: "when i feel her jump up and dance / i hear the music! my God / i'm talking about my nappy hair!" (*GW* 167). As the rest of the poem reveals, the black woman's hair is feisty, sexy, and inspirational. Joyce Johnson points out that the poem's verbs "capture the character and vitality of nappy hair; together with the word 'music,' they present images we readily associate with celebration, and thus, operate on two levels, as description and exultation."[13] The witty ending underscores the black woman's identification with her hair: "she can touch your mind / with her electric fingers and / the grayer she do get, good God, / the blacker she do be!" As in "there is a girl inside," this poem applauds the aging woman, but here the focus is on black women as proud representatives of both their race and gender. Using the exclamatory style of a gospel song, Clifton infuses wit into a poem of self-affirmation.

Nowhere is this more clear than in "what the mirror said," which immediately follows the two "homage" poems and precedes "there is a girl inside" in *Two-Headed Woman*. Clifton said that she wrote the poem after visiting Harvard University and noticing how different in appearance and age she was from all of the slender young women walking around Harvard Square.[14] The poem comically alludes to the talking mirror in "Snow

13. Johnson, 174.
14. *The Writing Life: Roland Flint Hosts Lucille Clifton*, VHS (Columbia, Md.: Howard County Poetry and Literature Society, 1991).

White," a fairy tale notably preoccupied with female beauty and skin color. Clifton's mirror, speaking in the black vernacular, affirms the black woman's pride in her body: "listen, / you a wonder. / you a city / of a woman" (*GW* 169). The poem goes on to detail the woman's complexity ("somebody need a map / to understand you") and to reassure her of her value ("you not a noplace / anonymous / girl"). Like the poems about hips and hair, this one marvels over the black woman's sexual power:

> mister with his hands on you
> he got his hands on
> some
> damn
> body!
>
> (*GW* 169)

The word "damn" adds zesty emphasis and turns a worthy "somebody" into a sexy body. The repeated references to black men in these lively poems typify Clifton's affectionate attitude toward the men of her race.

The black woman's resilience is the theme of "won't you celebrate with me," which appears in *The Book of Light,* thirteen years after the praise poems of *Two-Headed Woman.* But this one finds Clifton in a much more serious state of mind. Her speaker asserts that she "had no model" for her life: "born in babylon / both nonwhite and woman / what did i see to be except myself?" (*BL* 25). The woman seems to represent many generations; she is like the "wise elder" archetype that Eugenia Collier identifies in Sterling Brown's poetry, "whose heroism lies not in one magnificent gesture but in the lifelong struggle to Be, the struggle to maintain life and dignity and wholeness of self through the most arduous day-to-day effort, despite terrible losses."[15] Clifton's speaker is certain that her survival is a profound achievement. Rather than being a self-made woman, she views herself as a woman-made self:

> i made it up
> here on this bridge between

15. Eugenia Collier, "Message to the Generations: The Mythic Hero in Sterling Brown's Poetry," in *The Furious Flowering of African American Poetry,* ed. Joanne V. Gabbin (Charlottesville: University Press of Virginia, 1999), 28.

starshine and clay,
my one hand holding tight
my other hand; come celebrate
with me that everyday
something has tried to kill me
and has failed.

(*BL* 25)

Even as it recognizes the beauty and value of a hard-fought life, the poem strikes a plaintive note. The woman who must hold her own hand is surely lonely, in need of companionship. In Clifton's poems, self-reliance never sounds like much fun. Just as the narrator of "climbing" clings to the image of the woman with braids preceding her up the rope, the would-be hostess in "won't you celebrate with me" clings to the possibility of a party—a glad gathering of like-minded souls—and yet it seems that she is speaking into a vacuum, not really expecting the reassurance of a reply. Her ability to survive has put her at a remove from others; she is enviably strong but unenviably alone.

Clifton herself recognized the problem here. Bridging the divide between the lone woman and her desired companions, she began using "come celebrate with me" as a unifying poem during her poetry readings. In her recitation, from memory, she would change the poem's first-person pronouns in the concluding lines from singular to plural; "come celebrate with me" thus spoke for collective survival and involved her audience in the poignant celebration that the poem imagines.

Clifton's poems about womanhood are sometimes startling in their ambivalence. Consider, for example, the Kali poems in *An Ordinary Woman*. In these poems, Clifton draws on a Hindu vision of a powerful black woman, the Great Mother, who embodies destruction as well as creation. Her name meaning "Black One," Kali is typically portrayed in Western accounts as a terrifying, evil presence. The following depiction is representative:

[Kali] is the mother goddess in destructive aspect, devouring the life she has produced. The power of Kali abides in every woman. She is usually depicted with four arms. As life-giving mother, she is depicted with a golden ladle in her right hand, the bowl of abundant food in her left. . . . In her dual aspect she holds the symbols both of death and immortality:

the noose to strangle her victims, the iron hook to drag them in, the rosary, and the prayer book. She is sometimes pictured as a horrible, hungry hag who feeds upon the entrails of her victims.

In some Tantra texts she stands in a boat floating on an ocean of blood, drinking from a skull the lifeblood of the children she brings forth and eats back. In another Tantric depiction Kali is shown black as death with a necklace of heads; in her two right hands she holds the sword and the scissors of physical death; in her two left hands, the food-full bowl and the lotus of generation. She is strangely beloved in India as the life-giving, life-taking Mother.[16]

For Clifton, Kali's allure is not so strange. Reflecting Clifton's growing interest in feminist spirituality, Kali is portrayed in her poems as a natural female force, "only one aspect of the many-named, multiform Goddess," as Barbara Walker writes. "She was a truer image of the real world's variety and cyclic alternation than any of the images developed by patriarchy alone."[17] Describing Kali as "the permanent guest / within ourselves" and "dread mother" ("Kali," *GW* 128), Clifton expands the portrait over the course of a series of Kali poems in *An Ordinary Woman.* In "the coming of Kali," we see the terrifying black goddess as an inescapable dimension of the black female self: "i am one side of your skin, / she sings, softness is the other" (*GW* 135). Kali's "black terrible self" contrasts strikingly with the positive portrayals of black womanhood elsewhere in Clifton's body of work, yet the Kali poems are not about self-loathing or internalized racism or misogyny, nor do they contradict the composite portrait of the "ordinary woman" that emerges in this volume.

Instead, Kali extends Clifton's portrait of womanhood—specifically, black womanhood. Her fixation on the black goddess who alternately gives life and takes it away suggests that mothers are far from being one-dimensional, pure, and selfless beings. Kali is an emblem of self-involvement; rather than giving herself over to her children, she remains at the center of her own drama, drawing attention to herself rather than vanishing into her children's lives and identities. On a related note, Adrienne Rich writes in *Of Woman Born:*

16. *Funk and Wagnalls Standard Dictionary of Folklore, Mythology and Legend* (New York: Funk and Wagnalls, 1950), s.v. "Kali."

17. Barbara G. Walker, *The Crone: Woman of Age, Wisdom, and Power* (New York: Harper and Row, 1985), 72.

The "maternal" or "nurturant" spirit we want to oppose to rapism and the warrior mentality can prove a liability so long as it remains a lever by which women can be controlled through what is most generous and sensitive in us. Theories of female power and female ascendancy must reckon fully with the ambiguities of our being, and with the continuum of our consciousness, the potentialities for both creative and destructive energy in each of us.[18]

Both Rich and Clifton are interested in the full range of female experience—not just the positive, the good, and the obvious, but also the negative, the destructive, and the obscure. Their candor accommodates the complexity of actual feelings and experiences.

The very duality of Kali's powers of creativity and destruction explains why she is "strangely beloved" in India and why Clifton regards her with both awe and affection. The goddess makes tangible what many men fear in women and what many women fear in themselves—that is, an uncanny strength that may not always be marshaled for the good of others. In Clifton's poems, Kali becomes a metaphor for the needs and passions that women cannot easily explain or resolve, but she is also a projection of negative emotions—dissatisfaction, rage, and fury—that are all bound up in the culturally and biologically complicated role of the mother.

Throughout her body of work, Clifton argues that one must acknowledge the bad and destructive in one's self along with the good. Putting a separate face on those uncomfortable, "bad" feelings may make the acknowledgment a little easier. In "calming Kali," she begins,

> be quiet awful woman,
> lonely as hell,
> and i will comfort you
> when i can
> and give you my bones
> and my blood to feed on.
>   (GW 140)

The speaker may try to hush her feelings of loneliness as if they were quarrelsome children, but she knows that she will have to deal with her all-

18. Adrienne Rich, *Of Woman Born: Motherhood as Experience and Institution* (New York: Bantam, 1977), 290.

consuming emotions eventually. Kali is the neglected black female self who craves nurturing and maternal attention of her own. The speaker seems to think that nurturing herself, the Kali within, would amount to a self-sacrifice when it may be a matter of self-preservation. In the concluding line, "i know i am your sister," the speaker stops short of complete identification with Kali, but she does admit to a kinship that reinforces the theme of black sisterhood in *An Ordinary Woman*.

In "she is dreaming," also part of the Kali series, Clifton writes that

> sometimes
> the whole world of women
> seems a landscape of
> red blood and things
> that need healing,
> the fears all
> fears of the flesh; . . .
>
> (GW 138)

The lines conjure up images of menstruation, procreation, childbirth, and physical and emotional pain. The speaker sees female experience as all too frequently a matter of life and death, the blood symbolizing both a woman's life force and her profound vulnerability. The "flesh" that the poem speaks of becomes the emblem of womanhood, and that flesh is prey to its own ills as well as those that men impose on it:

> will it open
> or close
> will it scar or
> keep bleeding
> will it live
> will it live
> will it live and
> will he murder it or
> marry it.
>
> (GW 138)

Not too far removed from the chilling cynicism in Sylvia Plath's "The Applicant," this poem laments female suffering at the same time that it attempts to achieve distance from it. The female self is reduced to an imper-sonal, gender-neutral flesh—an "it"—that may or may not survive an injury, a rupture, a relationship gone sour. Though Kali is not mentioned by name, and we don't know whose dream is being recalled, this poem is of a piece with the other Kali poems. The physical and psychological dra-mas of survival, embodied in the figure of Kali, are as inescapable as they are routine.

While the poems discussed thus far may reflect Clifton's own experiences, they are not especially personal. Beginning with *An Ordinary Woman*, how-ever, Clifton has frequently published poems that are clearly autobio-graphical. These poems are about womanhood and more particularly about black womanhood, but they are also about being a black woman, born in 1936, known variously as Lucille, Lucy, Thelma Lucille, and Lu-cille Clifton. Clifton has often mined the derivation of "Lucille" from *light* for symbolic significance—for example, in "the light that came to lucille clifton" (both a poem and a section title in *Two-Headed Woman*) and her 1993 volume, *The Book of Light*, which opens with a poem titled "LIGHT." Clifton makes frequent use of her own name and includes unmistakable autobiographical details in numerous other poems. Sometimes she in-vokes her appearance: her large size, her one good eye, and the two extra fingers removed in her infancy. The defining characteristics of her body are integral to her self-exploratory verse.

We see this demonstrated in the humorous "lucy one-eye," where Clifton describes herself as a "big round roller" who sees "the world side-ways" (*GW* 145). The catalog of her idiosyncrasies ends with her assuring us, and herself, that "she'll keep on trying / with her crooked look / and her wrinkled ways, / the darling girl." Regarding the poem's surprising, cheerfully self-affirming last line, Clifton says that her editor at Random House, Toni Morrison, urged her to cut this line. She decided to keep it, however, because she liked it and was convinced that Morrison, for all of her literary expertise, didn't grasp poetry as well as she did prose.[19] No matter her age, Clifton is determined to remember and honor the "darling girl"—the "girl inside"—because that is a crucial part of her still-evolving identity.

19. *The Writing Life: Roland Flint Hosts Lucille Clifton.*

Any time the familial bond feels tenuous, however, Clifton grows uneasy, as in "speaking of loss." In this poem, she says, "i began with everything; / parents, two extra fingers / a brother to ruin" (*GW* 174). But now, bereft of those family members and "wearing a name i never heard / until i was a woman," she feels uncertain of her identity: "my extra fingers are cut away. / i am left with plain hands and / nothing to give you but poems." Though downplayed here, the poems Clifton writes are a consolation of enormous importance to her, because they help determine her identity and her relations to others. As a body of work, her poems will memorialize her corporeal self as well as her spirit.

Appearing in *An Ordinary Woman*, which was published the year that Clifton turned thirty-eight, "the thirty eighth year" explores the poet's identity as she heads into middle age. Perhaps indebted to Sonia Sanchez's "poem at thirty," a briefer, but similarly meditative self-reckoning, this poem illustrates all three themes discussed here. It is a definitive poem of womanhood, black female identity, and Clifton's own experience:

> the thirty eighth year
> of my life,
> plain as bread
> round as a cake
> an ordinary woman.
>
> an ordinary woman.
>
> i had expected to be
> smaller than this,
> more beautiful,
> wiser in afrikan ways,
> more confident,
> i had expected
> more than this.
>
> (*GW* 158)

In the opening stanza, Clifton asserts her gender but not her race. The fragments seem like private, even random thoughts, but the imagery deftly sketches a woman in her kitchen, the "ordinary" woman's domain. The opening imagery is homely but pleasant, since bread is life-sustaining and cakes are sweet. In the second stanza, the surprise and humor of the

admission "i had expected to be / smaller than this" come from the im-
probable syntax, but the rest of the carefully constructed litany implies
that this black woman is not without beauty or confidence, nor is she to-
tally lacking in knowledge of Africa. There is no reason, furthermore, why
she can't continue to grow emotionally and learn more about the home
of her ancestors.

The rest of "the thirty eighth year" continues to weigh hope against
disappointment, strength against vulnerability. Remembering her "very
wise / and beautiful / and sad" mother, who died young, Clifton feels the
winds of mortality swirling around her as she approaches forty. She can-
not help wondering whether her own life will end abruptly, in early mid-
dle age, as her mother's did. Midway through the poem, Clifton directly
addresses her deceased mother, an indelible presence in her poetry, and
then invokes the family's new generation of women: "i have taken bones
you hardened / and built daughters / and they blossom and promise fruit /
like afrikan trees" (GW 159). Having opted for motherhood, Clifton has
taken a typical path but one nonetheless filled with the wonderment of
blossoming daughters, the fruits of a new generation. Clifton's own
mother lives on in the daughter's memory and in the granddaughters'
genes. Interestingly, Clifton says that she has "built" her daughters,
thereby implying that she has consciously constructed them just as her
body, through its biological imperative, brought them into being. The
work of "building" daughters is not done in nine months; it is the work
of a lifetime.

The penultimate stanza is a prayer in which Clifton yearns for a dis-
tinct, comfortable identity of her own as she approaches "the final turn"
of her life, one that she hopes will lead her "out of my mother's life / into
my own. / into my own." Her daughters are not the only ones blossoming:
Clifton herself is still growing and preparing for the future, whatever that
future may hold. The poem finally emerges as a meditation on inner
strength rather than on shortcomings. By the time we read the words "an
ordinary woman" for the fourth time in the poem's conclusion, even this
seemingly bland expression has taken on a luminous resolve. "The strong
sense of general disappointment coupled with the sinking suspicion that
one's life has missed the mark strikes responsive chords in many readers,"
Wallace R. Peppers writes. "And worse still, from the speaker's point of
view, is the growing realization that this enormously unsatisfying condi-

tion is probably permanent."[20] The persistent repetition of "an ordinary woman," however, calls to mind its opposite as well as its literal meaning. The "ordinary" woman is on a profound journey, after all. Aware of her compounded identity as daughter and mother, as a black woman, and as an autonomous, ambitious self, the "ordinary" woman can truly come into her own, as the last lines suggest. The poem is not so much one of hopes dashed or dreams deferred as it is one of hopes tempered and dreams revised.

Clifton's late poems about womanhood are no less arresting than those she wrote during the prime of her life. Even in the wrenching lyrics about the illnesses she has suffered as an aging woman, such as "lumpectomy eve," she does not let her fears get the best of her:

all night i dream of lips
that nursed and nursed
and the lonely nipple

lost in loss and the need
to feed that turns at last
on itself   that will kill

its body for its hunger's sake
all night i hear the whispering
the soft

   love calls you to this knife
   for love   for love

all night it is the one breast
comforting the other

(TS 22)

Merely articulating her fear and sorrow is a victory of sorts; she will not be silenced by her illness or the pending surgery, nor will she pretend that her suffering is less painful than it is.[21] This late, difficult stage in her life

20. Wallace R. Peppers, "Lucille Clifton," in *Afro-American Poets since 1955*, ed. Trudier Harris and Thadious M. Davis, vol. 41 of *Dictionary of Literary Biography* (Detroit: Gale, 1985), 58.

21. The poet Audre Lorde, Clifton's contemporary, wrote about her experience with breast cancer in a prose work, *The Cancer Journals* (San Francisco: Aunt Lute Books, 1980).

will also be part of her career-long cycle of poems about womanhood. In the end, "lumpectomy eve" is a love poem for the speaker herself as well as an elegy for the lonely, love-starved, synecdochical breast. Characteristically for Clifton, this poem is itself comforted by other poems about her breast cancer in *The Terrible Stories*. After the lumpectomy comes the inevitable "scar," in which the speaker addresses the new "ribbon of hunger" on her body (*TS* 25). She begins, "we will learn / to live together," and the scar, in answer to a question that the woman puts to it, replies that it will call her "woman i ride / who cannot throw me / and i will not fall off." Though her body is inscribed with the vicissitudes of age and illness, the poet is still going forward, still coming into her own, long after her thirty-eighth year.

For Clifton, womanhood is a powerful, even awe-inspiring, foundation for the individual self. Her images of the female body are infused with tenderness and affection; her images of the female spirit radiate strength and humor. Although her poems admit to feelings of sorrow, vulnerability, and self-doubt, these emotions do not hold sway. Her own life provides the impetus for most of her poems, but like Whitman, she creates a wide-ranging, multitudinous self. As in "Song of Myself," a composite identity gradually emerges from Clifton's body of poetry, one that both absorbs and reflects the surrounding world. There are many women in her poems, but they all contribute to the black, female self that is Clifton, just as her clearly autobiographical poems contribute to our imagining of womanhood and black women. Her poems invite widespread identification across race and gender lines, though they are determinedly about women, especially black women, often Clifton herself. They fulfill what her friend Adrienne Rich hopes for in *Of Woman Born:* "We need to imagine a world in which every woman is the presiding genius of her own body. In such a world women will truly create new life, bringing forth not only children (if and as we choose) but the visions, and the thinking, necessary to sustain, console, and alter human existence—a new relationship to the universe."[22]

22. Rich, *Of Woman Born*, 292.

CHAPTER 4

Plath, Clifton, and the Myths of Menstruation

THE WOMAN WHO MENSTRUATES receives a monthly message from her body. Written in blood, the menstrual message is rich in meaning and metaphorical possibility. Although the authors of *The Curse: A Cultural History of Menstruation* may be overstating the case when they say, "Men cannot enter or even entertain the language of menstruation, with its fluidic periodicity, its mood-signaling, its cyclical reminder of the feminine real,"[1] menstruation does provide a natural subject for women's poetry. The twentieth-century American women who have taken up the challenge include Sylvia Plath, May Sarton, Anne Sexton, Marge Piercy, Ellen Bass, Ai, Sharon Olds, and Lucille Clifton.

Some of these women's poems concern fertility and childbirth; others take up the stigmas and taboos associated with menstruation; in still others the monthly blood is a source of pride and wonder. The moods run the gamut from joy to despair, and scanning even a partial list of titles reveals a wide-ranging response to this most intimate of subjects: "Maudlin" (Plath), "She Shall Be Called Woman" (Sarton), "Menstruation at Forty" (Sexton), "Tampons" (Bass), and "poem in praise of menstruation" (Clifton).[2] These poems attest to a willingness to write frankly about female sexuality, yet menstruation is not as pervasive a subject in American women's poetry as one might expect. Although many poets have written poems alluding to this bodily process, few have given it the thematic importance that we see in Plath and Clifton. By contrasting Clifton's menstrual poems with Plath's, we can contextualize the life-affirming view that Clifton's poems typically offer.

As the previous chapter has shown, Clifton concerns herself in poem

---

1. Janice Delaney, Mary Jane Lupton, and Emily Toth, *The Curse: A Cultural History of Menstruation,* rev. ed. (Urbana: University of Illinois Press, 1988), 81.

2. For an overview of pertinent poems, see "The Miracle of Blood: Menstrual Imagery in Myth and Poetry," in Delaney, Lupton, and Toth, 186–99.

after poem with the many conditions of womanhood. The same is true of Plath. Although Clifton's poems typically reflect her life as a black woman, neither she nor Plath speaks narrowly to members of one race or gender. Their poems about female sexuality, especially those about fertility, are highly revealing. The menstrual cycle inspires them both, yet the physical realities, emotions, and myths of menstruation lead them in decidedly different, if not totally incompatible, directions. Plath's fertility poems are characteristically ambivalent, even self-castigating, whereas Clifton's are gentler and more self-accepting. In Plath's *Collected Poems,* virtually any combination of blood, moon, and blossom spells trouble for the female persona. The omnipresent moon is a baleful witness to private suffering; a red flower, an excruciating reminder of one's own blood flow; and menstrual blood itself, the bright mark of mortality.

For Plath, the female body is a mythological template, and menstrual blood is the raw material from which poetry is made. For Clifton the stigmas associated with menstruation do not preclude an affirming mythos. While Clifton's poems may objectify the body, she typically views female attributes with grace and tenderness. Lest we think her a misty-eyed romantic, however, Clifton also acknowledges the hardships that attend menstruation. In her poems, the so-called curse is a mixed blessing.

Three years into her marriage to Ted Hughes, Plath wrote in her journal, "Great cramps, stirrings. It is still just period time, but I have even waves of nausea. Am I pregnant? . . . Maybe some good pregnant poems, if I know I really am."[3] The term "good pregnant poems" effectively merges two of Plath's strongest desires at that time in her life: to be pregnant and write good poems. As a pregnant poet, she would embody creativity, and if she wrote good poems about being pregnant, all the better. So the tardy arrival of her period came as a terrible disappointment: "Yesterday a nadir of sorts. Woke up to cat's early mewling around six. Cramps. Pregnant I thought. [No] such luck. After a long 40 day period of hope, the old blood cramps and spilt fertility."[4] Once she was menstruating, the prospect of

3. Sylvia Plath, *The Journals of Sylvia Plath,* ed. Ted Hughes and Frances McCullough (New York: Dial, 1982), 298.
4. Ibid., 298.

"good pregnant poems" swiftly receded: "I have a vision of the poems I would write, but do not. When will they come?"[5]

For Plath, a fertile mind seemed to depend on a fertile body. Given such a conviction, perhaps it was inevitable that the very idea of female fertility—including the menstrual cycle and all its symbolic implications—would be a creative wellspring for her. In Robert Graves's *The White Goddess,* a book Plath read for poetic inspiration, she encountered an elaborate mythology surrounding the menstrual cycle, and the mythological symbols were to become integral to her verse.[6] Primary among these symbols is the moon, one of Plath's signature images. As Judith Kroll has amply detailed in *Chapters in a Mythology,* the lunar cycle was central to Plath's mythologizing of female experience. Although the mystical belief that "the Moon, being a woman, has a woman's normal menstrual period . . . of twenty-eight days" is suggestive in itself,[7] Graves's elaboration on this primitive notion reveals the mind-boggling possibilities available to moon-gazing poets:

> The magical connection of the Moon with menstruation is strong and widespread. The baleful moon-dew used by the witches of Thessaly was apparently a girl's first menstrual blood, taken during an eclipse of the Moon. Pliny devotes a whole chapter of his *Natural History* to the subject and gives a long list of the powers for good and bad that a menstruating woman possesses. Her touch can blast vines, ivy and rue, fade purple cloth, blacken linen in the wash-tub, tarnish copper, make bees desert their hives, and cause abortions in mares.[8]

Such a bountiful catalog indicates that "spilt fertility" is not all bad. In her poetry, at least, Plath could turn a physical bane into a creative boon.

In poems written long before her great outpouring in late 1962, Plath was already integrating symbols available to her in *The White Goddess.*

5. Ibid., 299.

6. See Hughes's note in *Journals,* 221, and Judith Kroll, *Chapters in a Mythology: The Poetry of Sylvia Plath* (New York: Harper and Row, 1976), 39–41, for commentary on Plath's reading of *The White Goddess.*

7. Robert Graves, *The White Goddess: A Historical Grammar of Poetic Myth* (New York: Farrar, Strauss and Giroux, 1966), 170.

8. Ibid., 170.

These poems turn menstruation into an ominous drama, an end in itself. A case in point is the eight-line "Maudlin," which Plath wrote in 1956. Abounding with menstrual symbolism, the poem concerns a "sleep-talking virgin" lying "In a clench of blood" and muttering at the man in the moon.[9] Despite its linguistic ingenuity, "Maudlin" ends up sounding stilted and obscure. "Moonrise," appearing several years later, yields somewhat better results. The poem describes the moon ("Lucina, bony mother, laboring / Among the socketed white stars") watching over a mythologically resonant landscape (*CP* 98). Judith Kroll writes that this poem seems "built on a bit of information given by Graves: that the mulberry, which ripens from white to red to black, is sacred to the White Goddess, whose emblematic colors these are."[10] Indebted to Graves and probably Yeats's lunar imagery as well, "Moonrise" is more fully developed than "Maudlin." Both are important, however, in that they show Plath weighing the symbolic possibilities of a subject she knew both intimately and intellectually.

In "Barren Woman" and "Childless Woman," menstrual imagery conveys the psychic pain of infertility. Unable to escape the prisons that their uncooperative bodies have become for them, Plath's barren women give in to fear and self-loathing. Like "Lady Lazarus," they make spectacles of themselves. The narrator of "Barren Woman," which Plath wrote in 1961, describes herself as a "Museum without statues, grand with pillars, porticoes, rotundas" (*CP* 157). Her sterility is tantamount to an illness, bleakly confirmed by the moon's silent approbation. Like the grim moon-nurse who would appear in "Three Women" (1962), Plath's extended meditation on fertility and motherhood, the moon in "Barren Women" is a formidable, disturbing presence. As an emblem of the menstrual cycle, the moon seems to mock the woman's desperate desire to conceive a child. The lunar associations in "Childless Woman," written in 1962, are similarly ominous. But unlike the depressed but rational voice in "Barren Woman," the title character of "Childless Woman" sounds delusional. Addressing an indeterminate audience, she revels in her pathos: "Loyal to my image, / Uttering nothing but blood— / Taste it, dark red!" (*CP* 259). Given the

9. Sylvia Plath, *The Collected Poems*, ed. Ted Hughes (New York: Harper and Row, 1981), 51. Subsequent excerpts from this volume will be cited parenthetically as *CP*.

10. Kroll, 41.

depth of her despair, the visceral utterance of blood can mean only one thing to the speaker: her own funeral, as she asserts with an awful finality. In stark contrast to the fecund menstrual imagery in "Moonrise," this woman's blood is, at least in her mind, a harbinger of her death.

Plath lets go of textbook mythologies in these two poems and begins developing her own schema of moons and menstrual blood. The voices are more fully developed, and hence more memorable, than those in "Maudlin" and "Moonrise." We might even describe Plath's two barren personas as founding members in a morbid sisterhood. They are joined by the unhappy speaker in "Elm," who projects infertility onto the "merciless" moon, and the fragile narrator of "Poppies in July," who looks at red blossoms and sees "A mouth just bloodied. / Little bloody skirts!" (CP 192, 203). The "bloody skirts" are an obvious menstrual allusion, but even without that comparison the poppies have symbolic resonance. As the authors of The Curse point out, flowers in the Bible and in Greek myths sometimes symbolize menstruating women,[11] and as a source for opium, poppies represent the lure of oblivion and, by extension, the lure of death. In "Poppies in July," the poppies link menstruation with death.

Though neither of these latter poems explicitly concerns menstruation, in each case the insistent menstrual imagery feminizes the persona's anguish and renders unnecessary a title denoting the speaker's sex. It is certainly possible, as Kathleen Margaret Lant writes, that Plath was playing out personal conflicts in these poems: "Plath's view of herself as a writer was complicated by the fact that she condemned the weaknesses she and her culture associated with femaleness. Her desire to forge an identity as an artist was shaped—and in some ways distorted—by this conflict. What seemed most difficult for her to overcome was her very real awareness of the female body as vulnerable."[12] Yet that fully articulated awareness of female vulnerability is one of her poetry's great strengths. The menstrual blood trailing throughout Plath's poems forces us to acknowledge the way women's bodies are perceived by a patriarchal society as well as the way that hostility makes women feel about themselves.

Her harshest indictment of menstruating women occurs in "The Mu-

11. Delaney, Lupton, and Toth, 190–93.

12. Kathleen Margaret Lant, "'The Big Strip Tease': Female Bodies and Male Power in the Poetry of Sylvia Plath," Contemporary Literature 34, no. 4 (Winter 1993): 633.

nich Mannequins," a 1963 poem of chilling irony. In striking contrast to those of the "Barren Woman" and "Childless Woman," the title characters of this poem have chosen to be childless, and the poem, assuming a censorious tone, condemns them for their choice. Childless women may maintain figures as perfect as a mannequin's, but the poem argues that they do so at great expense to themselves. Their bid for "perfection" is a way of courting death (CP 262). By locating these women "In Munich, morgue between Paris and Rome" (CP 263), the poem isolates them, alludes to Nazism and the Holocaust, and implies that the women are a blight on society. The poem achieves its zenith of irony in the following lines: "The blood flood is the flood of love, / The absolute sacrifice. / It means: no more idols but me, / Me and you" (CP 263). The first two lines appear to reverse Plath's characteristically somber portrayal of menstruation. Momentarily, a woman's monthly blood seems a sign of holy grace, but the latter lines completely undercut that possibility. Though they may be fruitful, the mannequin women refuse to multiply.

The poem further implies that these women are figuratively digging their own graves, and the speaker's preoccupation with herself exposes her selfish motive. The deliberately childless woman places supreme value on her own sexual gratification; her lover's satisfaction is an afterthought, a byproduct of her own sexual self-idolatry. The men who consort with such women are consumed by their own pride and arrogance. Written in unrhymed couplets that are at once dreamy and starkly censorious, the poem condemns self-interested coupling.

Another 1962 poem, "Cut," also pursues the menstrual theme. Although the narrator's gender is not mentioned, the opening lines, describing a kitchen scene, and the pervasive menstrual imagery argue for a female persona. Like Plath's barren women, the defiant narrator of "Cut" cannot look at her body—in this instance, her bleeding thumb—without seeing a host of other images. And, in much the same manic spirit as "Lady Lazarus," she waxes sarcastic about her own suffering: "What a thrill—— / My thumb instead of an onion" (CP 235). In rapid succession, the image of her bleeding thumb metamorphoses first into a scalped pilgrim and then into a motley parade of characters, including "redcoats," a "Saboteur," a "Kamikaze man," a "Trepanned veteran," and a "Dirty girl" (CP 235, 236). The stream of metaphors finally concludes with the brusque, literal "Thumb stump" (CP 236).

Though "Cut" may have been inspired by a real-life kitchen mishap, it is hardly the "playful poem" that Anne Stevenson thinks it is,[13] since its main concerns are self-mutilation and bloodshed. The narrator's perverse fascination with her wound implies that perhaps it was not entirely unwelcome. We know that she has "taken a pill," but the poem's increasingly ambiguous phrasing suggests a suicide attempt as well as a desire to stem the localized pain in her hand. Then, in the highly compressed penultimate stanza, "The balled / Pulp of your heart / Confronts its small / Mill of silence" (CP 236). Much more than a thumb is at stake here.

One would not ordinarily expect a small cut to be fatal, but if we view the bleeding thumb as a menstrual symbol, then the persona's leap in logic becomes much more comprehensible. In the fifth stanza, the lines that compare blood to fleeing "redcoats" make use of a French euphemism for menstruating.[14] Plath may well have known the French euphemism, since she was living abroad (in England) at the time of "Cut." Her antipathy toward her estranged English husband would have heightened the significance of the fleeing "redcoats." Furthermore, as one of only two explicitly female metaphors in this thoroughly blood-soaked poem, "dirty girl" calls to mind both Christian and pagan injunctions against menstruating women. Like the kamikaze and the saboteur, the "dirty girl" is equal parts violation and vulnerability—and she is accountable for her own fate. But whereas her male counterparts' fates are determined by their occupations, hers is inherent to her sexuality: like it or not, the "dirty girl" is Everywoman.

The thumb in "Cut," moreover, appears synecdochic for the bleeding female body. While a nosebleed is a routine example of menstrual displacement, the more intriguing case of a bleeding thumb, in at least one instance, was diagnosed the same way. The Curse describes a nineteenth-century British woman, "Mrs. H., who was forty-one years old and weighed 254 pounds. She had profuse bleeding from her thumb; the bleeding had occurred simultaneously with her period for more than three years. The bleeding lasted three to five days; a bandage around it had to be changed frequently."[15] But "Cut" goes beyond the oddity of menstrual

---

13. Anne Stevenson, Bitter Fame: A Life of Sylvia Plath (Boston: Houghton Mifflin, 1989), 271.

14. Delaney, Lupton, and Toth, 116.

15. Ibid., 248–49.

displacement. Consider the unsettling conclusion: "How you jump—— /
Trepanned veteran, / Dirty girl, / Thumb stump" (*CP* 236). At first glance
it may seem that the speaker is cauterizing her penchant for eccentric
metaphors by returning to the literal image of the thumb. But the entire
stanza leaves itself open to a metaphorical reading. We can interpret the
jesting, almost flirtatious "How you jump——" as a description of a body's
last lurch of vitality. Such a reading would follow logically after the
deathly imagery of the penultimate stanza. But the word "jump" also
allows for intentionality. People jump, after all, because they are alarmed
or excited, and the woozy narrator of this poem expresses both emotions.
Confronted by a bleeding thumb, she figuratively jumps to her own
death—the moment when the "dirty girl" becomes a corpse, an inanimate
"thumb stump." Susan Van Dyne views the poem's final images as stark
evidence of the poet's pathology:

> Retrospectively, the darkening bloodstain that tarnishes the gauze wrap-
> ping evokes not just a wound but our sexuality. What is strangely disqui-
> eting for a female reader is that this final naming is itself a form of self-
> sabotage; we are pained by the alienation it produces and represents for
> us, by the evidence that the female speaker has necessarily internalized
> her culture's revulsion at female blood, sexuality, and domesticity. After
> all these male masquerades, the ebullient wit and rhyming agility of her
> performance, the woman writer who is confined to the role of scullery
> maid rewounds herself by unmasking the misogyny within.[16]

But in keeping with the outspoken narrative voices of "Daddy" and "Lady
Lazarus,""Cut" deploys social commentary via self-directed irony. If we
are pained by this poem, we are pained perhaps by its honesty above all
else. In "Cut" Plath unmasks a whole culture, not just one wounded char-
acter.

The same may be said of "Three Women," which Plath originally
wrote for a BBC radio broadcast that aired in August 1962. The public
performance, combined with the poem's ambitious length (it is the long-
est in her *Collected Poems*), suggests that "Three Women" was extremely
important to Plath, and its subject matter bears this out. Set in and around

16. Susan Van Dyne, *Revising Life: Sylvia Plath's Ariel Poems* (Chapel Hill: University of
North Carolina Press, 1993), 148.

a maternity ward, the poem concerns three unnamed women: the first woman (her marital status and occupation unspecified) will have a son; the second (a married secretary) will suffer a miscarriage; and the third (an unmarried university student) will give up her baby daughter for adoption (CP 176–87). By juxtaposing their individual experiences, the poem creates a three-way mirror of possibility for any woman of childbearing age. Plath's preoccupation with female fertility thus finds its fullest expression in "Three Women."

What we learn about these women, we learn only from their alternating interior monologues. Whether fertile or barren, the voices talk to themselves rather than each other. Though disembodied, they speak for their bodies; though isolated from each other, they share emotions of disillusionment and dread. Even the joy of the First Voice, who will keep her child, quickly gives way to feelings of violation: "I am the center of an atrocity. / What pains, what sorrows must I be mothering?" A few lines later, she describes the agonies of childbirth: "My eyes are squeezed by this blackness. / I see nothing" (CP 180). Such lines could well describe a death.

But the First Voice does not die in childbirth; she only feels as if she does. Her introspective thoughts remain troubled even as she cleaves to her newborn child: she is painfully aware of her blood loss and the coolly objective treatment she receives at the hospital. Coupled with this is a new anxiety about her role as protector: "How long can I be / Gentling the sun with the shade of my hand, / Intercepting the blue bolts of a cold moon?" (CP 185). Personified as female and bearing the full weight of mythical associations with menstruation, the moon in "Three Women" signals death rather than life. By assuming the powerful role of "a glaring white death-goddess,"[17] the moon taunts the women whose physical cycles it seems to control.

The Second Voice's ferociously metaphorical rendering of the moon magnifies the First Voice's aversion. Initially the Second Voice perceives a genderless emblem of her own failure to conceive: "There is the moon in the high window. It is over. / How winter fills my soul!" (CP 181). Attesting to the depths of her depression, the Second Voice sees death and images of emptiness wherever she turns. It is hard to know, in the ambig-

17. Kroll, 72.

uous lines that follow, whether she is imagining corpses or the pregnant women near her in the hospital ward: "These bodies mounded around me now, these polar sleepers— / What blue, moony ray ices their dreams?" (*CP* 181). It is clear, however, that the moon is a cold, invasive presence capable of tormenting the dead and the dreamers as well as the soul-sick insomniacs. The moon then evolves into an even more malevolent force, significantly acquiring a female gender along the way:

> I feel it enter me, cold, alien, like an instrument.
> And that mad, hard face at the end of it, that O-mouth
> Open in its gape of perpetual grieving.
> It is she that drags the blood-black sea around
> Month after month, with its voices of failure.
> I am helpless as the sea at the end of her string.
> I am restless. Restless and useless. I, too, create corpses.
>
> (*CP* 182)

In an alarming transition, the moon is first a speculum invading the female body, then a specter of grief and cyclical loss. For the profoundly isolated Second Voice, there is no comfort to be found in either her mind or the night sky: the moon only mocks her desires. Having projected the anguish of her failed pregnancy onto the powerful moon, the Second Voice nevertheless identifies with her nemesis: "I, too, create corpses." Taken together, all three voices confirm Adrienne Rich's observation that "Somewhere in the feelings, latent and overt, that women carry through menstruation, there is an association of the menstrual period with a profound ambivalence toward our impregnability, and toward institutionalized motherhood."[18]

Plath's ambivalence about motherhood provides the symbolic foundation for "Edge," one of her final poems (and perhaps the last one). Unlike the Second Voice, the dead woman in "Edge" has borne children, but this latter poem kills them off, thus obliterating whatever hopes they may have represented to their mother: "Each dead child coiled, a white serpent, / One at each little / Pitcher of milk, now empty" (*CP* 272). The dead woman slips irretrievably into mythology, as Judith Kroll writes:

18. Rich, *Of Woman Born*, 95.

Several details indicate that Sylvia Plath conceived the dead woman to be someone like Shakespeare's Cleopatra. Both are associated with Greece and Rome. The dead woman wears a Roman death-gown with the "illusion of a Greek necessity." Cleopatra, too, is identified with both Greece and Rome. . . . Further, the dead children, coiled serpents who lie at the breasts that once nursed them, recall the serpent (the asp) which Cleopatra put to her breast to kill herself, and which she spoke of as her child.[19]

When the woman dies, the powers of conception and creativity die with her. The poem portrays "this cessation," to borrow a term from "Three Women" (CP 181), like a film shown in reverse, as the children reenter the corpse like rose petals folding back into a bud. The bleak, sexualized blood imagery in "Edge" brings to mind "The Munich Mannequins" and "Poppies in July." As in those earlier poems, the menstrual metaphors in "Edge" are also deathly ones, but the horror of this poem lies in its preternatural calm. In "Edge" we look in vain for the subtext of survival throbbing at the heart of "Daddy," "Lady Lazarus," and even "Cut" and "Three Women." The living women in those poems who are so attuned to their shortcomings are very different from the dead woman in "Edge" whom a dispassionate narrator describes as "perfected" (CP 272). The speaker in this poem, whom Kroll identifies as "the dead woman's proxy,"[20] seems most closely aligned with the sorrowful Second Voice.

Recalling the Second Voice's terse pronouncement after her miscarriage, the statement "it is over" recurs in "Edge," now implying that it is the woman's whole life, not just her goal of conceiving and bearing a child, that has slipped irretrievably away. Perhaps inevitably, Plath's old nemesis the moon puts in a final appearance. As the individual woman's life vanishes from the poem, in sweeps the dry-eyed moon: a mourner who isn't sad, a watcher who sees nothing strange. Symbolizing death's triumph, the Plathian moon is the "O-mouth," always getting the last word.

In "Edge" and her other poems containing menstrual images, sometimes it is hard to say where an archetypal mythology ends and Plath's

19. Kroll, 145.
20. Ibid., 205.

personal pathology begins. Yet such a distinction is ultimately moot, since that blurring of boundaries is inherent to her poems' structure and meaning. In "Cut," "Edge," "Three Women," and her several short poems about barren women, Plath looks beyond the feminist dictum that was to take hold in the 1970s ("The personal is political") and finds that the personal is archetypal: one woman's experience is, often as not, the raw stuff of myth. One of her late poems, "Kindness," gives us a tantalizing glimpse of Plath's personal mythology. A private poem that resists definitive interpretation, "Kindness" nonetheless grips us with its stunning, double declaration about art and the poet's own life: "The bloodjet is poetry, / There is no stopping it" (CP 270).

Like Plath, Clifton is a mythologist whose gender contributes a great deal to her poetic sensibility. But while sorrow tempers many of Clifton's poems and she acknowledges the hardships of womanhood, her female personas do not court death as Plath's do, nor do they seem as vulnerable to the misogyny pervasive in Western culture. Clifton's poetry reflects a will to endure as well as a feisty feminist spirit. We see this right away in the titles of three collections that she published consecutively: An Ordinary Woman, Two-Headed Woman, and Good Woman: Poems and a Memoir, 1969–1980. This persistent emphasis on womanhood informs us that Clifton is not bashful about asserting her gender and using it as a thematic device. But even in her early publications, as Alicia Ostriker has observed, "Clifton is already maternal, daughterly, a voice at once personal and collective, rooted and relational."[21] Nowhere are Clifton's sustaining female powers more clear than in her poems about menstruation and fertility.

Four poems about menstruation appear in Quilting, Clifton's seventh book of verse. In the book's title poem, a woman and her daughter stitch a quilt while, elsewhere, "alchemists mumble over pots" (Q 3). This domestic scene "in the unknown world" is hopelessly at odds with the world where "science / freezes into stone." Though Clifton clearly allies herself with the quilters rather than the mumbling alchemists, the poem ends in consternation rather than confirmation:

> how does this poem end?
>   do the daughters' daughters quilt?

21. Alicia Ostriker, "Kin and Kin: The Poetry of Lucille Clifton," American Poetry Review 22, no. 6 (1993): 41.

do the alchemists practice their tables?
do the worlds continue spinning
away from each other forever?

(Q 3)

The questions are not merely rhetorical; they are unanswerable. As the antecedent to all the other poems in the volume, "quilting" pointedly suggests that we cannot grasp the larger patterns governing our fate. In such a world mothers and daughters who spend their time quilting, whether literally or metaphorically, are engaged in a supreme act of hope and faith.

The volume's five subtitles, the names of traditional quilting designs, give the book thematic unity. Each group of poems, like a carefully designed quilt, contributes to the conceit. The volume's first poem about menstruating, "poem in praise of menstruation," appears in "catalpa flower." The poem is in keeping with that section's preoccupation with creation and natural order. The other poems on this topic—"poem to my uterus," "to my last period," and "wishes for sons"—are in "eight-pointed star," where womanhood is the main focus. Appearing on successive pages, these three may be viewed as a sequence that, to reverse Robert Frost's famous maxim, begins in wisdom and ends in delight.

The self-consciously celebratory "poem in praise of menstruation" employs images that are wholly positive. In stark contrast to Plath's adversarial moon imagery, for example, Clifton's menstrual moon symbolizes a woman's kinship with the natural world. In the first three stanzas, a sensuous nighttime landscape merges with the female body: the menstrual flow becomes a river; the vagina, the river's delta. In the third stanza, the emotions and physical feelings associated with menstruating become the river's gushing current. With each successive stanza and with the repetition of "if there is a river," the poem gains momentum:

if there is a river
more beautiful than this
bright as the blood
red edge of the moon   if

there is a river
more faithful than this
returning each month

to the same delta   if there

is a river
braver than this
coming and coming in a surge
of passion, of pain   if there is

(Q 36)

In its periodic structure and enjambed lines, the poem embraces the men-
strual flow in form as well as content. Rather than signifying death or
failure—as it does in Plath's menstrual poems and Anne Sexton's elegiac
"Menstruation at Forty"—the female blood here inspires awe. The poem's
conclusion further exalts menstruation by placing it in a religious and
mythological context:

a river
more ancient than this
daughter of eve
mother of cain and of abel   if there is in

the universe such a river   if
there is some where water
more powerful than this wild
water
pray that it flows also
through animals
beautiful and faithful and ancient
and female and brave

(Q 36)

The fourth stanza alludes to God's remonstration of Eve: "I will greatly
multiply your pain in childbearing; in pain you shall bring forth children"
(Genesis 3:16). But rather than dwelling on the punitive legacy of men-
struation, the speaker recognizes that the enduring, "ancient" river of
blood necessarily links one generation to the next. Molding biblical my-
thology to a woman's biological necessities, Clifton finds beauty and won-
der within a subject many still consider taboo. In this way, she seems to

be carrying on the legacy of female blues singers who "summoned sacred responses to their messages about sexuality."[22]

The poem has a holistic, African sensibility to it, and it reflects affirming, matriarchal myths rather than the misogynistic ones recounted in The White Goddess. In civilizations of diverse origin (Greek, Hindu, Australian, Scandinavian, and Indian), Barbara Walker writes, the menstrual flow was cause for celebration and reverence:

> The esoteric secret of the gods was that their mystical powers of longevity, authority, and creativity came from the same female essence. The Norse god Thor for example reached the magic land of enlightenment and eternal life by bathing in a river filled with the menstrual blood of "giantesses"—that is, of the Primal Matriarchs, "Powerful Ones" who governed the elder gods before Odin brought his "Asians" (Aesir) out of the east.[23]

Other cultures have also used rivers as metaphors for menstruation: "The Sumerian Great Mother represented maternal blood. . . . From her belly flowed the Four Rivers of Paradise, sometimes called rivers of blood which is the 'life' of all flesh."[24] In Clifton's poem, the menstrual river likewise emerges as a harmonizing, all-powerful life force. In contrast to Plath's focus on the menstruating woman's vulnerability, Clifton develops the alternative notion that "menstrual blood carried the spirit of sovereign authority because it was the medium of transmission of the life of clan or tribe."[25] Clifton's lavish praise of women and their bodies, indicative of her interest in feminist spirituality, contrasts starkly with the irony and anguish in Plath's menstrual poems.

Her "poem to my uterus," however, illustrates a willingness to explore emotions other than joy and reverence. This poem about a hysterectomy is a self-elegy, to borrow Jahan Ramazani's term,[26] in that it antici-

22. Angela Y. Davis, Blues Legacies and Black Feminism: Gertrude "Ma" Rainey, Bessie Smith, and Billie Holiday (New York: Vintage, 1998), 9.

23. Barbara G. Walker, The Woman's Encyclopedia of Myths and Secrets (San Francisco: Harper and Row, 1983), 636.

24. Ibid., 638.

25. Ibid.

26. See Jahan Ramazani, Poetry of Mourning: The Modern Elegy from Hardy to Heaney (Chicago: University of Chicago Press, 1994).

pates the poet's loss of her procreative powers. Given her willingness to see menstrual blood as sacred blood, it is perhaps not surprising to see her mourning its absence. The poet who loves and respects her body will weep for its frailties, its irreversible changes.

Because of its subject matter, "poem to my uterus" invites immediate comparison with Anne Sexton's "In Celebration of My Uterus." The prospect of a hysterectomy is the premise for both poems, and it is instructive to see, in the following excerpt, how Sexton handles the topic:

> They said you were immeasurably empty
> but you are not.
> They said you were sick unto dying
> but they were wrong.
> You are singing like a school girl.
> You are not torn.
>
> Sweet weight,
> in celebration of the woman I am
> and of the soul of the woman I am
> and of the central creature and its delight
> I sing for you. I dare to live.[27]

First published in her *Love Poems*, this poem shows Sexton daring not just to live, but to love herself without reservation. When she writes, "There is enough here to please a nation" and, several lines later, "Many women are singing together of this,"[28] she is imagining a communal triumph of women's bodies and spirits. "In Praise of My Uterus" is that rare thing in Sexton's body of work: a truly happy poem. But such happiness depends on the woman's body remaining intact, untouched by predatory doctors. Should the doctors have prevailed, Sexton's poem would undoubtedly have taken quite a different turn, as Clifton's "poem to my uterus" does.

Faced with an imminent loss, Clifton cannot dismiss the doctors who hover menacingly over her future: "they want to cut you out / stocking i will not need / where i am going / where am i going" (Q 58). Her tone is

---

27. Anne Sexton, "In Celebration of My Uterus," in *The Complete Poems* (Boston: Houghton Mifflin, 1989), 181–82.

28. Ibid., 182.

plaintive and weary, and the phrase inverted into a question bespeaks
both a lack of purpose and a preoccupation with mortality. Her uterus is
an "old girl" (rather than "a school girl"), whose removal will foretell a
kind of death. Whereas Sexton's poem joyfully expands outward to en-
compass all women, Clifton's sorrowfully turns inward upon itself. The
frequent repetition of "you"—occurring seven times and echoed by the
word "uterus" appearing twice—gives the poem an aggrieved, even accu-
satory tone. We could call "poem to my uterus" a love poem, like Sexton's,
but this one is more precisely a breakup poem:

> my bloody print
> my estrogen kitchen
> my black bag of desire
> where can i go
> barefoot
> without you
> where can you go
> without me
>
> (Q 58)

The unsettling metaphors for the uterus echo Plath's aggressive objectifi-
cation of the body in "Cut," and for a moment it seems that this speaker
will risk a similarly macabre detachment from her own body. But Clifton's
sorrows come from her belief that body and soul are intimately bound
together. Surgery or no, her persona cannot imagine life without the
"bloody print" of menstruation; a woman and her body cannot be sepa-
rated one from the other. The poem's reflexive grammatical construction
suggests that physical self-awareness is the very essence of self-knowledge.
The poet who writes "in praise of menstruation" is not going to give up
easily on her own claims to fertility.

Like "poem to my uterus," Clifton's "to my last period" also addresses
the speaker's body and makes use of female personification, but here we
see the poet making her characteristic turn toward self-reconciliation:

> well girl, goodbye,
> after thirty-eight years.
> thirty-eight years and you
> never arrived

> splendid in your red dress
> without trouble for me
> somewhere, somehow.
>
> (Q 59)

The blood flow becomes a "red dress" and the personified menstrual proc-
ess is a persistent source of difficulty. Stoicism combines with humor to
make these lines sympathetic rather than cloying. In the concluding
stanza, the speaker develops the metaphor in a way that is poignant as
well as amusing:

> now it is done,
> and i feel just like the grandmothers who,
> after the hussy has gone,
> sit holding her photograph
> and sighing, *wasn't she*
> *beautiful? wasn't she beautiful?*
>
> (Q 59)

The scandalized "grandmothers" who would label a mischievous young
woman "a hussy" nevertheless enjoy reminiscing about her, for the beauti-
ful troublemaker has provided them with a vicarious thrill. She represents
what they might have been (and perhaps were) long ago. As an emblem
of female sexuality, the menstrual period may also be more gratifying to
remember than to deal with firsthand. Even so, the woman who has had
a hysterectomy or experienced menopause may mourn the passing of her
childbearing years, the diminishment of sexual appetite, and the inescap-
able intimations of mortality. This poem involves both a definitive loss
and a recognition of a milestone achieved. Ever attuned to the paradox of
growing through loss, Clifton assuages her own pain, and that of her read-
ers, by acknowledging the dual nature of the experience.

While "poem to my uterus" and "to my last period" align female sexu-
ality with individual identity, the slyly titled "wishes for sons" projects the
humiliations of menstruation onto the opposite sex. In its series of
"wishes" or curses, the poem redirects the biblical curse: "i wish them
cramps. / i wish them a strange town / and the last tampon. / i wish them
no 7–11" (Q 60). With remarkable economy, Clifton sums up two immedi-

ately recognizable travails. Yet the poem is not just about the inconve-
niences menstruation can cause:

> i wish them one week early
> and wearing a white skirt.
> i wish them one week late.
>
> later i wish them hot flashes
> and clots like you
> wouldn't believe.   let the
> flashes come when they
> meet someone special.
> let the clots come
> when they want to.
>
> (Q 60)

Were a man to experience these dilemmas, the poem makes it clear that
he would acquire a new humility as well as a new intimacy with his body.
In the next stanza, the image of menopausal hot flashes again links the
menstrual cycle with embarrassment, and the accompanying blood clots
illustrate the unpredictability of menopause, the horror of the body aging
and changing according to its own implacable schedule. The final lines
provide an illuminating social critique: "let them think they have
accepted / arrogance in the universe, / then bring them to gynecologists /
not unlike themselves." Pointedly addressed to "sons," this poem is a crisp
indictment of men who, for reasons both anatomical and cultural, have
no idea of the humiliation their mothers, sisters, and partners experience
on a regular basis. Like many of Plath's poems, "wishes for sons" asks us
to confront an essential difference between women and men and to ac-
knowledge the way that difference has shaped men's views of women and
women's views of themselves.

In light of the legacy Plath has left to other poets addressing menstru-
ation in their verse, we can say that Clifton's poems offer not so much a
competing mythology of the menstruating woman as an alternative, com-
plementary one. As Chapter 3 demonstrated, Clifton often speaks through
a female persona who loves and honors her own body. In her poems about
menstruation and a woman's reproductive parts, this love of the female
takes on several different guises. She sometimes strikes an elegiac chord

in her menstrual poems, but her characteristic resilience of spirit still comes through. In the meditative "poem to my uterus," there is a flash of wit as well as pain in the startlingly direct address, and the metaphor of the hussy in "to my last period" is bound to surprise and amuse. The conceit in "wishes for sons" is funny because it is so boldly unsympathetic to men while so frank in its collation of inconveniences peculiar to women. Clifton is not merely flaunting a talent for feminist jest, though. Her "poem in praise of menstruation" celebrates all living creatures, while causing us to reconsider and perhaps set aside the tiresome stigmas attached to menstruation. She seems intent on honoring all of the different stages of the female life cycle. In doing so, she acknowledges the mortal limitations while praising the mythic beauty of womanhood.

Although they approach the female body and its special powers from notably different perspectives, both Plath and Clifton are forthright and provocative poets whose strong, definitively female voices demand our close attention. They are both bracingly honest, drawing on their different backgrounds and philosophical outlooks to create a poetic analogue to their own experiences as women. The contrasting visions we find in Plath and Clifton ultimately complement one another. Together, they suggest the myriad of emotions most women feel when contemplating the intimate experience of menstruation and the messages it embodies.

CHAPTER 5

The Biblical Poems

STARTING WITH PHILLIS WHEATLEY'S poetry in the eighteenth century, continuing through the slave narratives and spirituals of the nineteenth century, and taking on increasingly sophisticated and ironic significance in Harlem Renaissance works and later twentieth-century novels and poetry, the Bible has always been an inspiration and catalyst for African American literature. Lucille Clifton's use of biblical narrative and metaphor is in keeping with this tradition. Brought up in a Southern Baptist church in Buffalo, Clifton often cited good preaching as an early influence on her poetry, and she thought she "would have been a good preacher."[1] Because there is so much biblical material in her poetry and such a strong moral emphasis throughout her body of work, one could say that she is something of a preaching poet. Certainly, her knowledge of the Bible is integral to her identity and her verse.

Such an identification is especially evident in her repeated linking of "Lucille" and light. As noted earlier in this study, Clifton finds metaphorical and spiritual significance in her own name, which means light. This opens up lots of interesting possibilities, but the further connection of Lucille with Lucifer, which also has an etymological connection to light, is serendipitous for a spiritually questing poet who delights in word play. But Clifton makes a point of saying that, despite the biblical emphasis in her poems and her references to her own name, she does not want to be categorized as a Christian poet or even as a religious one:

> I don't think I'm religious because that has such a definite meaning among readers: religious will always mean Christian. I am well aware of the atrocities committed in the name of Christianity. Though I was raised as a Southern Baptist, one set of my godchildren is Jewish-Catholic, and the other set is Hindu. I've been to all those places of worship. In my house, I have a Bible, a Bhagavad-Gita, a Torah, and the Bahai book. My

---

1. Glaser, 312.

husband was a Yogi. I do believe in spirit and the world of spirits, but I don't think of myself as Christian because that word is so laden with baggage. A theologian at St. Mary's College said that I was post-denominational. I said, "Okay, thank you, now I understand."[2]

A Baptist by training but a pluralist by inclination, Clifton does not write biblically oriented poems strictly in the service of Christian beliefs. Instead, the Bible's stories and characters provide her with a spiritual frame for her ideas. She has speculated that writing poems may be "how I worship. Perhaps this is my meditation, my way of exploring the sacred."[3] The Bible's archetypes and metaphors inform that meditation and exploration.

Because the Bible invites literary interpretation even as it provides moral instruction, it has been a natural point of departure for many poets. Its diverse histories, tales, parables, poems, and proverbs are effective in large part because of the way they are written. The medium is part of the message. No paraphrase of the Twenty-third Psalm, for instance, could ever do justice to the original. While the same may be said of all good poetry, it seems especially relevant to Clifton's body of work. In Clifton, we see not only an effective synthesis of medium and message but also a fusion of the literary and the sacred and of the canonical and the radical. Although done with little fanfare, this is nonetheless a sweeping accomplishment, as Akasha Hull points out: "Clifton succeeds at transforming the Bible from a patriarchal to an Afrocentric, feminist, sexual, and broadly mystical text."[4] She achieves this transformation in various ways and with varying degrees of emphasis on the Bible's content. By surveying a sampling of her biblically inspired poems, we can see how her reading of the Bible and her poetic vision inform one another.

The Bible's thematic importance to Clifton's poetry first asserts itself in *Good News about the Earth,* her second book. The section titled "some jesus" consists of sixteen poems employing biblical personas. Among the most striking of these is "john," in the voice of John the Baptist. As is true of many of the poems in this volume, "john" implicitly commemorates

2. Somers-Willet, 75.

3. Ibid., 75.

4. Akasha (Gloria) Hull, "In Her Own Images: Lucille Clifton and the Bible," in *Dwelling in Possibility: Women Poets and Critics on Poetry,* ed. Yopie Prins and Maeera Shreiber (Ithaca: Cornell University Press, 1997), 293.

the Civil Rights movement of the 1960s. Although Martin Luther King Jr. is never mentioned by name, "john" invites us to consider the parallels between Christ and the activist-minister assassinated in 1968. Written in a stylized black vernacular, the poem commemorates the preaching Clifton heard as a child, yet it is remarkably ambiguous in its evocation of the savior:

> somebody coming in blackness
> like a star
> and the world be a great bush
> on his head
> and his eyes be fire
> in the city
> and his mouth be true as time
>
> he be calling the people brother
> even in the prison
> even in the jail
>
> i'm just only a baptist preacher
> somebody bigger than me coming
> in blackness like a star
>
> (GW 98)

Like the nineteenth-century spirituals, whose "genius . . . rested in their double meaning, their blending of the spiritual and the political,"[5] this poem invites multiple interpretations. The vernacular dialect and the Afrocentric imagery together create a black Christ, a sixties-style radical "coming in blackness" and wearing "a great bush" of an Afro. Symbolizing the savior's importance to the world, the image of the star alludes not only to the star of Bethlehem, but perhaps also to the North Star guiding nineteenth-century slaves toward freedom. Hardly the blue-eyed, straight-haired Christ whose portrait hung on Sunday School walls in the 1960s and 1970s, Clifton's Christ remains true to the spirit of biblical prophecy. Her poem may be subversive, but it is also genuine in its enthusiasm and reverent in its evocation of the savior.

5. Gates and McKay, *Norton Anthology of African American Literature*, 135.

That savior may be either Jesus Christ or Martin Luther King Jr. Once we begin thinking about King, the persona's witty description of himself as "a baptist preacher" alludes to King's own religious denomination, and "blackness" in the first and last lines signifies King's race, not just night-time or the spiritual void that the savior is entering. Such an interpretation is in keeping with a poem in *Good Times*, "the meeting after the savior gone," which is subtitled "4/4/68," the date of King's assassination. In Clifton's typology, Jesus Christ and Martin Luther King Jr. are closely identified, the one's life figured in the other. Like her African American forebears, who Clifton does not conform to any one creed but rather finds in the Bible a system and a symbolism that can be adapted to her own spiritual needs and artistic goals.

The poem "john" thus alludes to both Christ and Martin Luther King Jr. Clifton's symbiosis is further exemplified in the poem's syntax. While the vernacular use of "be" suggests that the speaker is African American, the parallel structure of "john" owes a debt to Hebrew poetic style. In the books of Psalms, Proverbs, and Lamentations, the use of parallel syntax creates order and instills a ritualistic quality. A variation in this syntax—such as an unexpectedly short line, with two stressed syllables instead of three—can convey a disturbance and heighten the poem's drama. In "john" there is an example of this incomplete parallelism in the first stanza, which ends on a truncated, obliquely mournful note. Moving on to the space separating the two stanzas, we subconsciously register an absence. The impact is akin to that of the missing beat effectively deployed in Hebrew poetry. The editors of the *Oxford Annotated Bible* explain, "The unequal metrical pattern 3 + 2 is known as the Qinah ("lament") meter, because it is the prevailing meter used in the book of Lamentations and occurs frequently in laments, although it is not confined to this type of composition. The unfulfilled expectation of a third beat in the second stich creates a peculiarly haunting effect."[6] In "john" the seemingly fore-shortened first stanza evokes the foreshortened life of the savior, evidenced in both Christ's crucifixion and King's assassination.

Many of the other poems in the "some jesus" section also reflect a

6. Herbert G. May and Bruce M. Metzger, "Characteristics of Hebrew Poetry," in *The New Oxford Annotated Bible with the Apocrypha*, ed. Herbert G. May and Bruce M. Metzger (New York: Oxford University Press, 1977), 1526.

contemporary African American consciousness. Sometimes this consciousness is expressed through a yearning for Africa, as in "the raising
of lazarus." Like "john," this poem has the ring of prophecy, even as it
contemplates the past: it looks simultaneously backward to its biblical
sources and forward to historical events in the lives of African Americans.
In the Bible, the story of Jesus bringing Lazarus back to life symbolizes
the spiritual rebirth available to all who believe in Jesus, but in "the raising
of lazarus" the story has special implications for African American slaves
and contemporary blacks continuing the fight against racial oppression:

> the dead shall rise again
> whoever say
> dust must be dust
> don't see the trees
> smell rain
> remember africa
> everything that goes
> can come
> stand up
> even the dead shall rise
> 　　　　　(GW 102)

The poem accrues meaning when considered in relation to the other
poems in *Good News about the Earth* about the Civil Rights movement and
the legacy of slavery. Dedicated to the memory of African Americans
killed in race conflicts—"for the dead / of jackson and / orangeburg / and
so on and / so on and on" (GW 53)—*Good News about the Earth* posits
Clifton's own typology. For her, as for many of her African American forebears, the Bible prefigures African American history, and African American life continually retells and expands upon the archetypal stories of the
Bible. Akasha Hull explains that, in Clifton's poetry, "transforming biblical figures into plain black folks is a move that simultaneously levels and
elevates. It brings the Bible's inhabitants down to earth, while it imparts
to black people some of the status of universal heroes and heroines."[7]

　　Clifton's biblical poems also reflect an awareness of the Black Theol-

---

7. Hull, "In Her Own Images," 281.

ogy movement, which sought to make Christianity more relevant and meaningful to blacks.[8] The tenets of this theological development, which paralleled the Black Arts Movement, clarify Clifton's perspective. Black theology can be defined as "a hardheaded, practical, and passionate reading of the signs of the times in the white community as well as the black. It is an elucidation of what we have understood God to be about in our history, particularly in the history of our struggle against racial oppression."[9] The same could be said of many of Clifton's biblical poems, especially those that speak directly to blacks seeking solace after the deaths of King and Malcolm X. The fact that Clifton appears to be addressing a black audience, while not necessarily excluding nonblacks, brings a biblical precedent to mind. In the parable of the sower, recounted in the book of Mark, Jesus explains the art of theological interpretation to his disciples: "'To you has been given the secret of the kingdom of God, but for those outside everything is in parables; so that they may indeed see but not perceive, and may indeed hear but not understand; lest they should turn again, be forgiven'" (Mark 4:11–12). Clifton's biblical poems often feel like parables built on parables; their secrets reveal themselves to readers open to the secrets of African American self-salvation.

The title *Good News about the Earth* is itself an allusion to Jesus's message in the Gospels: "'The spirit of the Lord is upon me, because he has anointed me to preach good news to the poor. He has sent me to proclaim release to the captives'" (Luke 4:18). It has a topical referent as well, since the "Good News" Bible, adapted into contemporary English, was a popular edition during the 1970s. Clifton's appropriation of "good news" might seem a wholly ironic commentary on the widespread upheaval of the late 1960s and early 1970s. But another look at Black Theology puts Clifton's usage in context. Citing the "good news" passage in the book of Luke, James H. Cone writes, "In the process of rereading the Bible in the light of black history, black clergy radicals . . . began to refer to God as the liberator of the oppressed Hebrew slaves in Egypt and to Jesus as the new liberator whom God has anointed" to spread the Gospel's good news to

8. Major J. Jones, *The Color of God: The Concept of God in Afro-American Thought* (Macon, Ga.: Mercer University Press, 1987), 2.

9. G. S. Gilmore and James H. Cone, *Black Theology: A Documentary History* (Maryknoll, N.Y.: Orbis Books, 1979), 4, quoted in Jones, 3.

the downtrodden.[10] With this in mind, we can view Clifton's *Good News about the Earth* as a meditation on the principles that Black Theology upholds. She, too, is arguing for spiritual liberation grounded in a specifically African American understanding of Christianity in general and Jesus in particular. The possibility of that liberation comes through in "God send easter," "easter sunday," and "spring song," all of which radiate hope and spiritual vitality. Here is "spring song," the book's last poem:

> the green of Jesus
> is breaking the ground
> and the sweet
> smell of delicious Jesus
> is opening the house and
> the dance of Jesus music
> has hold of the air and
> the world is turning
> in the body of Jesus and
> the future is possible
>
> (*GW* 106)

Clifton finds the joy of springtime in Jesus and the joy of Jesus in the resurrected landscape; there is no boundary separating the two. This juxtaposition of a Christian symbol with a sensual celebration of life on earth represents the symbiotic world view that becomes increasingly central to her poetry in later years. She is like "the preacher-as-creator [who] recovers Jesus and places Him within the fresh water of the black experience. . . . Stepping out on space and time, he brings color and excitement and intensity to an often colorless Judeo-Christian religion."[11] Clifton, as a poet-preacher, suggests in "spring song" that Jesus is a joyful state of consciousness available to all who recognize the beauty and sensuality of the natural world.

During the next decade, the focus of Clifton's biblical poems shifts from Jesus to the Virgin Mary. In *Two-Headed Woman,* she imbues Mary

10. James H. Cone, *For My People: Black Theology and the Black Church* (Maryknoll, N.Y.: Orbis Books, 1984), 80, quoted in Jones, 4.

11. Dolan Hubbard, *The Sermon and the African American Literary Imagination* (Columbia: University of Missouri Press, 1994), 12.

with complex emotions and desires that the Gospels do not explore. Further complicating the portrait, the Mary poems appear in a section titled "two-headed woman," a reference to a supernatural figure of African origins. The two-headed woman, like the mother of Christ, looks within her own heart even as she looks out at the world. Although this would seem to be a positive, truly insightful way to approach life, Clifton is not talking about insight as we typically think of it. Instead, she is exploring the phenomenon of "second sight" or clairvoyant perceptions. This is intimated in the poem introducing the collection's "two-headed woman" section. Like Sylvia Plath's persona in "Lady Lazarus," Clifton anticipates the curiosity and approbation attending a woman who does not fit societal norms: "see the sensational / two-headed woman / one face turned outward / one face / swiveling slowly in" (GW 185). But whereas Plath's Lady Lazarus is furious at the world and herself, Clifton, who identifies with the two-headed woman, seems to be working toward self-acceptance, grounded in both her race and her gender, as well as attempting to understand the spiritual world.

Because Clifton went through a spiritual transformation in the late 1970s, when she felt that her deceased mother was speaking to her, she had reason to feel that she was both a second-sighted clairvoyant and something of a "two-headed" freak, at least in the eyes of those who scoff at communication with the world of spirits. But this was not just an isolated experience in her life. Her later poems, such as "evening and my dead once husband" in *The Terrible Stories*, indicate that Thelma Sayles was not the only one who would speak to Clifton from beyond the grave. When the voices first started coming to her, Clifton has recalled, she thought she was "cracking up and taking the children with me."[12]

To tell people that she had been in touch with the dead would be to invite startled scrutiny, and as it happened, even her mother's spirit seemed to think that Clifton was turning away from a normal life. After she had begun receiving unbidden messages from Thelma Sayles while

12. Akasha (Gloria) Hull, "Channeling the Ancestral Muse: Lucille Clifton and Dolores Kendrick," in *Female Subjects in Black and White: Race, Psychoanalysis, Feminism*, ed. Elizabeth Abel, Barbara Christian, and Helen Moglen (Berkeley: University of California Press, 1997), 340. Much of the material about Clifton in "Channeling the Ancestral Muse" is reprinted, in slightly different form, in Hull's *Soul Talk*.

playing with a Ouija board, Clifton decided to experiment with automatic writing, a spontaneous technique that has long fascinated authors in search of divine inspiration.[13] Akasha Hull writes, "When she [tried automatic writing], she received automatic messages faster. On one occasion, her pen wrote, 'Stop this. You're having conversations with me as if I'm alive. I am not alive. Go. Conversations are for live people.'"[14] But Clifton was apparently not alone in her mystical experiences; she said that her children also felt Thelma's presence. Gradually the family got used to the newly charged atmosphere in the household. According to Clifton, the family "incorporated the nonvisible into our scheme for what is real. It worked for us."[15]

Her supernatural visions were full-body experiences making Clifton keenly aware of her untapped potential as a poet and spiritual being. She began to write poems that drew on her own visionary experiences while also building on the spiritual practices of her African and African American forebears. Like black female authors of nineteenth-century spiritual narratives, such as Rebecca Cox Jackson and Jarina Lee, she sought to represent a complex realm that Christianity alone could not adequately address. Doing so involved her in an Africanized, symbiotic way of seeing things—a world view typical of African American mystics.[16] She gradually grew more comfortable with her intermediary role as a poet sorting through ambiguous messages and deciding which ones to share with others. Clifton, an American woman of African ancestry now in her early forties, seemed to be following in the tradition that says that "[o]ne is not born a 'mystic' in Africa; one becomes one."[17] If communicating with disembodied spirits was to be part of her life experience, then she would embrace it.

Accepting, if not ever fully understanding, a world beyond the visible

13. In addition to Clifton, Alice Walker, Toni Morrison, Sonia Sanchez, Toni Cade Bambara, and Dolores Kendrick are among the black women writers who have experienced some form of "second sight." See Hull, Soul Talk.

14. Hull, "Channeling the Ancestral Muse," 340.

15. Ibid., 340.

16. Mullen, 634.

17. Dominique Zahan, "Some Reflections on African Spirituality," in African Spirituality: Forms, Meanings and Expressions, ed. Jacob K. Olupona (New York: Herder and Herder, 2000), 20.

and the known enabled Clifton to get on with her life and her poems. In *Two-Headed Woman* Clifton identifies not only with the Virgin Mary but also Joan of Arc. By associating herself with Mary and Joan, Clifton imagines a spiritual sisterhood (thus expanding on the theme of sisterhood in *An Ordinary Woman*) in which her communications with her mother can be illuminating, even holy. That is not to say that such contact is not terrifying and isolating for the woman in touch with forces beyond the visible world. These daring poems blend fear and courage, self-doubt and self-discovery, as Clifton attempts to understand divine powers through her mortal perceptions.

Clifton's poems about the Virgin Mary envision her as a child working at her mother's side, as a young woman anticipating Jesus's birth, and as an old woman looking back on her experience. This female trinity subtly alludes to "the 'Thousand-Named Goddess' whose images were embedded in the cultures of the whole Eurasian land mass."[18] Barbara Walker explains: "This many-named Goddess was the first Holy Trinity. Her three major aspects have been designated Virgin, Mother, and Crone. . . . The same trinitarian pattern can be traced in all the Goddess figures of India, Arabia, Egypt, the Middle East, Aegean and Mediterranean cultures, and among Celtic and Teutonic peoples of northern Europe."[19] By embedding goddess symbolism into her three-way portrait of Mary, Clifton skews the traditional Christian view of the Holy Virgin as a one-dimensional icon seen from a worshipful distance. There is a historical precedent, however, for representing Mary herself as a trinity:

> We find early Christian writings that identify all three Marys at the crucifixion with one another, as if they were one more version of the ancient female trinity. There was a Virgin Mother, a Dearly Beloved (Magdalene), and a third, more shadowy Mary. The Coptic *Gospel of Mary* said they were all one. Even as late as the Renaissance, a trinitarian Mary appeared in the *Speculum beatae Marieae* as Queen of Heaven (Virgin), Queen of Earth (Mother), and Queen of Hell (Crone).[20]

Clifton contributes to the mythologizing of Mary in her sequence, but her portrayal seems mainly designed to bring us closer to Mary, and Mary

18. Walker, *Crone*, 21.
19. Ibid.
20. Ibid., 24–25.

closer to us. Her Mary is one we can easily relate to, a mortal woman who speaks openly about her fears.

For Clifton, imagining the so-called Virgin in the sex act is the ultimate means of humanizing a sacred icon. We see this in "holy night," for instance, where Mary struggles to understand the relationship between the flesh and the spirit:

> joseph, i afraid of stars,
> their brilliant seeing.
> so many eyes. such light.
> joseph, i cannot still these limbs,
> i hands keep moving toward i breasts,
> so many stars. so bright.
> joseph, is wind burning from east
> joseph, i shine, oh joseph,   oh
> illuminated night.
>
> (GW 200)

Mary appears possessed by the spirit of God, but the poem also describes sexual intercourse, the act that, despite widely credited reports to the contrary, probably brought Jesus into the world. Afraid of divine censure as well as her body's orgasmic shudders, Clifton's Mary reaches out to Joseph for comfort and reassurance. In the penultimate line the poem achieves a dramatic and sexual climax. The "illuminated night" in the final line suggests that Mary herself has been illuminated by a new understanding of herself and her body. The poem shows Mary contemplating the power of the Holy Spirit, symbolized by the stars. While the idiosyncratic use of "i" hints at Mary's initial discomfort with the sex act, the "i" is also a homonym with the "eyes" of the watching stars. Mary and the stars are in effect watching one another, and the identity of one seems to mirror the other. The rhyming of "light," "bright," and "night" adds further unity to the poem, implying that the opposites complement and define one another.

This Mary is an active, questioning woman rather than a passive vessel of God's will. Her womanhood complicates things for her even as it makes Jesus—and all of Christianity—possible. It is not until the end of the poem that she understands her own body and its relation to the spiri-

tual world. But in that climactic moment of self-understanding, the famil-
ial triad of Mary and Joseph and Jesus parallels that of Father, Son, and
Holy Ghost. The trinity (shadowing the trinity of Marys in the sequence)
is structurally apparent in the poem's division into three stanzas of three
lines each, while the total of nine lines represents the human gestation
period. More than just a vessel delivering Jesus to the world, Mary is the
essential female component in this creation story. Clifton's emphasis on
Mary's womanhood makes the persona more real and her story more im-
mediate. Interestingly, the Mary in "holy night" has a race as well as a
gender. Clifton has said that these poems are "written in a kind of Rasta-
farian dialect"; this is yet another way that Clifton makes a biblical charac-
ter "racially black."[21] Doing so connects Mary with the other biblical char-
acters in Clifton's pantheon and draws the persona closer to Clifton
herself, one black female mystic pondering, and speaking through, an-
other.

In both *An Ordinary Woman* and *Two-Headed Woman*, Clifton struggles
with her own experience with divine insight. The etymological connec-
tion between "Lucille" and light enables her to express the visceral experi-
ence of self-illumination. It is a deeply personal experience and, for her,
a metaphorical rebirth best understood in matrilineal terms. In an un-
titled poem in *An Ordinary Woman*, she allies herself with the foremothers
whom she loves and reveres:

> light
> on my mother's tongue
> breaks through her soft
> extravagant hip
> into life.
> lucille
> she calls the light,
> which was the name
> of the grandmother
> who waited by the crossroads

21. "Lucille Clifton—Reading," Lannan Foundation Audio Archives, 8 December 1999,
www.lannan.org/audio/audioABCD.htm (accessed 22 February 2004); Hull, "In Her Own
Images," 284, 280.

in virginia
and shot the whiteman off his horse,
killing the killer of sons.
light breaks from her life
to her lives . . .

mine already is
an afrikan name.

(GW 148)

The shooting of the "whiteman" alludes to a family story central to Clifton's memoir, *Generations*. Biographical details are not essential, however, to this poem's sacred rendering of family history. The poem makes it clear that her gender, race, and relationship with her mother are all integral to her understanding of the "light" in her name and her life. Furthermore, we can see in this poem, among others, that "[w]hile Christianity strongly influences African-American spirituality, it is also evident that the visionary tradition allows within its spiritual matrix a space for a syncretic African-based spirituality or diasporic consciousness"[22] that accommodates more than one belief system. For instance, Clifton's reverence for her foremothers carries implications of African ancestor worship. She takes divine solace in thoughts of the strong women whose minds and bodies enabled her to come into existence. The absence of a male godhead from the poem is significant. The poem posits an alternative, feminist spirituality and suggests that her great-grandmother's killing of a "whiteman" was a necessary sacrifice.

The biblical allusions to light in her poetry are inescapable, but it is useful to turn once again to Barbara Walker for a lesson in the diverse mythologies that inform feminist spirituality and contribute to the complexity of Clifton's conceit:

Our patriarchal Bible predictably attributes to the male God the invocation *Fiat lux* (Let there be light). However, earlier images of the Goddess bore titles showing that she was the original light bringer, like Mater Matuta, "mother of the First Dawn." Egyptians said the light of the sun rose on earth for the first time from the womb of the Goddess. Under

22. Mullen, 631.

her Roman title of Juno Lucina, "bringer of Light," she not only mothered the light of the world but also "opened the eyes" of newborn children with her gift of sight.[23]

Clifton, for her part, seems to be engaged in an internalized call and response between the Bible she studied as a child and the matriarchal mythologies that perhaps better suit her evolving spirituality. The tension between the two makes for compelling, mysterious poems.

Like the persona she creates in "mary," Clifton both fears and craves illumination. In "the light that came to lucille clifton"—the last poem of the "two-headed woman" section—she objectifies her experience by using the third-person: "she closed her eyes, afraid to look for her / authenticity / but the light insists on itself in the world; / a voice from the nondead past started talking" (GW 209). Unwilling to confront the light, Clifton is nevertheless unable to escape its message: "she closed her ears and it spelled out in her hand / 'you might as well answer the door, my child, / the truth is furiously knocking.'" Initially afraid of divine illumination, Clifton gradually comes to realize, as Mary does, that it is nevertheless her human birthright.

In *Two-Headed Woman*'s final section, we see the poet coming to terms with her destiny and finally embracing it. Titled "the light that came to lucille clifton," this section expands on the scene sketched in the preceding poem of the same name. The first poem, "testament," is representative. Here, Clifton's persona appears vulnerable but self-accepting; her mystical contact with her mother has now been universalized into an experience of divine illumination. Rather than feeling like she is leaving sanity behind, Clifton imagines herself at the beginning of a newly enhanced spiritual life:

> in the beginning
> was the word.
>
> the year of our lord,
> amen. i
> lucille clifton
> hereby testify

23. Walker, *Crone*, 28.

that in that room
there was a light
and in that light
there was a voice
and in that voice
there was a sigh
and in that sigh
there was a world.
a world a sigh a voice a light and
i
alone
in a room.

(GW 213)

The biblical vocabulary transforms Clifton's persona into a religious prophet and makes her experience archetypal rather than merely personal. We see this in the opening stanza, which borrows from the first verse of John: "In the beginning was the Word, and the Word was with God, and the Word was God" (John 1:1). The long second stanza can be read as both an oblique description of divine communication and the poet's internalizing of the book of John, which repeatedly represents light as the divine illumination manifested in Jesus. We see this in John 1:9: "That was the true Light, which lighteth every man that cometh into the world." By putting her name in her poem, Clifton makes sure we know this is a woman's mystical transformation, not just the experience of "every man."

Because of her clairvoyant experiences, Clifton's faith in the Light is quite strong. For her, it represents a clarity of vision infused with love. According to Akasha Hull,

> Once [Clifton] asked her supernatural source, "What is God?" and was told that "God is Love is Light is God." She continues: "I don't say God particularly because it's too externally defined, so I talk about the universe, but for me the universe is sort of like Light, big L. And I believe that there is a Light, whatever that means—and it is like that, it is like the making clear what has not been clear, being able to see what has not been seen. I just feel an instinctive trust in that."[24]

24. Hull, "In Her Own Images," 288.

Although the communication Clifton received is couched in the Bible's language and metaphor, the direct transmission of the insight gave it personal relevance and urgency. Hearing about Love and Light from a disembodied spirit is different, after all, from sitting down and reading the book of John or even finding solace in feminist theology. In her biblical poetry from this phase in her life, we see her struggling to understand her relationship with the spiritual world and her own mystical powers. The apparent paradox of Clifton's faith is that it finds expression in biblical rhetoric and public declamation even as she maintains that it is very much a private, intuitive, and idiosyncratic affair.

The feeling that faith is ultimately an individual experience is not unique to her, however. Meditative souls typically leap from the individual to the universal with scarcely a glance at the prevailing categories of the day. Like Blake and Yeats, as well as her contemporaries Alice Walker and Toni Morrison, Clifton does not turn away in fear from spiritual realms she cannot totally grasp. Her perceptions are not portraits of God but rather self-portraits, and these, enigmatic though they may be, give us one more point of departure in our own attempts to understand the holy and the human.

Given her comments about Light, it is not surprising that in "testament" the divine light is not identified by either name or gender. The name "lucille clifton," however, does have a gender, and, for those who read the poem in the context of her other work, a race and specific personality attached to it as well. Such layers of meaning suggest ways in which Clifton finds self-affirmation in her poetry and her spiritual life. This is self-affirmation in a very broad sense, since Clifton's name does not exclude others from her poems or the situations she describes. The intimacy in her biblical poems comes from the emotions that her poems provoke in us as we think in new ways about the biblical Creation story, spirituality, and our own identities.

In *Two-Headed Woman,* her alliance with Mary and Joan of Arc reveals that she has actively looked for, and found, kindred spirits. Though each of our lives poses a unique set of problems, the questions we ask in attempting to solve our problems are much the same. Clifton's poems alluding to her contact with the dead implicitly ask: What happens after we die? What is the nature of the world we cannot see? And how much control do we have over what we feel and believe? For a poet whose writing exhibits a great deal of forethought and self-control, this last question would seem to present special difficulty. To write meaningfully about experiences that are beyond one's control paradoxically requires a great deal of self-control. In plumbing her own spiritual depths, Clifton finds a subject naturally, even preternaturally, well suited to her chosen verse form. A lyric poem is an epiphany in verse, a luminous moment. By grouping poems about female visionaries and visionary experiences, Clifton creates a panoramic view of spiritual epiphany. This is one way of exacting control over a seemingly uncontrollable subject.

In the section titled "the light that came to lucille clifton," we see Clifton repeatedly weighing fear and self-doubt on one hand against self-acceptance on the other. In "perhaps" she wonders whether she is going blind or deaf, "or going away from my self," but there is also the possibility that "perhaps / in the place of time / our lives are a circular stair / and i am turning" (GW 216). A fuller recognition of her own identity seems possible here as her fears and self-doubts ultimately become part of the self she accepts. Such a transformation is the more convincing for being portrayed repeatedly, from different perspectives and with different degrees of conviction, over the course of *Two-Headed Woman*.

The Bible does not play a significant role again in Clifton's poetry until the 1991 publication of *Quilting*. In returning to the Bible for poetic inspiration, Clifton seems to find her center again. Appearing at the end of the volume, where Clifton typically places her biblical poems, the "tree of life" section contains ten poems that are akin to the panels in a narrative quilt recalling biblical stories in vibrant imagery. Clifton's poems concern the relationships between Adam and Eve, Eve and Lucifer, and Lucifer and the angels in heaven. In contrast to their presentation in the Bible and Milton's *Paradise Lost*, Clifton's portrayal of these characters is affirming and affectionate, especially where Lucifer is concerned. A quote from Isaiah 14:12 provides the epigraph for the first poem in the sequence: "How art thou fallen from Heaven, O Lucifer, son of the morning?" (Q 71). Clifton makes one small but significant change here: she replaces the exclamation point in the King James version with a question mark, thereby suggesting that this is a real query, not a scathing assessment. Throughout the sequence, she consistently views Lucifer as a character worthy of thoughtful interrogation. Never referring to him as "Satan" or "the devil," she regards him in *Quilting* as an appealing mischief-maker akin to an African trickster or even to Puck in Shakespeare's *A Midsummer Night's Dream*. By identifying her persona as Lucifer, Clifton not only plays upon the etymological association between light and Lucifer; she also sidesteps the racist connotations often associated with the word devil. For her, Lucifer is a manifestation of humanity's inherent flaws: "I've said that I know there's Lucifer in Lucille, because I know me: I can be so petty, it's amazing! And there is therefore a possibility of Lucille in Lucifer. Lucifer was doing what he was supposed to do, too, you know? It's too easy to see Lucifer as all bad. Suppose he were merely being human."[25]

Although Clifton says in the same interview, "I believe that if we face up to our responsibility and the possibility of evil in us, we then will understand that we have to be vigilant about the good,"[26] her poems about Lucifer and the Creation story are not about evil. Rather, they look at man and woman in their allegedly "fallen" state as sexually aware adults who have Lucifer to thank for their newly raised consciousness. Unlike Milton's Satan, whose evil emerges as a powerful, infectious force, the Lucifer of *Quilting* is primarily the herald of human sexuality. He introduces Adam and Eve to sex, and Clifton—never one to shy away from sensual delights—cheers him on. Such a conception of Lucifer is in keeping with African American folklore in which the devil "is a powerful trickster who often competes successfully with God."[27] He may even be an emblem of insurgent black power, for folklorist Zora Neale Hurston strongly suspected "that the devil is an extension of the story-makers while God is the supposedly impregnable white masters, who are nevertheless defeated by the Negroes."[28]

Throughout the "tree of life" section of *Quilting*, sexuality is a form of illumination, and Lucifer is the bearer of this particular form of self-knowledge. The angels mourn Lucifer's departure from heaven, while Lucifer determines that he is God's servant "doing holy work" on earth ("lucifer understanding at last," Q 75). Exhibiting an elegant wit, he observes that "if the angels / hear of this / there will be no peace / in heaven."

---

25. See Chapter 9, 188.

26. Ibid., 187.

27. Zora Neale Hurston, *Mules and Men* (1935; reprint, New York: Perennial Library, 1990), 47.

28. Ibid.

In such a mythos, Lucifer really is doing God's work, and those who are outside his ken have an incomplete grasp of the divine. For Clifton, sex is a divine idea that manifests itself in human pleasure. As Hull sees it, "Ultimately, Clifton seems to be saying that sexuality is life, or the way of and to life—or that wrestling with it determines what life is about. Literally, sexual connection is the means by which life is propagated and continues."[29] These observations are confirmed in "eve's version," in which Eve delights in her own body and appears to merge with Lucifer at the end of the poem:

> it is your own lush self
> you hunger for
> he whispers   lucifer
> honey-tongue.
>
> (Q 74)

The alignment of "lush self" and "lucifer" creates a visual pun, suggesting that Eve and Lucifer are allies.

Clifton implies that Lucifer is acting out of necessity, a necessity that will be for the good of humanity. As the "light-bringer / created out of fire," he announces, "illuminate i could / and so / illuminate i did" ("lucifer speaks in his own voice," Q 80). Beneath this blunt declaration Clifton asserts herself as a black poet sharing her epiphanies with the world. Known as both the Prince of Darkness and the Light Bearer, Lucifer embodies the same polar opposites as does Clifton. A dark-skinned poet whose first name means "light," she knows something of the paradox the light-bearing Lucifer experiences as the so-called Prince of Darkness.

The "tree of life" poems reveal a rejuvenated Clifton, once again drawing strength from the Bible, especially the Creation story. These works are humorous and sensual, and they bear out Alicia Ostriker's observation that the biblical revision being done by contemporary women poets contains "a tremendous outpouring of comedy, shameless sexuality, an insistence on sensual immediacy and the details belonging to the flesh as holy, an insistence that the flesh is not incompatible with the intellect."[30] For all of the comedy, however, "lucifer understanding at last,"

29. Hull, "In Her Own Images," 292–93.

30. Alicia Suskin Ostriker, *Feminist Revision and the Bible* (Cambridge: Blackwell, 1993), 81.

"eve's version," and "adam thinking" are far from irreverent. The human thoughts and feelings that Clifton ascribes to Adam and Eve and especially to Lucifer make them accessible and engaging characters. Rather than mocking the Bible or the progenitors of the human race, she is reinterpreting the ancient stories and in effect adding her own chapters to the Bible. In these later biblical poems, she views Adam and Eve and Lucifer as residents of a First Community, where everyone's actions have an impact on everybody else. As each one imagines a response to every other, we see that this community exists largely within each character's mind. It is in the mind, after all, that relationships really take hold and help determine who we are. In a similar fashion, Clifton's long-time relationship with the Bible is integral to her identity. Writing about Adam and Eve and Lucifer ultimately becomes a way for Clifton to write about herself and humanity.

Nowhere is this more clear than in *The Book of Light,* the title indicating a commentary on the book of John or even an addendum to the Bible. The book culminates in "brothers," an eight-part sequence poem returning to the Creation story and once again taking up Lucifer's point of view. Because this poem is a watershed achievement in Clifton's career, it will be addressed separately in the next chapter. The poem represents the culmination of Clifton's thoughts on Lucifer as a symbol of a flawed human with a keen awareness of the divine.

In *The Terrible Stories,* the clear vision of *The Book of Light* gives way to somber meditations on loneliness and lyrical expressions of the dread and sorrow of breast cancer. In the concluding section, "From the Book of David," Clifton assumes the persona of David, the Old Testament's most celebrated warrior, leader, lover, and poet. Clifton seems to take some consolation in this alter ego, who offers her an escape from her own troubles and a way to reframe the human suffering that absorbs her attention. Since all of his relationships are charged with drama and emotion, David is an apt persona for a poet so interested in the complexities of human experience. Clifton speaks through him in poems such as "son of jesse," "david has slain his ten thousands," "bathsheba," "oh absalom my son my son," and "what manner of man." This group is a variation on the theme that evolves over the course of her many biblical poems. David's activities provide her with a new set of scenarios, but the exploration of identity is similar to what we see in other Clifton poems. She projects her own wondering self onto an archetypal persona in order to question the order of the universe and make sense of her own mind and soul. Though David is male and does not appear to be black like most of her other biblical characters, he is nevertheless another of her kindred spirits. He has his own terrible stories, stories of love and pain and sacrifice to which we can all relate, and his questions are not so far removed or so different from those of anyone alive today.

In the book's final poem, "what manner of man," David asks, "how can this david love himself, / be loved (i am singing and spinning now) / if he stands in the tents of history / bloody skull in one hand, harp in the other?" (*TS* 69). Clifton herself is very much present, assessing both David's character and her own role as a poet aspiring to be both celebratory and elegiac. The parenthetical comment—"(i am singing and spinning now)"—makes it sound as if Clifton is not speaking through her persona so much as she is speaking in tandem with him. She, too, craves love, as many of the personal poems in *The Terrible Stories* make clear. Yet a keen awareness of mortal suffering and a preoccupation with art can make love hard to come by. David's final song is an elegy for all the singing, spinning visionary poets who vanish into their art, trailing their mortal questionings after them.

Of the nineteen new poems in *Blessing the Boats: New and Selected Poems, 1988–2000,* five contain biblical imagery: "lazarus (first day)," "lazarus (second day)," "lazarus (third day)," "grief," and "report from the angel of eden." Their sadness is in keeping with the somber mood of the other new poems. In contrast to the Afrocentric political message of "the raising of lazarus," in *Good News about the Earth,* the sequence about Lazarus in *Blessing the Boats* concerns the uncertain boundary between life and death. As Clifton anticipates her own death, she imbues her personas with a stark awareness of mortality, and they explore possibilities that are evidently much on her mind. In the first poem of the Lazarus sequence, for instance, Lazarus describes the liminal state he was in when he was brought back to life: "i found myself twisting / in the light for this / is the miracle, mary martha; / at my head and at my feet / singing my name / was the same voice" (*BB* 26). The light symbolizes a divine force at work in both the mortal and immortal realms. The miracle, the poem asserts, is the presence of this divinity on both sides of the human passage from living to dead. But Lazarus's new knowledge sets him apart from everyone else, as the second poem suggests; he is not so much brought back to his old life as he is given a new one: "what entered the light was one man. / what walked out is another" (*BB* 27). In the third poem, Lazarus appears ready to return to the realm he briefly entered. The poem concludes, "sisters stand away / from the door to my grave / the only truth i know" (*BB* 28). It is not just the ultimate certainty of death that Lazarus strains toward; it is also the long perspective that the experience of death has already given him, a perspective that makes life on earth perhaps less compelling than it once was. The valedictory tone of the sequence is representative of the other biblical poems in *Blessing the Boats* and, indeed, of all the volume's new poems.

The poems "grief" and "report from the angel of eden" have an end-of-millennium feel to them, both apocalyptic and emotionally exhausted, in keeping with the symbolically significant year of their publication. They lack the ebullience of the biblical poems in *Good News about the Earth*. But these new poems do exhibit the elegiac strain consistently present in her poetry, and they use the Eden myth to critique American society, in keeping with a recurring pattern that J. Lee Greene has traced in African American fiction.[31] In "grief," Clifton imagines "the pain / of the grass / that bore the weight / of adam," and "the original bleeding, / adam moaning / and the lamentation of the grass" (*BB* 30). Further into the poem, she mourns "the myth of america" and "the girl / with twelve fingers / who never learned to cry enough / for anything that mattered." Clifton is that girl grown old, her extra fingers removed at birth, and her lamentation stands in for all of her unshed tears. In "report from the angel of eden," the angel is not identified by name, but the persona may be Lucifer yet again, full of fear this time. Watching the human angels coupling— "the nubs of their / wings were flush under their skin" (*BB* 32)—the angel realizes "they could do evil / with it and i knew / they would." This is a significant departure for Clifton, who in the past characterized the sex act as one of necessary joy. Here, however, sex seems to be not evil in itself but the means to an evil end, and it is that human potential for evil that the poem contemplates. With this terror in mind, the angel-speaker anxiously asks, "what now becomes . . . / of Paradise." The unpunctuated,

---

31. See J. Lee Greene, *Blacks in Eden: The African American Novel's First Century* (Charlottesville: University Press of Virginia, 1996).

unanswerable question hangs with foreboding at the end of the new poems in *Blessing the Boats*.

By adapting biblical stories to African American experience in *Good News about the Earth*, Clifton gives the Bible new cultural and political relevance while elevating her people's recent history to archetype. Neither suffers by way of comparison as Clifton applies her holistic logic to every dimension of her biblical writing, seeing the sacred in the topical and the topical in the sacred. Likewise, her poems about the Virgin Mary in *Two-Headed Woman* cause us to look anew at Mary, female sexuality, and feminist spirituality. Clifton's Mary is a courageous woman whose self-doubts do not prevent her from changing history. Her sexuality is neither her whole identity nor a discreet function designed to service God and man. It is, instead, one integral part of a complex self. In Clifton's poems, Mary's holiness extends implicitly to all women, their bodies being holy temples for human spirits.

In *Quilting, The Book of Light, The Terrible Stories,* and *Blessing the Boats*, Clifton explores biblical themes as a way of universalizing her own experience and exploring the nature of God and humanity. Although she resists the label of a "religious" or "Christian" poet, there is much in her poetry that is religious and a great deal that is Christian. Her love of her fellow humans and her spirit of forbearance are certainly in keeping with Jesus's teachings. Yet Clifton's special vision refocuses much of what we read in the Bible. Her faith, as Alicia Ostriker writes, "is intensified rather than dissipated by its independence of dogma, its syncretism, and its ability to represent women as central to sacred drama."[32] In keeping with her prevailing stance on race, moreover, Clifton makes sure that we recognize the role of black people, female and male, in this drama. Although she does not always posit a race for the characters in her biblical poems, she does so often enough that we get the drift. Spirituality cannot realistically be separated from the personal realities of race and gender.

That said, it is interesting to note that Clifton's meditations on light have a significant, rather ironic, antecedent in Jonathan Edwards's "A Divine and Supernatural Light" (1734): "This spiritual light is the dawning of the light of glory in the heart. There is nothing so powerful as this to support persons in affliction, and to give the mind peace and brightness

32. Ostriker, *Feminist Revision and the Bible*, 85.

in this stormy and dark world."[33] The distance between the eighteenth-century Puritan minister and the contemporary African American woman poet is not so great as one might suppose. Still, in Clifton's poetry, the Christian mythos exists primarily as a means of framing questions rather than definitively answering them. She does not insist that her stylized interpretations of the Bible are the right ones or the only ones; they are just hers. "Poetry and art," she says, "are not about answers to me; they are about questions."[34] The questions she poses in her poems are there for us to ponder, amplify, and answer if we can. What Clifton identifies as the human "desire / to reach beyond the stars" (*BL* 70) involves reaching within ourselves, plumbing our own spirits' depths, and attempting to grasp the ungraspable. For her, understanding the divine and understanding one's own humanity are ultimately two halves of the same endeavor, one reenacted time and again in the Bible and in her poems.

33. *Selected Writings of Jonathan Edwards,* ed. Harold P. Simonson (New York: Continuum, 1990), 87.

34. See Chapter 9, 194.

CHAPTER 6

Diabolic Dialogism in "brothers"

LUCIFER, THE LIGHT-BEARING Prince of Darkness, appears to be Lucille Clifton's favorite alter ego, a talkative angel with human flaws. The life of the primordial party, Lucifer brings Adam and Eve the glad tidings about sex in the "tree of life" sequence in *Next*. Lucifer's role in the grand upheaval explains his appeal to Clifton, long fascinated by biblical characters' flaws and foibles. Her humanizing of Lucifer is in keeping with her belief that the human and the divine are intertwined, our understanding of the one contingent upon an awareness of the other. Although this is evident in all of her biblical poems, the theme is elevated to the level of theodicy—a defense of God's enigmatic silence—in "brothers," the culminating eight-part sequence written from Lucifer's point of view in *The Book of Light*, the 1993 volume following *Next*.

A great deal of interesting context surrounds the Eden myth at the heart of "brothers." J. Lee Greene has argued persuasively in *Blacks in Eden: The African American Novel's First Century* that a radical refashioning of this myth is integral to African American literature. Regarding Phillis Wheatley's "On Being Brought from Africa to America," Greene notes that "Wheatley uses biblical allusions to treat tropologically and dialogically African Americans' marginal status in American society."[1] Like Wheatley and the later African American novelists Greene analyzes, Clifton writes with full awareness of an Anglo-American literary tradition begun during colonial times. "Building upon the image of America as a New Eden," says Green, "Anglo-Americans from the colonial period onward appropriated, transformed, and conflated passages from the Judeo-Christian Bible to justify their exclusion of Africans and descendants of Africans from the American family." Clifton, however, is among those black writers "who have proffered a view of American history that on the whole inverts the pervasive paradigm of Anglo-American literature."[2] As

---

1. Greene, 1.
2. Ibid., 1–2, 6.

Chapter 5 demonstrated, she repeatedly juxtaposes poems about African American life with portraits of biblical characters in order to expand our understanding of both.

Clifton is not just reimagining the figure of Lucifer as described in the Bible, though the Bible is her primary source. Nor is she merely retooling *Paradise Lost,* though Milton's epic poem is an important reference point. Explaining why she took on the Creation story in her poetry, she remarked, "If Milton can do it, so can I!"[3] Clifton's jesting acknowledgment of her towering precursor indicates that the Bloomian anxiety of influence is alive and well among contemporary poets. But like Charles Chesnutt in the nineteenth century and Clifton's friend Ishmael Reed, Clifton honors Milton even as she challenges his authority. Though she does not regard him in the same worshipful way that Phillis Wheatley did—even in her last, impoverished years, Wheatley "did not sell her valuable edition of *Paradise Lost;* it was sold in payment of her husband's debts after her death"[4]—Clifton clearly respects his epic precedent even as she appropriates the story of the Fall. Her sequence of short poems about Lucifer ironically invokes Milton's lengthily described Satan,

> Squat like a Toad, close at the ear of Eve;
> Assaying by his Devilish art to reach
> The Organs of her Fancy, and with them forge
> Illusions as he list, Phantasms and Dreams,
> Or if, inspiring venom, he might taint
> Th' animal spirits that from pure blood arise.[5]

Clifton's eight-part meditation, "brothers," comprises a mere 114 lines, a pithy rejoinder to the 258 pages of "*English* Heroic Verse without Rime" that make up *Paradise Lost.*[6]

---

3. See Chapter 9, 188. For an analysis of four other black authors (Phillis Wheatley, John Boyd, Charles Chesnutt, and Ishmael Reed) who respond to Milton, see Carolivia Herron, "Milton and Afro-American Literature," in *Re-membering Milton: Essays on the Texts and Traditions,* ed. Mary Nyquist and Margaret W. Ferguson (New York: Methuen, 1987), 278–300.

4. Herron, 286.

5. John Milton, *Paradise Lost,* in *Complete Poems and Major Prose,* ed. Merritt Y. Hughes (1957; reprint, Indianapolis: Odyssey, 1980), 297.

6. Ibid., 210.

In addition to the Bible, *Paradise Lost*, and the African American literary tradition responding to Anglo-American versions of the Eden myth, her portrayal of Lucifer has important antecedents in African and African American religion and folklore. During the eighteenth and nineteenth centuries, African Americans' concept of the devil was not strictly grounded in Christian notions of sin and evil, perhaps because the idea of original sin was unknown to their African ancestors. As Dominique Zahan explains, "Traditional African religion is devoid of the notion of original sin. . . . The destiny of the African is linked neither to the original drama in which the primordial ancestor played the leading role nor to the tragedy of redemption in which the essential role is played by God himself."[7]

The devil that African American slaves and their descendants imagined was an intriguing trickster who could be inspirational at times. According to Melville Herskovits's account in *The Myth of the Negro Past*, the devil's good qualities can be traced to "that character in Dahomean-Yoruba mythology, the divine trickster and the god of accident known as 'Legba'; the deity who wields his great power because of his ability to outwit his fellow gods."[8] Since they had a vested interest in the abolition of slavery, it follow that the slaves would project their fondest desires on a trickster god capable of outsmarting his adversaries.

The myth of Legba enabled African American slaves to construct a devil more useful to them, allegorically speaking, than the evil Satan that white Christian ministers propagated. Zora Neale Hurston's anthropological research in the 1930s supports this notion. Among southern blacks, many of whom were descended from slaves, Hurston found that "The devil is not the terror that he is in European folk-lore. He is a powerful trickster who often competes successfully with God."[9] The widespread belief that the devil was black no doubt heightened African American interest in this compelling figure. Many Europeans had long believed the devil to be "a blackfaced, clubfooted man with cloven feet, claw-like hands, and fiery red eyes, who had a ball and chain attached to his leg and a pronged fork in his hand."[10] This racist fantasy, conjuring up a nightmare vision of

7. Zahan, 3.

8. Melville J. Herskovits, *The Myth of the Negro Past* (1941; reprint, Boston: Beacon Press, 1958), 253.

9. Hurston, 248.

10. Jon Michael Spencer, *Blues and Evil* (Knoxville: University of Tennessee Press, 1993), 21.

a slave-beast, held sway in the United States well into the twentieth century. Such a horrifying image, mingled with the trickster influences of Africa, made the devil a tantalizing figure for African American ministers and musicians alike. "There is little question that the devil was a principal player in African-American religious belief and lore and therefore in the mythologies of the blues," Jon Michael Spencer writes in *Blues and Evil,* "and it is most probable that the emphasis on devil-lore among southern blacks was an early modern Europeanism dating back to the thirteenth century."[11]

Born at the end of the Great Depression, Lucille Clifton came of age in an era when devil tales were still an integral part of African American religion and culture. The devil was a common discussion topic at the Macedonia Baptist Church, which her family attended in Buffalo, and she also heard about the devil at home. According to Clifton, her father called the devil "the forky-tailed man."[12]

Her recurrent, often ironic, rendering of key episodes in the book of Genesis brings to mind the blues and its musical and cultural antecedents, and Clifton grew up listening to the music of Mamie Smith and Billie Holiday.[13] In the lyrics of Smith, Holiday, and other female blues singers, the sacred and the secular come together in a fusion of African and Christian perspectives. Sex, sexuality, and liberation are frequent subjects of blues songs by both men and women, but the religious consciousness found in the blues suggests the genre's connections to gospel music and its origins in African American spirituals. As Angela Davis explains, "Blues make abundant use of humor, satire, and irony, revealing their historic roots in slave music, wherein indirect methods of expression were the only means by which the oppression of slavery could be denounced. In this sense, the blues genre is a direct descendant of work songs, which often relied on indirection and irony to highlight the inhumanity of slave owners so that their targets were sure to misunderstand the intended meanings."[14]

Like the slaves' spirituals, Clifton's biblical poetry prior to *The Book*

---

11. Ibid.
12. Conversation with the author, 24 June 2000.
13. Ibid.
14. Davis, *Blues Legacies and Black Feminism,* 26.

of Light brings together Christian doctrine and an African ethos in a liber-
ating, African American message about self and universality and the divin-
ity implicit in sexuality. In "brothers," her previous meditations on the
Bible provide a context and counterpoint for a poem of a different order.
The sequence has elements in common with her other biblical poems,
but it is more detailed in its theological intent and more probing in its
questionings. Though it is not her last poem making use of the Eden myth,
"brothers" feels like a culmination, a summing-up of many years of spiri-
tual searching.

The poems comprising "brothers" are short lyrics, written in Clifton's
characteristic lowercase style. The parenthetical note at the beginning of
the sequence establishes the biblical frame of reference: "(being a conver-
sation in eight poems between an aged Lucifer and God, though only Luci-
fer is heard. The time is long after)" (*BL* 69). This minimalist description
pays glancing tribute to the prose "Argument" preceding each book of *Par-
adise Lost*. But whereas Milton lays out the plot of the blank-verse poetry
that will follow, Clifton only hints at the paradoxes to come. Although the
Bible does not tell us much about the relationship between God and Luci-
fer "long after" the Fall of Man, Clifton imagines that Lucifer, at least,
would want to keep the dialogue alive. As an "aged" character in this
poem, Lucifer is immediately humanized, and, over the course of the se-
quence, he is a proxy for Clifton and her own questions about God. Unlike
Milton, she is not so much telling a story as she is setting forth an age-
old dilemma. Lucifer's one-sided conversation with God enables her to
address the theological problem of God's silence in the face of human suf-
fering. Through the figure of Lucifer, Clifton gradually comes to terms
with this silence and affirms her faith in a higher power and the redemp-
tive grace of poetry.

All of the poems in the sequence make imaginative use of archetypal
Judeo-Christian imagery. At the outset, for instance, Lucifer recalls Eve's
birth as a wondrously organic event: "the sweet / fume of the man's rib /
as it rose up and began to walk" (BL 69). Alluding to the account in Gene-
sis in which God creates Eve from Adam's rib, these lines emphasize the
magic of Eve's supernatural transformation from inanimate rib to ani-
mated spirit. African American mysticism enters into the poem as the fa-
miliar outline of the biblical story gives way to what feels like a folk tale
bubbling up from our collective subconscious mind. While the "sweet

fume" brings to mind the feminine scent of perfume, there is also the zesty aroma of barbecue in the "fume of the man's rib." Clifton thus makes room for soul food in her Creation story.

The story in Genesis is further transformed in Lucifer's recollection of the animal kingdom: "the winged creatures leaping / like angels, the oceans claiming / their own." This polymorphic blurring of birds, fish, and angels allows for a variety of origin myths. A subsequent image—the "hum of the great cats / moving into language"—subtly alludes to scientific theories of evolution even as it acknowledges the biblical account of Man's giving "names to all cattle, and to the birds of the air, and to every beast of the field" (Genesis 2:20). In those great purring cats, Clifton once again invokes African American history: maybe the lions and tigers of Eden were the original hep cats, African animals swaying to the beat and humming the prelapsarian blues.

We may also recognize colloquial African American speech in the sequence's title, which raises the intriguing possibility that God and Lucifer are true soul brothers. Through her intertexual identification with Lucifer and her use of a first-person persona in "brothers," Clifton makes it clear that this is not only an African American version of the archetypal tale: it is her own version, and Lucifer, the so-called Prince of Darkness, is an ironically fitting conduit for a dark-skinned poet whose name means light. Clifton's humanizing of Lucifer suggests that he would be the logical character to pose the questions haunting everyone, perhaps even God. When Lucifer says to God, "let us rest here a time / like two old brothers / who watched it happen and wondered / what it meant," it is obvious that there is no other "brother" he would rather visit. The poem presupposes that they have now reached a point at which they can at last talk freely.

The second poem, "how great Thou art," continues to develop Clifton's personal mythos:

> that rib and rain and clay
> in all its pride,
> its unsteady dominion,
> is not what You believed
> You were,
> but it is what You are;

in Your own image as some
lexicographer supposed.

(BL 70)

The poem thus implies that the language in Genesis may be more symboli-
cally appropriate than its original author and subsequent translators and
interpreters (i.e., the "lexicographer") realized. The point is not that Man
literally looks like God, or that, for lack of a more appealing model, we
imagine God in our own image. It is, rather, that man and woman are
enfolded within our understanding of God or the universe or some all-
encompassing self. A knowledge of the Earth has given Clifton's Lucifer
insight into the divine. This is a distinctly human insight, one that we
see frequently in Clifton's poetry, especially her biblical poems. The poem
further implies that the human ambition and desire to know and under-
stand "God" are also part of "God." Such a view may call to mind Emer-
son's Over-soul, a spiritually unifying concept absorbing and uniting all
souls. But Clifton is making an epistemological point, distinct from Emer-
son's claims for the Over-soul's unifying properties, that becomes increas-
ingly important to the sequence's overall meaning.

A look at Bakhtin's concept of dialogism is useful here. Just as dialo-
gism "exploits the nature of language as a modeling system for the nature
of existence,"[15] so Clifton implies that the complementary relationship be-
tween language and silence parallels the relationship between the human
and the divine. She uses grammar and syntax, moreover, to represent the
plurality of the universe, the enfolding of the human within the divine.
We are visually reminded, for example, in the assertion that human desire
"is You. all You, all You," that the second-person pronoun can be plural
as well as singular. The triple iteration brings the Holy Trinity to mind,
but Clifton seems more interested in suggesting that the concept of God,
defined in terms of both unity and infinity, accommodates the multiplicity
of men and women, just as the idea of Lucifer embraces the reality of
Lucille.

In order to make her argument work, Clifton must assert her own
presence within the persona of Lucifer, and she does so in "as for myself,"
a title that deftly invokes both poet and persona. Here, Lucifer/Lucille

15. Eric Holquist, *Dialogism: Bakhtin and His World* (New York: Routledge, 1990), 33.

identifies not only with God but with Eve as well. Establishing his human-
ity from the outset—"less snake than angel / less angel than man"
(*BL* 71)—Lucifer initially seems perplexed by his own insight: "how come
i to this / serpent's understanding?" He nevertheless manages to ally him-
self with both Woman and God. Likening himself to a pregnant woman,
Lucifer announces, "i too am blessed with / the one gift you cherish; / to
feel the living move in me / and to be unafraid." Just as a woman holds
her unborn child within her and God holds the living within His universe,
so does Lucifer in his guise as snake hold the living within him. The image
has a literal basis because snakes can and do eat some creatures whole,
and the victim may appear to be alive as it moves through the snake's
body.

Symbolically, this image calls to mind the Hindu mythologizing of
snakes, especially the figure of Ananta, an enormous snake representing
eternity in its embrace of the globe. There is also a hint of the supreme
Haitian snake god, Damballa Ouedo Onedo Tocan Freda Dahomey, whose
name is linked to Dahomey, Africa,[16] the birthplace of Caroline Donald,
Clifton's great-great-grandmother. When seen in these non-Western con-
texts, Lucifer's claims in "as for myself" become more comprehensible and
far-reaching: flexing his own Africanized, mythological muscle, Lucifer is
a shape shifter on a grand scale, and his malleability expands "brothers" to
include faiths other than the Christian one providing its narrative frame.

In the fourth poem, "in my own defense," Lucifer declines to take
responsibility for Adam and Eve's introduction to sex and mortality. Not
only does he absolve himself, but he absolves Adam and Eve as well: "they
whose only sin / was being their father's children" (*BL* 72). It is God's
responsibility, Lucifer declares, to rectify any damage done: "only You
could have called / their ineffable names, / only in their fever / could they
have failed to hear." This poem obliquely poses the central riddles of the
Fall of Man: Why did God set up his human children for failure? Why did
he allow the Earth to harbor evil, mischief, carnality, if He didn't approve
of such things? At the very least, why didn't He guide Adam and Eve away

16. Zora Neale Hurston quoted in Blyden Jackson, *A History of Afro-American Literature*,
vol. 1, *The Long Beginning, 1746–1895* (Baton Rouge: Louisiana State University Press, 1989),
218–19.

from certain doom? What is interesting about "in my own defense" is that
Lucifer does not try to explain his role in the Fall of Man. Instead, he
defends his decision, and Adam and Eve's, to leave behind the idyllic plea-
sures of the Garden of Eden. Lucifer thus implies that the Fall of Man was
about a fundamental breakdown in communication rather than mortal
vulnerability to evil. As Lucifer tells it, there may still have been a chance
for a human reinstatement in Paradise, but God did not call Adam and
Eve back, and even if He had, they would not have heard. The story of the
world since then, Clifton implies through her rhetorically savvy persona,
has revolved in large part around frustrated human attempts to reestablish
a conversation with God. Caught up in the "fever" of their mortal lives,
people continue to have difficulty hearing what, if anything, God has to
say.

But Lucifer is not at a loss for words. Picking up on the passage in
Genesis in which Eve experiences "delight" upon eating the apple of the
Tree of Knowledge, the next poem explores the beauty of the mortal,
earthly world. The title sets up the beginning of the poem:

the road led from delight

into delight. into the sharp
edge of seasons, into the sweet
puff of bread baking, the warm
vale of sheet and sweat after love,
the tinny newborn cry of calf
and cormorant and humankind.

(BL 73)

Then, alluding to God's punishment of Man and Woman and the serpent,
Lucifer acknowledges "pain, of course," and "the bruising of his heel, my
head, / and so forth." Lucifer nevertheless insists that suffering is not the
whole story, and he asks, a bit truculently, for a chance to celebrate the
sensuous joys of food and rest, lovemaking and life-making: "forbid me
not / my meditation on the outer world." In this version of the Fall of
Man, the emphasis is on domestic pleasures and the shared life cycle of
man, beast, and bird. "The rest of it"—the pain and suffering forming the
inevitable backdrop for all that is good—is dismissed as a topic for another
day. By focusing on the beauty of the world and dismissing all of human

suffering with a few offhand phrases, the poem attempts to restore balance to a story that dwells unfairly on sorrow and pain. In doing so, the sequence revisits a theme of the "tree of life" poems—that is, the pleasures accompanying the Fall of Man. Here, however, Clifton does not focus on sex alone. In a few phrases, Lucifer sums up earthly joy and beauty; the playfulness of the "tree of life" section has given way to a serene satisfaction with all the good things, all the sensual pleasures, of life on earth.

Clifton's luciferous alter ego has plenty of doubts and questions, however, as the next poem reveals. "'The silence of God is God,'" draws its title from a line in Carolyn Forché's poem "The Angel of History."[17] The Forché poem, also a sequence, is a meditation on the horrors of war. Clifton's Lucifer is likewise concerned with war, though her poem is sufficiently ambiguous to encompass trouble of all kinds, including racial and sexual oppression. The poem asks God to explain why He neither stopped nor ignored the devastation: "tell us why / You watched the excommunication of / the world and You said nothing" (BL 74). The word "excommunication," typically denoting expulsion from the Catholic Church, in this context implies that a world containing so much cruelty warrants divine censure, regardless of whether God actually articulates it. With the poem's emphasis on "tongues bitten through / by the language of assault," the term might be taken another way as well: Perhaps the very lack of communication—or, more precisely, the movement away from spiritual communion—is at the root of the world's troubles. The expression of cruelty (the "tongues bitten through") is itself excruciatingly painful, an assault on one's own being. In any case, Lucifer articulates an age-old complaint against God: Why doesn't He do something when things go so terribly wrong?

Yet God's silence does not necessarily mean that he is absent or uninterested. Lucifer comes to that conclusion in "still there is mercy, there is grace." As the sequence moves toward its denouement, this poem takes refuge in the thought of a merciful God. The poem, responding to its own title, begins, "how otherwise / could i have come to this / marble spinning in space / propelled by the great / thumb of the universe?" (BL 75). The

17. Carolyn Forché, "The Angel of History," in The Angel of History (New York: HarperCollins, 1994), 5.

marble imagery is playful, and the tone is much less dire than in the previous poem. Lucifer's question implies that divine grace had a hand, or at least a thumb, in placing him on Earth. The poem continues in the same rhetorical mode, "how otherwise / could the two roads / of this tongue / converge into a single / certitude?" Picking up on the familiar image of the serpent's forked tongue, which tradition tells us is a sign of the creature's deceitful ways, these lines move toward a self-reconciliation in which faith wins out over doubt. The poem's ending initially appears to be a question paralleling the others, but it quickly resolves itself into a statement of Lucifer's newfound certainty: "how otherwise / could i, a sleek old / traveler, / curl one day safe and still / beside You / at Your feet, perhaps, / but, amen, Yours." Here we see a domesticated Lucifer, more of a dog than a serpent, nestling close to his master. Though he may want to imply equality by saying he is "beside" God, he then admits that he is actually beneath Him, at His feet. The important thing for Lucifer at this juncture, it seems, is that he has found an identity within God's universe and within God's reach. His doubts have at least temporarily abated.

Clifton's all-too-human Lucifer is wrestling with issues that have special significance for African Americans. The resolution in "still there is mercy, there is grace" is hard won, especially when we see it in the context of Clifton's many poems about African American life. According to the theologian Major J. Jones,

> For the Afro-American, hope has always been a kind of restlessness filled with protest. It seemed patient only on the surface; but it was ever a deep troubling beneath the calm that would not be stilled. Faith must not only be a consolation in suffering and times of evil but also a protest of divine promise against suffering and evil. For one to be sustained by hope in times of great stress, that person must be assured that God is fighting not only with the individual but also against evil and suffering, that God is able to help one overcome all odds.[18]

Although Lucifer might seem an unlikely mouthpiece for this viewpoint, voiced in "still there is mercy," he is an appropriate persona for "brothers," since Clifton delights in the dialogic opposition between Lucifer and

18. Jones, 36.

God. For Clifton, Lucifer speaks for human suffering rather than evil. Because of his once-privileged place in heaven and his fallen status, his perspective is longer and broader than anyone else's. Suffice it to say that a theodicy formulated by Lucifer will carry special weight.

That becomes clear in the concluding poem, which bears the enigmatic title ". . . . . is God." This alludes to Forché's line "The silence of God is God," but it opens up other possibilities as well. Maybe anything is God, or everything is God, or maybe God remains undefined or undefinable. As we read the poem, we see that for Clifton's Lucifer, God's ambiguous silence puts the onus of speech on everybody else. "Your tongue" is "splintered into angels," and Lucifer the light-bearing angel claims, "even i, / with my little piece of it / have said too much" (*BL* 76). The act of questioning is now dismissed as a sign of faithlessness: "to ask You to explain / is to deny You." The existence of this capitalized "You" is found in the silence preceding and surrounding human utterance. The concluding lines refer to John 1:1, "In the beginning was the Word, and the Word was with God, and the Word was God." But that is not the only allusion. For Clifton's Lucifer, "before the word / You were. / You kiss my brother mouth. / the rest is silence." (*BL* 76). Lucifer's last words are Hamlet's last words as well. By giving this brief, profound line to Lucifer, Clifton not only allies herself with Shakespeare but also establishes her persona as a tragic hero who recognizes, belatedly, divine justice at work: God's silence calls human speech into being. That silence is the background on which human utterance makes its imperfect mark. Rather than questioning what appears to be an inexplicable void, Lucifer now knows that God is speaking through him. As an emissary of God, a questioner sprung from the ultimate, unknowable answer, Lucifer glimpses the divine page beneath the human poem and knows that their coexistence is what creates meaning. And it is out of that organically evolved meaning, not out of a complete knowledge of all God's ways, that faith emerges. Major J. Jones provides this helpful meditation on the subject:

> If our knowledge of God were absolute, our choices would be limited and faith would not be free. An objective justification of faith, moreover, would have the same effect: Faith must be subjective, because if an objective proof of faith were possible at all, all free decisions made in faith-knowledge would be eliminated. Human beings would no longer be free

to say "yes" or "no" to God, just as we do not say "yes" or "no" to gravity. If God could be proved, like a law of nature or a mathematical formula, but in the personal sphere, then faith in God would become a law and a formula and God would become a demanding master over his faith-slaves.[19]

The beauty of faith, as Clifton's Lucifer realizes, is that it is a supreme act of free will demonstrating knowledge of one's self. Faith is the means by which ordinary mortals can approach God.

The interdependence of language and silence, word and page, enables us to wonder about God and ourselves and to frame those wonderings into speeches, sermons, and poems. The kiss is a manifestation of brotherly love, a priestly yet sensual act bringing to mind God's love for all of humankind embodied in the New Testament's Jesus. That love is all-encompassing, all-forgiving—and all-silencing. In the face of such love, language finally yields. Interestingly, in a volume titled *The Book of Light* by a poet for whom light is a signature motif, Clifton's Lucifer never says that God is love, or that God is Light, but that is because the message is implied throughout the sequence. A unifying, clarifying love has been present all along, "before the word," and the attempts to fill the silence with words or imbue the silence with meaning are in themselves defining human activities.

Clifton's dialogue between a silent God and a talkative, aged Lucifer asks us to meditate on the mutually defining components of the human and the divine. By using the Bible's stories of Creation and the Fall of Man as the text of her "conversation," she seems to agree with Bakhtin that

> there is neither a first word nor a last word. The contexts of dialogue are without limit. They extend into the deepest past and the most distant future. Even meanings born in dialogues of the remotest past will never be finally grasped once and for all, for they will always be renewed in later dialogue. At any present moment of the dialogue there are great masses of forgotten meanings, but these will be recalled again at a given moment in the dialogue's later course when it will be given new life. For nothing is absolutely dead: every meaning will someday have its homecoming festival.[20]

19. Ibid., 27.
20. Mikhail Bakhtin quoted in Holquist, 39.

We see this enacted in "brothers," in which God's silence is the explicit subject of two component poems and the implicit subject of the entire sequence. Clifton raises the topic of divine silence and then returns to it in the final poem, complicating it anew and confirming our intuition that this silence has been her main subject all along. The sequence is in itself a contribution to the endless, pancultural dialogue questioning God's character and will; in this reenvisioning of the Eden myth, the poet is creating a "homecoming festival" for all of the meanings attached to this myth.

The shifting meanings in this sequence of poems speak to the larger world that Bakhtin describes. The multiplicity of meanings and their inevitable, seemingly cyclical resurrection give credence to a host of redemptive mythologies. In "brothers" in particular and in Clifton's overall body of work, the language of poetry has a redemptive, life-affirming power. Poetry mirrors the organic relationship between mortal questionings and divine certitude; the lines of a poem and its surrounding white space are mutually defining, inseparable to the point of being a paradoxically self-contained but infinitely large whole: in short, the Universe.

Speaking through Lucifer in the closing sequence of *The Book of Light,* Lucille Clifton is herself a fallen angel addressing the ultimate Light source. Along the way, she is merging English, Anglo-American, and African American literary traditions in a poem that reclaims and revivifies the myth of Eden. The always-relevant story of Creation does not belong to the Judeo-Christian tradition alone, nor must its retelling by a contemporary African American woman merely refute the canonical version found in English and Anglo-American literature. In "brothers" Clifton is comfortable in the company of Milton and Shakespeare, her "brothers" in the art of writing poetry. Just as attuned to them as she is to the rich and dynamic legacies of African and African American literature and folklore, she writes in a spirit of cooperation rather than competition. She is never one to shrug off the importance of canonical white male poets—the epigraphs in *Generations* from Whitman's *Song of Myself* are a case in point—and in taking on the enormous problem of God's silence, she recognizes that this concern is not hers alone.

Her self-assurance enables her to address a profoundly enigmatic Supreme Being and make sense of the divine silence. When her persona says "even i, / with my little piece of it / have said too much," Clifton is weighing the meaning of her poem against the abundant mysteries of divine silence. Perhaps language, no matter how poetic, cannot do justice to God, and perhaps asking the questions that this poem asks amounts to a denial of God. But this poet's persona has been kissed by God, an indication that He loves the Lucifer in Lucille, and that kiss makes it possible for the Lucille in Lucifer to give God the last word.

CHAPTER 7

Elegies for Thelma

FOR LUCILLE CLIFTON, WHAT FREUD called the work of mourning has been a lifelong work in progress. She is naturally drawn to the elegy, a fluid form that enables her to meditate on both life and loss. Her memoir, *Generations*, and most of her poems are elegiac in nature. Her poems about deceased family members and assassinated black leaders are obvious examples of elegies, but she has also written elegies for herself, her body, the black community, and American society. The pervasive elegiac strain provides an important counterpoint to the joyful resilience that attracts many readers to her writing.

In Clifton's poetry, we quickly find that the pain of loss and the hard-won victory of survival are virtually inseparable. Almost any handful of her poems could illustrate her handling of the elegy, but because her relationship with her mother has proven so important to her life and writings, the elegies for Thelma Sayles can illustrate Clifton's use of this emotionally charged and historically significant form.[1] Clifton has written about her mother throughout her career as a professional writer. In *Generations: A Memoir,* she declares that "Mama's life was—seemed like—the biggest waste in the world to me, but now I don't know, I'm not sure any more" (*GW* 273). Definitive only in its ambivalence, this disarming admission is characteristic of Clifton's complex commentary on the parent whose memory she valiantly seeks to preserve. In death, Thelma seems to be always with Clifton, in the form of an unanswerable riddle continuously rephrasing itself at the edges of the poet's consciousness. Her conflicting emotions seem only to heighten Clifton's desire to fashion with words an umbilical cord leading back to the prelapsarian safety of the womb, where the maternal bond is incontrovertible and absolute.

1. For analysis of the modern elegy, see Ramazani. For a concise historical overview of the elegy, see Morton W. Bloomfield, "The Elegy and the Elegiac Mode: Praise and Alienation," in *Renaissance Genres: Essays on Theory, History, and Interpretation,* ed. Barbara Kiefer Lewalski (Cambridge: Harvard University Press, 1986), 147–57.

In 1969, the year that she published her first book of poetry, she also published "The Magic Mama" in *Redbook* and "Christmas Is Something Else" in *House & Garden,* essays about Thelma that provide enlightening context for the elegies to come. Although *Redbook* labels it as fiction, "The Magic Mama" is actually a memoir. The piece captures the painful, powerful emotions her mother inspired in Clifton and forecasts the importance of Thelma to her daughter's elegiac body of work. Recalling her mother's epilepsy, Clifton writes:

> The thing to do, then, is to watch her. Always, every move. And to be afraid if she should go out of the house until finally she stops going. And worry her all the time with Mama you okay and Mama what's the matter until she would stay home to get away from the children's fear and shame. Shame of Mama. At night, listening for the animal sounds and rushing in to hold her arms down and try to protect her tongue; lying awake and listening so that I can rush right in and let the Daddy and kids rest, not be disturbed. Then one night, hearing and turning over and pushing the arms against the ears and trying to go on to sleep anyhow, why don't she stop by herself, why don't she leave me alone. Pause. And oh, Lord, rushing up and in and being extra careful, extra gentle, crying, begging the gone-away-for-a-minute lady to forgive this daughter. Again.[2]

This fluid rendering of love, sorrow, and guilt reveals the depth and complexity of Clifton's devotion to her mother. Thelma Sayles died in 1959 at age forty-four, when Clifton was only twenty-two. Thelma had collapsed in a hospital, where she was finally being tested and treated for epilepsy. The timing of the essay's publication, in the year that Clifton made her public debut as a poet and children's book author, suggests that she was weighing her abundantly promising life against her mother's foreshortened, constricted one. "The Magic Mama" is an elegy in prose, a précis for the poems Clifton would go on to write both for and about her mother.

Thelma is also the subject of "Christmas Is Something Else," published in the December 1969 issue of *House & Garden.* An unusually somber choice for the magazine's Christmas issue, this essay describes Thelma as both the quiet center around which the household revolves and the embodiment of the family's pathos. On Christmas Eve, she prepares food

2. Lucille Clifton, "The Magic Mama," *Redbook,* November 1969, 89.

for her husband's annual open house but does not attend the party: "Sitting in her chair by the window, rocking, humming 'Precious Lord,' she would smile as the friends stood dutifully before her for a minute, making dutiful small talk, saying hello to Thel. But the party would soon arrange itself all through the downstairs, and we children upstairs in our beds would hear Mama vanishing into hers."[3] Unable or unwilling to join in the festivities, she retreats to her bed, and neither her husband nor the party guests seem to mind. It is only Clifton, remembering her childhood perceptions, who mourns the strangeness of her mother's retreat.

It seems that Thelma is in this family but somehow not entirely of it. She is a poignant and beloved figure, whose opinions matter, even though she is so passive and retiring. She is the one the young Lucille runs to when Santa Claus has brought only ill-fitting coats and comic books:

> "Was we bad? we wasn't bad, was we?"
> "No baby, you all are good children." She shook her head again. Then she lay back in her bed as if everything was going to be all right. I saw, and was calmed.
> "That's all right, baby, Santa Claus must of forgot you all. In the morning Mama will take you all to Sears and buy you all the toys you want." She closed her eyes.[4]

Clifton reports that her mother did not in fact take the children shopping after Christmas. We are left to surmise that Lucille is both wounded and subtly enlightened by her mother's fib. There is no Santa Claus for them to believe in, and much worse, Thelma's credibility is damaged. Despite her promises and desires, she cannot right all the wrongs of her children's young lives; she, too, is flawed and mortal.

In the final scene, Clifton recounts the family's annual Christmas pilgrimage to Thelma's unmarked grave: "We were silent, angry, furious that Christmas would dare to come with Mama gone."[5] Thelma's importance to the family very nearly defies words. But once Clifton catches up with the others at the grave, she discovers that her father is talking to Thelma as if she were still alive: "'Back again,' he said; 'it's Christmas and we're

---

3. Lucille Clifton, "Christmas Is Something Else," *House & Garden* (December 1969), 70.
4. Ibid., 71.
5. Ibid., 115.

all back together again. But this ain't all. Look, Lue got the baby. Merry Christmas, Thel.'"⁶ The new baby is that unexpectedly wonderful gift that can make Christmas special. But as it is portrayed here, the occasion is bittersweet at best. Thelma is gone, and the continuation of the family line cannot erase the painful fact that this gentle woman, who may have been better suited to the role of grandmother than that of mother, never got to see her grandchild. Echoing the scene in which the guests greet Thelma before going in to the Christmas party, her husband and children now pay their respects at Thelma's unmarked grave. In death as in life, she is the keeper of the family's pride and sorrow, the one who defines what the rest of them are—and are not.

In both "The Magic Mama" and "Christmas Is Something Else," Thelma's early death is a traumatic touchstone. Although Clifton is more explicit in "The Magic Mama" about her subsequent feelings of guilt and anguish, both works detail the unmitigated pain and shock of the loss. They form the elegiacal backdrop for the poems in which Clifton figuratively reunites with Thelma while often staking a claim to an identity distinct from her mother's. The poems, though obviously the work of a grieving spirit, are often startling in their frank acknowledgment of the deceased woman's frailties and the daughter poet's continuing desire to wrest autonomy away from Thelma. Clifton sees herself in her mother and her mother in herself; the refracted images are not always flattering to either.

The single poem about Thelma in *Good Times* is an ambiguously worded elegy, a highly distilled version of Clifton's 1969 prose commentaries on her mother. The untitled poem criticizes Thelma for dying young and leaving her unprotected family members behind to fend for themselves:

> my mama moved among the days
> like a dreamwalker in a field;
> seemed like what she touched was hers
> seemed like what touched her couldn't hold,
> she got us almost through the high grass
> then seemed like she turned around and ran

6. Ibid., 116.

right back in
right back on in
            (*GW* 16)

As in Clifton's magazine essays, Thelma is an elusive presence in this poem. She is a "dreamwalker" (rather than an ordinary sleepwalker) lost in her impenetrable reveries. The middle lines imply that she has a strong hold on the people around her, though they may not grasp her, either literally or figuratively. In the end, Thelma is a disappointing protector, a fallible guide. The final image calls to mind escaping slaves and perhaps Harriet Tubman's role in their liberation. But the comparison falls deliberately short, as Clifton complains, obliquely, that her mother fell prey to fears and frailties that she should have overcome. The figurative language encapsulates the poet's feelings of betrayal. She is both grieving and aggrieved.

Later elegies return again and again to Clifton's relationship with her mother, a relationship that did not end with Thelma's death. In what can only be described as an extraordinary development, Clifton says that during the mid 1970s her long-dead mother began speaking to her from beyond the grave. Akasha Hull writes: "This unsought, unexpected supernatural contact with [Thelma] inaugurated Clifton's conscious recognition of the spiritual realm. Her next volume of poetry, *Two-Headed Woman* (1980), charts the turbulence of this awareness, but ends with a calm acceptance of the truth that she has come to know."[7] Feeling that she was in direct contact with her mother opened the elegiac floodgates. Clifton told Hull that in her supernatural communications "there was a progression for her from the slow Ouija board, to automatic writing, to not particularly having to write because she could hear—'but writing and hearing were almost like the same thing.'"[8]

Though such visions are unusual, Clifton is not alone among writers and artists in having this sort of experience to draw on in her work. William Blake, William Butler Yeats, and Allen Ginsberg all claimed to have had visionary experiences, and Sylvia Plath and Ted Hughes experimented with a Ouija board. Even more germane to Clifton's racially inscribed

7. Hull, "Channeling the Ancestral Muse," 330.
8. Ibid., 341.

body of work, nineteenth-century African American women such as Rebecca Cox Jackson, Harriet Tubman, and Sojourner Truth all had life-altering visions. As Hull has documented, Clifton's contemporaries Dolores Kendrick and Sonia Sanchez also claimed to have had contact with their deceased mothers, and both draw on visionary experiences in their writing.[9]

For women writers, perhaps especially for African American women, communication with one's deceased mother holds social and political as well as personal significance. The poet who writes down her deceased mother's words is making the matrilineal line part of her art as well as her life. Since blacks were so long denied the right to literacy in the United States, and women and blacks the world over continue to battle oppression on many different fronts, the black female visionary poet who acknowledges her mother's continuing presence in her life is insisting on a unique female strength and wisdom passed down from generation to generation. Given the means of transmission, such strength and wisdom defy pervasive attempts to stifle black women and suggest a resilience beyond the ordinary ken. Such is the case with Clifton, who has long paid tribute to both the enduring power and the complexity of black women.

Since Clifton was "hearing" from her mother and transcribing her mother's words, it was not surprising that she chose to write back. *Two-Headed Woman* contains a series of poems directly addressed to Thelma: "to thelma who worried because i couldn't cook," "poem on my fortieth birthday to my mother who died young," and "february 13, 1980." These brief, rather startling poems conform to Peter Sacks's definition of the elegy "as a *work,* both in the commonly accepted meaning of a product and in the more dynamic sense of the working through of an impulse or experience—the sense that underlies Freud's 'the work of mourning.'"[10] Interestingly, these elegies dwell on Thelma's weaknesses and shortcomings. It is as if Clifton, spiritually and metaphorically back in touch with her mother, is "working through" the meaning of Thelma's early death as well as the sorrows that Clifton herself may well be prone to experience.

In "to thelma who worried because i couldn't cook," the complicated

9. For more information on spiritual writers, see Mullen.

10. Peter M. Sacks, *The English Elegy: Studies in the Genre from Spenser to Yeats* (Baltimore: The Johns Hopkins University Press, 1985), 1.

title immediately places mother and daughter in opposition to one an-
other. By using her mother's first name, Clifton speaks to her deceased
mother on equal terms rather than as a deferential daughter acknowledg-
ing her past (and perhaps continuing) incompetency. She is recalling one
of her mother's concerns about her, which, in the context of this poem,
is a metaphor for Thelma's fear that her daughter would have trouble at-
tracting a man:

> because no man would taste you
> you tried to feed yourself
> kneading your body
> with your own fists. the beaten thing
> rose up like a dough
> and burst in the oven of your hunger.
> madam, i'm not your gifted girl,
> i am a woman and
> i know what to do.
>
> (GW 175)

The first line immediately signals that cooking and eating will symbolize
female sexuality. Whereas in "the thirty eighth year" Clifton uses bread
imagery to describe her own seemingly unexceptional female self—"plain
as bread / round as a cake / an ordinary woman" (GW 158)—here, bread-
baking is equated with Thelma's sexual frustration. Thelma is both bread
and ravenous baker, destroying herself even as she attempts to satisfy her
cravings. The lines "kneading your body / with your own fists" pun on
her need for physical affection while conflating self-gratification with self-
loathing. The rejected female body is finally a "beaten thing," whose
bloated size testifies only to Thelma's overheated, unsatisfied desires, "the
oven of your hunger."

The conclusion turns away from this pathetic image and makes three
abstract declarations. Coolly addressing Thelma as "madam," the poet as-
sumes a Miltonic formality before effectively disavowing her mother's
hold on her. She can no longer countenance the affectionate label of
"gifted girl," since she sees herself not as an intellectually precocious
daughter but as a fully matured woman. She has learned from Thelma's
example—but perhaps not what Thelma wanted her to learn.

The poem seems to be yearning toward the form of a blank-verse sonnet. Its rhetorical development brings the sonnet form to mind—the beginning setting up a dilemma, the middle elaborating on it, and the last two lines providing closure—but this poem accomplishes in nine lines what a sonnet does in fourteen. In keeping with Thelma's abbreviated, misshapen life, it feels both sped up and truncated. The poem's brevity also comments on the poet's state of mind, the abrupt turn in line 7 marking her brusque rejection of her mother, and the exaggerated finality of the last lines suggesting a child's headstrong desire to be taken as a grownup. The repetition of "i"—literally, an "i" rhyme—further indicates her preoccupation with herself.

The other echoes and rhymes in "to thelma" also contribute to our understanding of mother and daughter. The assonance of "feed," "kneading," and "beaten," gives these words a cumulative force, at one with Thelma's insatiable longing, and the explosive alliteration of "body," "beaten," and "burst" underscores both Thelma's pained physicality and the daughter poet's equally pained rebellion against her deceased mother. The end words in lines 1 and 5, "you" and "dough," identify Thelma with her implacable body. The rhymes of the first, middle, and concluding lines also dramatize the poet's desire to distance herself from her mother. Finally, ending the poem with "do"—the first two letters of "dough"—implies visually and aurally that the daughter has extracted what she needs from her mother in order to shape her own life. By her own estimation, she is a self-directed, grown woman who knows "what to do" rather than a pathetic mound of female dough.

This devastating portrait undercuts the characterization of Thelma in *Generations,* where Clifton reminiscences about her mother's baking skills and sympathetically recounts the sexual rejection Thelma suffered at the hands of her husband, Samuel Sayles. But in this poem, the insistent focus on womanhood recalls Sacks's belief that "one of the most profound issues to beset any mourner and elegist is [her] surviving yet painfully altered sexuality. Although it is crucial for the mourner to assert a continued sexual impulse, that assertion must be qualified, even repressively transformed or rendered metaphorical, by the awareness of loss and mortality."[11] The metaphorical rendering of Thelma as throbbing dough

11. Ibid., 7.

simultaneously represses and releases a sexual impulse. It is as if Clifton, confident of her own prowess, tries on the problem of sexual dysfunction and then quickly discards it. The bread imagery is not just a metaphor for Thelma's sexual dysfunction, however; it is also a trope for her dying. In rejecting Thelma's model, Clifton champions her own life and sexuality. Just as her truculent claiming of womanhood presupposes the power of sexual repression, so does the embracing of life assume mortality's iron grip on everyone. In its elliptical way, then, the poem exposes the pain of Clifton's loss even as it projects that pain onto Thelma. For there is no mistaking the poet's agonized love for her mother or her own desperate desire to live and thrive. The poem thus fulfills Coleridge's observation that the elegy "'must treat of no subject *for itself,* but always and exclusively with reference to the poet himself. As he will feel regret for the past or desire for the future, so sorrow and love become the principal themes of elegy.'"[12] In writing about her mother, Clifton fairly bursts with the emotions Coleridge describes.

The second poem in this sequence, "poem on my fortieth birthday to my mother who died young," is another link in Clifton's elegiac chain. This is a self-consciously occasional poem, one that simultaneously commemorates the daughter's life and the mother's death. Since the poet has reached the age of forty, she is positioned to outlive her mother chronologically, and this prospect is the poem's real occasion. Although this poem is not as damning as "to thelma," it continues to set Clifton's strengths against her mother's frailties. Echoing "my mama moved among the days," this poem's conceit implies that Thelma, in dying young, literally fell short of her daughter's expectations:

> well i have almost come to the place where you fell
> tripping over a wire at the forty-fourth lap
> and i have decided to keep running,
> head up, body attentive, fingers
> aimed like darts at first prize, so
> i might not even watch out for the thin thing
> grabbing toward my ankles but
> i'm trying for the long one mama,

---

12. Samuel Taylor Coleridge, *Table Talk,* 12 October 1833, quoted in Bloomfield, 148.

running like hell and if i fall
i fall.

(GW 176)

Written as one long sentence, this heavily enjambed poem is like a runner in its unwillingness to stop. Significantly, it is not a run-on sentence betraying a confusion of purpose but a grammatically complete one evincing direction and order. This is commensurate with the poet's expressed determination. As Fabian Clements Worsham points out, "Here the tone is not at all melancholy; rather than growing more abject as the fateful date nears, Clifton (perhaps drawing upon the emotional resources she has inherited and cultivated) seems to rally as she approaches the homestretch. Defiant, strong, goal-oriented, she informs her mother that she intends to keep running."[13] But her misgivings about approaching the age at which her mother died are clearly still on her mind. She is bound to fear that she, too, is headed toward a premature demise, and that would make the milestone fortieth birthday that much harder to face: "The vortex of her mother's death continues to pull her into its spiral."[14]

The poem's metaphor for death is a trip wire, a malevolent "thin thing / grabbing toward my ankles." Much more insidious than a cumbersome but clearly visible hurdle, the wire indicates that this particular race is designed to fell even the strongest competitors. Just as the runner who assumes the proper attitude and posture—"head up, body attentive"—is unlikely to notice wires in her path, the person who lives boldly does not typically anticipate misfortune. Of course, tenacity of will cannot stave off death forever, as the poem's ending acknowledges. The colloquial phrase "running like hell" obliquely conjures up thoughts of death and makes it sound, for the first time, as if Clifton is running away from something. No matter how much she throws herself into living, she cannot completely forget or ignore her own mortality. That, after all, is the opposition in this race. Yet even if she were to block out morbid thoughts entirely, a huge paradox would remain, for the life lived bravely and joyfully still

13. Fabian Clements Worsham, "The Poetics of Matrilineage: Mother and Daughters in the Poetry of African American Women, 1965–1985," in *Women of Color: Mother-Daughter Relationships in 20th-Century Literature,* ed. Elizabeth Brown-Guillory (Austin: University of Texas Press, 1997), 123.

14. Ibid., 123.

ends in death. Every "fall" into mortality is as inevitable as Adam and Eve's, an inevitability that the syllogistic "if i fall / i fall" makes abundantly clear.

Like "to thelma," this poem has the skeletal structure of a sonnet. The problem of outliving Thelma is introduced and developed, and then the word "but" at the end of line 7 turns the poem toward its resolution. The last two lines function as a couplet, neatly drawing things to a close while contributing enormously to the poem's meaning. Although there is no set meter, the visual length of the lines draws our attention to key words. Because the first line is noticeably longer than all of the others lines, "fell" hangs precariously off the poem's right edge. Likewise, "thin thing" dangles at the end of a long line, evoking the danger of falling. In the last two lines, the word "fall" echoes "hell," causing us to perceive the one in the other, and the repetition of "i fall" gives these words extra weight. The conditional "if i fall," moreover, teeters above the truncated last line. There, the independent clause "i fall" huddles against the left margin. Graphically and grammatically, Clifton emphasizes the inherently conditional nature of life and the definitive nature of death.

Both "to thelma" and "poem on my fortieth birthday" purport to be about separation and coming into one's own, but they are also studies in separation anxiety. It is only in the sequence's third poem, "february 13, 1980," that the poet admits the degree to which her life is bound to her mother's. On the surface, this sorrowful confession undercuts the bravado of "to thelma" and the panicky joie de vivre of "poem on my fortieth birthday," but it is ultimately the sequence's most forthright expression of her feelings for her mother.

The title marks the twenty-first anniversary of Thelma's death. Like that of "poem on my fortieth birthday," however, the occasion being marked is more of an ongoing process than a fixed moment in time. Having lived without her mother for twenty-one years, Clifton acknowledges that the loss is itself a growing presence in her life:

> twenty-one years of my life you have been
> the lost color in my eye. my secret blindness,
> all my seeings turned grey with your going.
> mother, i have worn your name like a shield.
> it has torn but protected me all these years,

now even your absence comes of age.
i put on a dress called woman for this day
but i am not grown away from you
whatever i say.

(GW 177)

The poem has three distinct parts, each with its own unifying metaphor. In the first three lines, the metaphor of blindness conveys a dramatically altered world view as Clifton admits how much Thelma's absence has affected her life. Though few may notice it, her "secret blindness" conveys her private feelings of helplessness. In the next three lines, the poet alludes to her own name, Thelma Lucille, which literally allies her with her mother. The ambiguous description of the shield allows for a couple of interpretations. It may be that the name-shield has torn—that is, Clifton has begun to move beyond an all-consuming identification with her mother even though she can still take refuge in that identity when she wants. It may also be that Clifton herself has felt torn between autonomy and a continuing dependence on her mother. The concluding lines allow for both of these possibilities. "Her complex feelings are apparent," Worsham writes, "when she notes that the shield has both ripped her up and safeguarded her."[15] Here, as in "to thelma," Clifton asserts her own womanhood, which for her is always a statement of autonomy. She does so "for this day" as she marks the figurative coming of age of Thelma's absence. Like a child reluctant to leave home, Clifton admits for the first time in this sequence that she remains very much attached to her mother. Her autonomous appearance belies a soul still enmeshed in her mother's lost life.

As the last and most explicitly mournful of the three poems, "february 13, 1980" casts the whole sequence in a traditionally elegiac light. The contradictory impulses in the first two poems give way to a conscious awareness of internal conflict. The concluding triple rhyme ("day," "away," "say") indicates that the pieces of the puzzle are finally falling into place. The now-familiar assertion of womanhood no longer obscures Clifton's attachment to her mother. And by declaring "i am not grown away from you" rather than "i *have* not grown away from you," further-

15. Ibid., 123.

more, she appears to be coming to terms with her own complicated identity. Now we see that the poet's identification with her mother underlies all of her declarations, all of her poems—"whatever i say." This concluding phrase occupies only a fraction of the space filled by every previous line, and in its lonely brevity, it is like the last line of "poem on my fortieth birthday." In the one, the white space following the words represents the silence following a death; in the other, it brings to mind the unspoken messages hovering around any utterance.

For Clifton, at the time these poems were published, much was still to be said—and left unsaid—on the subject of Thelma, whose death brought with it the pain of silence and, many years later, the shock of a seemingly supernatural communication. Hull has noted, "Clifton's communications with her mother have slackened in recent years, and the number of poems about her (never that large, considering her general impact on Clifton's life) has likewise decreased."[16] Her later elegies for Thelma, however, are no less fervent than the ones appearing in *Two-Headed Woman*. They reflect Clifton's continuing relationship with her mother, a relationship that can be both nurtured and codified in poetry. Their increasing empathy continues the pattern begun in "february 13, 1980," and along with her earlier poems for Thelma, they represent the longest running series in Clifton's body of elegiac verse.

In *Next*, multiple elegiac strands form a tapestry of mourning as Clifton writes about African slaves, contemporary and historical victims of war, and people close to her who died young, including her husband, Fred, who died of cancer at age forty-nine. In her ongoing work of mourning, Clifton now juxtaposes an elegiac sequence about Thelma with sequences about Crazy Horse (one of Clifton's longtime heroes), Fred Clifton, and a young family friend who died of leukemia. These poems illustrate a desire not only to articulate feelings of loss and longing but also to give the lost ones their own voices. Assuming Thelma's persona—perhaps the logical next step after automatic writing—enables Clifton to gain new insight into her living self.

Each of the four sequences begins with a poem about the subject's death and ends with a poem delivering that person's "message." In these elegies, Clifton seems to address herself, as well as her readers, through

16. Hull, "Channeling the Ancestral Muse," 346.

the persona of the deceased. The use of such a persona deflects some of the emotional isolation that accompanies grief and loss and insists on a connection between the living and the dead. In this way, the poems build on the spiritual foundation laid in *An Ordinary Woman* and *Two-Headed Woman*. Through her choice of personas, Clifton appears to be collaborating with the dead in order to bring important messages to the living. A brief look at the poems that share space with the Thelma poems shows the extent to which the elegy as a form has permeated Clifton's body of work.

A longtime advocate of Native American rights, Clifton views the nineteenth-century Indian leader Crazy Horse as a personal hero. This is not surprising, since Crazy Horse's mysticism, courage, and passion seem to parallel Clifton's own. Here is Dee Brown in *Bury My Heart at Wounded Knee* (1971) recounting the origin of the Indian warrior's name:

> Each time he went into the Black Hills to seek visions, he had asked Wakantanka to give him secret powers so that he would know how to lead the Oglalas to victory if the white men ever came again to make war upon his people. Since the time of his youth, Crazy Horse had known that the world men lived in was only a shadow of the real world. To get into the real world, he had to dream, and when he was in the real world everything seemed to float or dance. In this real world his horse danced as if it were wild or crazy, and this was why he called himself Crazy Horse. He had learned that if he dreamed himself into the real world before going into a fight, he could endure anything.[17]

Like the Bible's King David, another of Clifton's heroes and the subject of a sequence in *The Terrible Stories*, Crazy Horse is a warrior and mystic. His willingness to fight for what he believes in contributes to his appeal for Clifton, who writes in "the death of crazy horse,"

> remember my name, Lakotah.
> i am the final war chief.
> father, my heart,
> never defeated in battle,

17. Dee Brown, *Bury My Heart at Wounded Knee: An Indian History of the American West* (New York: Holt, Rinehart and Winston, 1971), 289.

father, my bones,
never defeated in battle,
leave them at Wounded Knee

and remember our name. Lakotah.
i am released from shadow.
my horse dreams and dances under me
as i enter the actual world.

(N 47)

The "actual" world is the spiritual world where Crazy Horse's soul will live on. Like Clifton herself, he is a visionary whose conception of the world transcends the visible and the known.

In contrast to the Crazy Horse poems, the other sequences that make up "or next" grow out of Clifton's personal knowledge and experience. In the nine poems about Joanne C. (whom Clifton has identified as a family friend who came from the island of Grenada), the subject of the sequence fights a valiant battle before dying of leukemia at age twenty-one. The opening poem, "the death of joanne c.," is a ten-line cry of agony. In it, the narrator sees her disease-ravaged body as "the battleground that / shrieks like a girl" (N 54). Making imaginative use of a Civil War image, she calls herself "gettysburg" and declares that "i host the furious battling of / a suicidal body and / a murderous cure." The conceit is continued in the sequence's closing poem, "the message of jo," in which the dying girl says, "my body is a war / nobody is winning" (N 62).

Her mental illness demands a cataclysmic metaphor. Acquiescence becomes the only tenable posture, as Jo's message finally makes clear: "my blood is a white flag, / waving. / surrender, / my darling mother, / death is life." Jo's family and friends must surrender along with her to the inevitability of her dying so young. The loss that cannot be reconciled must still somehow be accepted. The "darling mother" seems to represent all mothers witnessing the death of a child. As in Generations, when Clifton identifies so strongly with Caroline's excruciating loss of her daughter, this poem recognizes the maternal bond even as it insists on the finality of death.

The Joanne poems are among Clifton's bleakest. Greg Kuzma has persuasively analyzed the sequence's arrangement:

A different poet might have grouped all the poems about Joanne's death from leukemia together in one or two longer poems, but Clifton leaves them to make what seems a casual assortment. Where each of the poems as we read might well be the last, we become unusually alert and attentive, only to find on the next page another Joanne poem taken from a slightly different perspective. . . . Clifton in effect re-creates some of the anxiety and tension that accompany any long terminal illness. Life progresses day by day from terror to remission, from moments of anguish to moments of calm and insight and a suspension of hostilities. Any day offers a fresh perspective, or may, or holds out hope for the kind of seeing that may bring an ultimate and healing knowledge.[18]

The five poems about Fred Clifton likewise imply that healing knowledge can be culled from a painful loss. These latter poems echo the Crazy Horse poems in their ethereal nature and preoccupation with names and identity. They also call to mind the stories of *Generations,* especially Samuel's memory of Caroline, Clifton's great-great-grandmother, refusing to reveal her African name—the imagined key to understanding the whole family's African origins. In "i'm going back to my true identity," Fred's persona declares, "i was ready to return / to my rightful name" (N 65). The name symbolizes Fred's spiritual identity, which cannot be articulated or fully known on earth. Clifton imagines that Fred, now deceased, has an important message for her: "tell her there is no deathless name / a body can pronounce." As his "living wife," Clifton relies on language as a means of describing and reclaiming her husband, but this poem argues that there is a realm beyond language where human names do not and cannot exist.

Such an argument might seem to fly in the face of the Romantic notion of the poet, who, in Emerson's terms, "is the Namer or Language-maker, naming things sometimes after their appearance, sometimes after their essence, and giving to every one its own name and not another's."[19] If Fred Clifton has slipped beyond the grasp of language and human names, then he would seem to have eluded his living wife once and for all. But for both Emerson and Clifton, that very elusiveness gives credence

18. Greg Kuzma, "Women Hoping for Rain," review of *Next,* in *Georgia Review* 42, no. 3 (Fall 1988): 630.

19. *Selected Essays, Lectures, and Poems of Ralph Waldo Emerson,* ed. R. E. Spiller (New York: Washington Square, 1965), 16–17.

to the idea of a spiritual realm underlying the poetic one. Emerson writes, "This expression or naming is not art, but a second nature, grown out of the first, as a leaf out of a tree. What we call nature is a certain self-regulated motion or change; and nature does all things by her own hands, and does not leave another to baptize her but baptizes herself."[20] Fred Clifton's "true identity," the deathless name beyond the poet's ken, is the essence of selfhood which language can only attempt to describe.

Set against the lyrical mysticism of the Crazy Horse poems, the raw devastation of the Joanne C. poems, and the intellectualized yearning of the poems for Fred Clifton, the elegiac sequence about Thelma reaches for the middle ground of reconciliation. Although Clifton is still mourning the loss of her mother, she finds solace in the thought that she embodies some of Thelma's strengths. When the poet assumes Thelma's voice in "the death of thelma sayles" and "the message of thelma sayles," she appears to be responding to her own reproachful questions in "my mama moved among the days." The later poems describe the legacies of love, maternal strength, and poetic inspiration that Thelma passed on to her daughter. These poems, which seem quite aware of their status as elegies, are both for and, rhetorically speaking, *by* Thelma. In "the death of thelma sayles," Clifton writes:

> i leave no tracks so my live loves
> can't follow. at the river
> most turn back, their souls shivering,
> but my little girl stands alone on the bank
> and watches. i pull my heart out of my pocket
> and throw it. i smile as she catches all
> she'll ever catch and heads for home
> and her children. mothering
> has made it strong, i whisper in her ear
> along the leaves.
>
> (*N* 51)

Its conceit revisiting and revising that of "my mama moved among the days," this poem suggests that Thelma did not retreat in fear of her re-

---

20. Ibid., 17.

sponsibilities to her family but rather completed a journey still beyond her daughter's understanding. Here we see Clifton's desire to stay in contact with her mother, even after her mother's death, and the mythological allusions to the underworld suggest that Clifton's relationship with her mother is not just personal but archetypal. Sacks notes that "the elegy follows the ancient rites in the basic passage through grief or darkness to consolation and renewal."[21] We see that progression here, as Clifton reconciles herself to her mother's death and acknowledges, through the persona of Thelma herself, the powerful gift of maternal love. The poem pays glancing tribute to the Persephone myth, with the figure of the daughter accomplishing what Sacks calls "an initiate's descent to and ascent from a crisis of mysterious revelation."[22] Thelma's heart symbolizes the continuing life of the family and the regenerating strength of motherhood. Thelma lives on in her daughter's own mothering of children.

Another important part of Thelma's legacy comes through in "the message of thelma sayles." Here, Clifton has her mother speak from the bedroom, where Thelma was spurned by Samuel and then suffered epileptic fits. What was mystifying might well have been mystical: "the first fit broke my bed. / i woke from ecstasy to ask / what blood is this? am i the bride of Christ? / my bitten tongue was swollen for three days" (N 53). Speaking to herself through the persona of her mother, Clifton continues, "i thrashed and rolled from fit to death. / you are my only daughter." At this point the focus shifts from Thelma's life to Clifton's own. No longer the watchful little girl of the previous poem, she is an adult worried about her own mortality.

Thelma's admonition in the poem provides a way for the grown daughter to reconcile her fears: "when you lie awake in the evenings / counting your birthdays / turn the blood that clots on your tongue / into poems. poems." Writing a poem, like rearing a child, is an act of hope and love; it is a way to give voice to the many selves welling up within and a means of exploring, if not solving, the mysteries of human life. Unlike Thelma, Clifton preserved and published her poetry. Thelma's example helped point Clifton toward this particular vocation and thus provided her daughter with yet another source of strength. The woman who has borne poems *and* children is doubly creative.

21. Sacks, 20.
22. Ibid.

In "The Magic Mama," Clifton tells us more about her mother's writing of poetry. Although she has remarked during readings that Samuel denied Thelma the opportunity to publish her work, here Clifton lays the blame on the whole family:

> A book of verse she wrote was accepted by a publisher but the family didn't approve; we don't want everybody reading about our Mama, you ain't no poetry writer, you a mother; and so she burned it. After that she wrote no more. Except after the arrogant daughter, the poet daughter, showed her some poems celebrating misunderstood youth, she said, I'm gonna show you how to write a poem, baby, that ain't no poem. And she wrote one.
>   Forgive.

Although no one forced Thelma to burn her poems, Clifton belatedly assumes responsibility for her mother's rash act. She is "the poet daughter" who swiftly picks up the tradition her mother felt forced to drop. In the wake of her mother's death, she determines that her own writing—and all of her life-affirming acts—will be a form of penance: "Everything for her, everything, all poems, all movings-up, all goodnesses, everything begging, begging, Mama, Mama of Magic, forgive. Forgive. Forgive."[23] Living her life in this way may assuage the guilt she feels for having outlived her mother and outstripped her as a poet; it is also a means of motivating herself as a writer.

Even if Thelma had not been Clifton's mother, the dynamics of mourning a poet who died young would be complicated enough. "The death of the poet," Eric Smith writes, "cannot but bring to mind the poetic purpose and the future death of that other poet who is now writing."[24] It follows that the death of a poet *and* mother would be even more profound, ineluctably heightening the daughter poet's consciousness of her own creative and procreative powers. We see this particular drama of mourning played out in "fury," a poem with the dedication *"for mama"* in *The Book of Light:*

23. Clifton, "Magic Mama," 89.

24. Eric Smith, *By Mourning Tongues: Studies in English Elegy* (Totowa, N.J.: Rowan and Littlefield, 1977), 11.

remember this.
she is standing by
the furnace.
the coals
glisten like rubies.
her hand is crying.
her hand is clutching
a sheaf of papers.
poems.
she gives them up.
they burn
jewels into jewels.
her eyes are animals.
each hank of her hair
is a serpent's obedient
wife.
she will never recover.
remember. there is nothing
you will not bear
for this woman's sake.

(BL 45)

In this retelling, we do not learn of the events leading up to Thelma's burning of her poems. Instead, the poem dwells on Thelma's pain, comparing the sacrifice of her writing to a literal destruction of the self from which "she will never recover." The complex image of her hair conjures up a woman who is part furious Medusa and part submissive spouse. The implication is that Thelma, no matter how much it enrages her to burn the written record of her selfhood, has willingly complied with her husband's wishes.

The directive to "remember" at the beginning and end involves the reader as well as the poet in the act of self-immolation. Although the dedication clarifies the relation between poet and subject, Thelma is described in the poem's body only as "this woman." To remember Thelma is to salvage and then reconstruct her sacrificed selfhood. Though only a substitute for the deceased, the poem is a powerful substitute, for it embodies the art central to the dead woman's identity. The poem's closing entreaty emphasizes this point. The line "remember. there is nothing" marks the absence where the mother poet's poems should have been. The sentence completed in the last two lines suggests that no amount of self-sacrifice will equal Thelma's, so the daughter poet must stoically bear her own burdens. Because the word "bear" can denote giving birth as well as withstanding pain, the last lines also imply that the daughter poet's creations—her poems and her own children—will pay tribute to Thelma.

Coming nearly twenty-five years after the heart-wrenching avowals in "The Magic Mama," the declaration indicates that Clifton, in 1993, still believes that her lengthening life and well-received volumes of verse must somehow make up for Thelma's premature death, the ashes of her poems. Poignant because it can be neither proven nor entirely discounted, such a belief helps explain the elegiac nature of Clifton's poetry. In her 1999 interview with Charles Rowell, Clifton further elucidated her endeavor: "[W]hen my brother died, I started asking myself who was going to remember my mother as a young woman. . . . [I]f the last person who remembers is gone, what is left? What will be left of my mother? I must stay alive so that in a way my mother stays alive."[25]

Clifton's work of mourning is the work of her life and her art. As we have seen in the poems for her mother, her elegies express numerous emotions, including defiance, fear, and faith. In keeping with the Romantic notion of the elegy, these works strive toward self-understanding and self-acceptance even as they embrace the sorrows of loss. Yet the elegies for Thelma are only a core sample of a largely elegiac body of work, as her poems about Crazy Horse, Joanne, and her husband have illustrated here. We see a similar entwining of love and sorrow, pleasure and regret, in Clifton's elegies for still other family members and friends, and even for her own body as she endures the losses of uterus, breast, and kidney. The elegiac strain is especially prevalent in her prose memoir *Generations*, as the next chapter will demonstrate.

25. Rowell, 57–58.

CHAPTER 8

Concentric Circles of Selfhood in *Generations*

LUCILLE CLIFTON PUBLISHED *Generations: A Memoir* in 1976, the year of the American bicentennial. During a time of widespread reflection on the nation's past, Clifton focused on her African and African American ancestors' lives in both slavery and freedom. She was, of course, not alone in this endeavor; in the same year that *Generations* came out, Alex Haley's *Roots* caused a national sensation. Haley's book spurred many Americans to trace their genealogies and take pride in their family origins. Its eventual transformation into an enormously popular TV miniseries illustrates just how accessible *Roots* was to a mass audience. Haley told a riveting story, and later reports that parts of his book were plagiarized did little to diminish mainstream enthusiasm for his accomplishment.

In contrast to the bold, novelistic storytelling of the 688-page *Roots*, Clifton's 54-page narrative of her paternal family lineage is meditative, elliptical, and elegiac. *Generations* may be seen as a collage of "mourning stories," to use Karla Holloway's term,[1] in its preoccupation with the deaths of family members, but it is a book of praise as much as one of grief and lamentation. Because Clifton, like Haley, finds strength in her family's past and a great deal of hope in its future, one does not come away from *Generations* feeling either depressed or falsely reassured. As in her poetry, Clifton bases her cultural critique on her own and her ancestors' experience while maintaining a deep faith in the power of the human spirit to outlast adversity. *Generations* is a signal achievement in African American literature as well as an invaluable aid in understanding Clifton's poetry.

The work's stylistic elegance and implicit epistemological concerns distinguish it not only from *Roots* but from memoirs of the same era by other black women poets, such as Gwendolyn Brooks's *Report from Part One* (1972) and Maya Angelou's *I Know Why the Caged Bird Sings* (1970).

---

1. Karla F. C. Holloway, "Cultural Narratives Passed On: African American Mourning Stories," in Napier, *African American Literary Theory*, 655.

Although those two books contribute to their authors' larger poetic endeavors, they do not aspire to the same goals that Clifton's memoir does. In addition to telling one African American family's story, *Generations* causes us to contemplate the many ways we receive, imagine, and write about the past. It is interesting to note that Toni Morrison was Clifton's editor at Random House, the original publisher of *Generations*, and Clifton said that Morrison encouraged her to tape-record the stories as a way to begin the project.[2] Like Morrison's *Beloved* (1987), *Generations* addresses the myriad connections between memory, slavery, and African American family life. The memoir's meaning transcends the particulars of the lives it recounts.

The death of Samuel Sayles and Clifton's journey with her husband and brother to her father's funeral provide the book's opening chapters with a narrative frame. *Generations* commemorates both deceased and living family members, and the sections about the trip to Samuel's funeral alternate with sections in which Samuel himself provides family history. The long dead, the recently deceased, and the still living coexist in Clifton's narrative; *Generations* acknowledges the truth of this coexistence—this borderless cohabitation—in its elliptical telling.

The deceased span four generations, beginning with the family matriarch: Clifton's paternal great-great-grandmother, Caroline Donald Sale, who was captured as a young child in Dahomey, Africa, and brought to New Orleans to be a slave. At the age of eight in 1830, according to Sayles family lore, Caroline walked from New Orleans to Bedford, Virginia, where she grew up in slavery, the property of Bob Donald. After working in the fields throughout her youth, she was purchased by John F. Sale at the behest of a slave in his possession, Louis Sale, who wanted Caroline to be his wife.

Though Louis was a great deal older than Caroline, the two were married, and she remained in the Sale household until the end of the Civil War. Caroline became a well-respected midwife in Bedford and had children of her own. Among those children was Clifton's great-grandmother, Lucy Sale. Once grown, Lucy became involved with a white northerner, Harvey Nichols; for reasons apparently known only to her, she shot him dead one night when Harvey had come to see her. The result of Lucy's

2. Rowell, 56.

union with Harvey Nichols was Gene Sayle, a free spirit born with a withered arm. He was the father of Samuel Sayles, a proud, overbearing man eager to discuss his family's history. Samuel's wife (and Clifton's mother), Thelma Moore Sayles, is also memorialized in the book. A shy, loving woman who suffered from epilepsy, Thelma died at age forty-four.

Over the course of these storied generations, the family name evolves from Sale to Sayle to Sayles. After Emancipation, the black Sales added the y to their name as a means of distinguishing themselves from their former owners. This subtle but significant alteration announced a new distance but preserved the old connection. Samuel Sayle later decided to add an s to his name as an indication that "There will be more than one of me" (*GW* 243). He wanted it to be known that the family was not only a distinct entity but also a growing clan that would thrive and multiply.

The connection to the slaveholding family is still embedded in the name, however, a point Clifton makes on the first page of *Generations*. An elderly white woman named Sale, who has compiled a family history, calls in response to Clifton's notice in a Bedford, Virginia, newspaper soliciting information about the Sale/Sayle family. The woman does not recognize the name of Samuel Sayles, her contemporary, but, writes Clifton, "she tells me that the slave cabins are still there at the Sale home where she lives, and the graves of the slaves are there, unmarked. The graves of my family. She remembers the name Caroline, she says, her parents were delivered by the midwife, Mammy Caroline. The midwife Mammy Caroline" (*GW* 227). Caroline left an indelible impression on both families, and as mother and midwife she helped deliver both families into the present world that Clifton and her white counterpart occupy. The fact that she had an African name lost over time makes Caroline all the more important to this family and Clifton's narrative. Calling to mind the lines "before the word / you were" in "brothers" (*BL* 76), Caroline the Dahomey-born woman has an existence preceding that of the name she is known by in the United States, and her meaning to future generations continues long after her death. *Generations* is in many ways an extended elegy for Caroline.

The living family members described in *Generations* fulfill Samuel's prophecy. They include the poet Thelma Lucille Sayles Clifton; her brother, Sammy, and two half-sisters, Jo and Punkin; her husband, Fred Clifton; and the Cliftons' four daughters, Sidney, Fredrica, Gillian, and

Alexia, and their two sons, Channing and Graham. The book is thus true to its expansive title: at the same time that it eulogizes Clifton's parents and her paternal ancestors, all of whom were affected by the soul-deadening institution of slavery, it also commemorates the family's living generations and the future manifested in the Clifton children. Like her poetry, the memoir oscillates between elegy and praise song. The dead are recalled, and the living are commended.

With her heightened awareness of mortality, Clifton seems to realize that the story she is telling in *Generations* is essentially the story of all families, the complex narrative behind the poignant snapshots found in any family album. The family photos included in the memoir drive home this point, as Cheryl Wall demonstrates in her discussion of the relationship between the pictures and text in *Generations*.[3] In the black-and-white image of Samuel Sayles, for instance, he stands between two houses, with his suit jacket in one hand and his vest flapping in a long-ago breeze. Probably taken by his wife or one of his children, the picture shows a strong, self-confident man in the prime of his life. Like all photographs of the now-deceased, the image commemorates both a presence and an absence. Although the faces vary from album to album, the mingled emotions of love and sorrow that such pictures inspire are familiar to virtually everyone.

One comes away from *Generations* feeling, then, that the Sayleses are a representative American family, but their African origins and passage through slavery give them special insights into this country's history. *Generations* emphasizes slavery's impact on the family, even as Clifton endorses her parents' view that slavery was a temporary aberration in the history of a strong, free people. By placing the family's stories in the historical context of slavery in America, Clifton makes *Generations* an archetypal tale. Although she is writing about her own family, *Generations* is illustrative of many families that have endured and even triumphed in the face of enormous obstacles. Once in her father's voice and again in her own, Clifton tells of "[t]he generations of Caroline Donald, born free among the Dahomey people in 1822 and died free in Bedford Virginia in 1910" (*GW* 230). The litany of names that follows this preamble positions

---

3. See Cheryl Wall, "Sifting Legacies in Lucille Clifton's *Generations*," *Contemporary Literature* 40, no. 4 (Winter 1999): 552–74.

Clifton's genealogy alongside those in the Old Testament. Readers of *Generations* who know her poetry will recognize Clifton's transformation of African American experience into something both universal and sacred. This universalizing of experience, via an African matriarchal lineage, means that the text may hold lessons for present-day readers, no matter what their race or ethnicity. Just as the Bible is "concerned to remember the past for what it has to say to the present," so, too, is *Generations*.[4]

In addition to the Bible, the source so crucial to Clifton's poetry, the genre of the slave narrative is an important antecedent to this memoir. Like many of the slave narratives, the tales and anecdotes making up *Generations* started out as oral history. Her strong-willed father, an inveterate storyteller whose persona is so important to this book, provides her with the raw material for *Generations*. Since her father had little formal education and could not write more than a few words, the very act of writing down Samuel's stories must have felt empowering and ennobling. Like the slaves and ex-slaves whose stories made the dramatic leap from word-of-mouth to words in print, Samuel would leave a permanent record, via his daughter's book, for future generations to contemplate. And since Clifton prepared for the writing of the book by reciting family stories into a tape recorder, she was in effect continuing the oral tradition so important to her family in particular and to the transmission of African American history overall.

Furthermore, while Clifton's multigenerational memoir is very different in style and organization from a classic slave narrative like the *Narrative of the Life of Frederick Douglass*, it does tell the story of a slave, Caroline. As in a traditional slave narrative, the book traces Caroline's life from slavery to freedom. Though Caroline is long dead, Clifton humanizes her ancestor's plight so that readers cannot help empathizing with the African child who became an American slave and finally evolved into a freed African American matriarch. Much more than a one-dimensional victim of her times, Caroline is a living presence in the minds of her descendants. Put another way, she is the core around which much of the family's self-knowledge revolves. We find, in fact, that a sort of gender parity results from the attention that *Generations* gives to Caroline. It is as if Clifton is

---

4. Herbert G. May and Bruce M. Metzger, "How to Read the Bible with Understanding," in May and Metzger, *New Oxford Annotated Bible with the Apocrypha*, 1516.

not only helping her talkative father keep Caroline's spirit alive, but also countering his style of storytelling—and Douglass's—by placing her enigmatic great-great-grandmother at the center of a family circle as well as at the beginning of a genealogical line.

Clifton makes this point by telling Samuel's and Caroline's stories practically at the same time. Her rhetorical balancing act can be usefully compared to what Douglass does in his 1845 autobiography. Robert B. Stepto has analyzed Douglass's use of syncretic phrasing, his uncanny "ability to startlingly conjoin past and present and to do so with images that not only stand for different periods in his personal history but also, in their fusion, speak of his evolution from slavery to freedom." One example of this, Stepto points out, occurs in Douglass's description of his physical suffering as a slave. When Douglass imagines placing his pen in the gashes left by the frostbite he suffered as a child in slavery, he figuratively and literally "takes measure of the wounds of the past."[5]

By way of comparison, consider the opening vignette in *Generations*. Here, the poet describes the telephone conversation with the white woman who has responded to Clifton's notice in the Bedford newspaper. Upon questioning, it becomes clear that this woman's compilation of the Sale family history does not acknowledge the family slaves, who also bore the name of Sale. We learn that the slave graves on the Sale family property are not even marked. *Generations* clearly seeks to right these wrongs. Though she has no further conversations with the Bedford woman, the connection remains, as Clifton explains:

> Yet she sends the history she has compiled and in it are her family's names. And our family names are thick in her family like an omen. I see that she is the last of her line. Old and not married, left with a house and a name. I look at my husband and our six children and I feel the Dahomey women gathering in my bones.
>
> "They called her Ca'line," Daddy would tell us. "What her African name was, I never heard her say. I asked her one time to tell me and she just shook her head. But it'll be forgot, I hollered at her, it'll be forgot.

5. Robert B. Stepto, "Narration, Authentication, and Authorial Control in Frederick Douglass's *Narrative* of 1845," in *African-American Autobiography*, ed. William L. Andrews (Englewood Cliffs, N.J.: Prentice Hall, 1993), 31.

> She just smiled at me and said 'Don't you worry, mister, don't you
> worry.'" (*GW* 228)

In these paragraphs, we hear Clifton, Samuel, and Caroline—three voices
spanning 150 years. The call-and-response among them is a variation on
the syncretic phrasing that we see in Douglass. As in the passage from the
Narrative mentioned above, Clifton's juxtaposition of voices connects past
and present lives and indicates that individual identities grow out of col-
lective experience. By quoting her father, who is quoting his great-grand-
mother, Clifton posits what we might call a concentric approach to self-
hood: each member of a generation inevitably, though often unwittingly,
embraces and embodies all preceding generations. While she never denies
the existence of a distinct chronological line, Clifton's conception of fam-
ily—and, by extension, all humanity—expands in circles, organically and
holistically. This is in keeping with the African tradition she honors in
Caroline's memory.

A concentric vision of history does not make the past any more acces-
sible or understandable, of course. Again and again, Clifton yearns for
facts out of which she can fashion salient truths. In this respect, she seems
to have taken after her father, whose memories of his childhood cluster
around his conversations with Caroline. A curious and precocious child,
Samuel tries valiantly to get Caroline to talk about her past. He persis-
tently pumps her for information: How had she been captured in Africa?
How did she feel when she and her mother were permanently separated
from each other? The answers to these questions belong to a hidden self,
one that presumably lurks somewhere inside Caroline. We don't know
why she won't respond to Samuel's queries, but given her obvious love for
him and her willingness to talk to him about the legendary Dahomey
women of Africa, it may be that she is trying to spare him knowledge of
the pain she endured. To Samuel's credit, he divines that Caroline's reve-
lations as well as her secrets are important to the family history he is pass-
ing on to his daughter:

> She talked like she was from London England and when we kids would
> be running and hooping and hollering all around she would come to the
> door and look straight at me and say "Stop that Bedlam, mister, stop that
> Bedlam, I say." With a Oxford accent, Lue! She was a dark old skinny

lady and she raised my Daddy and then raised me, least till I was eight years old when she died. When I was eight years old. I remember everything she ever told me, cause you know when you that age you old enough to remember things. I remember everything she told me, Lue, even though she died when I was eight years old. And then I knowed about what she remembered cause that's how old she was when she got here. Eight years old. (*GW* 230)

By connecting his age at the time of Caroline's death to her age at the time of her arrival in the United States, Samuel insists on a continuity in the family history: his memory of his first eight years links him to the eight-year-old Caroline's memories of Africa. He cannot know all of Caroline's story, as much as he might like to, but he knows that she brought bits and pieces of Africa with her to the United States. In this regard, Cheryl Wall writes, "The insistent repetition of the age indicts the system of slavery that robs generations of childhood, even as it honors the spirit that enabled the child Samuel to remember fragments of the past." Because he remembers a great deal from his early childhood, he believes that Caroline did, too. Her memories of Africa infiltrated his childhood and influenced his identity as a grown man. "Samuel Sayles carried with him a recollection of a past more distant than slavery," Wall points out. "For this family, the heroic memory of the ancestral journey from Dahomey to America, then from New Orleans to Virginia, becomes a talisman for later generations to stave off pain and grief."[6] Though secondhand, that African influence will be part of his legacy to his children, a legacy crucial to Clifton's poetry.

The complex realities of slavery clearly preoccupy Samuel. This is especially apparent in his recollection of Caroline's marriage to a slave many years her senior. Though there is no indication that her marriage was unhappy, she had no choice in her mate. Samuel sums up the paradox of whatever happiness Caroline may have found in this unsought domestic life: "'Oh slavery, slavery,' my Daddy would say. 'It ain't something in a book, Lue. Even the good parts was awful'" (*GW* 237).

Caroline's silence on the subject of her African name is a frightening part of her story because it cannot be analyzed or rationalized in any de-

6. Wall, 561, 554.

finitive way. Still, her admonition to her great-grandson—"Don't you worry"—implies that the family will live on, regardless of which names show up in the record books. These words, which show up again at the end of the memoir, create a verbal touchstone, one of several in *Generations* that appear to represent Clifton's own world view. The blank space where Caroline's African name should be, the unmarked graves in Bedford, the white Sale woman's version of history—though disturbing, none of these negates the reality of Clifton's own life with her husband and children, nor will the omissions prevent the poet from contemplating and recording her own version of the family history. The omissions, in fact, will spur her on. They are like the white spaces around lines in a poem, the lacunas that make the written words stand out.

The first four chapters of *Generations* alternate tales of Clifton's paternal ancestors with an account of the events immediately following Samuel's death. This organization pays tribute to the deceased father who passed the family history on to his daughter. But because Samuel knew his aged great-grandmother Caroline, he is present in both strands of the narrative. The most basic facts do not dispel the impression that Samuel and Caroline are somehow always at the center of things. As Clifton explains, "My father was born in Bedford Virginia in 1902. His father Gene Sayle had died when he was a little boy and his mother had gone to work in the tobacco factory, leaving my father and his two brothers and one sister in the care of her dead husband's grandmother. My father's great-grandmother, who had been a slave" (*GW* 243). Samuel cannot be extricated from the telling of Caroline's story, nor can she be removed from an account of his life. The memoir's epigraphs from "Song of Myself" reinforce the idea that the lives of different generations inevitably contain and continue one another. Clifton quotes the following from Whitman:

> They are alive and well somewhere,
> The smallest sprout shows there is really no death,
> And if ever there was, it led forward life, and does not wait at
>   the end to arrest it,
> And ceas'd the moment life appear'd.
>
> (*GW* 263)

To tell Caroline's story is to tell Samuel's; to tell Samuel's is to tell Caroline's and Clifton's. And to quote Whitman, in *Generations,* is to quote

Clifton. As Edward Whitley writes, "Clifton's response to Whitman's 'Song of Myself' speaks with a double voice as she embraces the Whitmanian spirit of inclusion and celebration, but replaces the autonomous individuality informing so much of 'Song of Myself' with a collective, generational sense of self based around an expanding African American family."[7]

That collective sense of self and the overlapping narratives in *Generations* provide us with a useful model for understanding the way history works. Like much of Clifton's poetry, this book implies that history is all about the connections between people and between generations. These connections provide continuity, and it is that regenerative continuity that gives us hope for the future. Furthermore, the interlocking parts of any story, or history, create an impression of organic wholeness. Seen from Clifton's perspective, stories find their natural place within larger stories; text becomes context. As Clifton puts it, "[O]ur lives are our line and we go on. I type that and I swear I can see Ca'line standing in the green of Virginia, in the green of Afrika, and I swear she makes no sound but she nods her head and smiles" (*GW* 276). Caroline and Clifton were not acquainted, but through Samuel and their shared faith in him, the two women can at least figuratively believe in and approve of each other.

All of this reclamation does not come without a price, however, and that price is tallied in the suffering writ large in some of the most sacred of family stories. We see this in the account of Lucy, Clifton's grandmother, who shot and killed the white father of her child. As a result, Lucy allegedly became the "'First Black woman legally hanged in the state of Virginia'" (*GW* 240). The murder of Harvey Nichols would seem to be a horrible blot on the family history, but when Samuel recollects this apocryphal episode, Clifton notes, with seeming amazement, that "he would be looking proud" (*GW* 240). He is so proud of his grandmother Lucy that he names his daughter Thelma Lucille. It is hard to be certain what impresses Samuel more: the audacity of Lucy's crime or the dubious honor of her legal trial and execution.

Imagining how Lucy and Lucy's mother must have felt, Clifton naturally associates emotions other than pride with her great-grandmother's hanging. For her, the story is about the pain and disgrace visited on Caro-

7. Edward Whitley, "'A Long Missing Part of Itself': Bringing Lucille Clifton's *Generations* into American Literature," *MELUS* 26, no. 2 (Summer 2001): 48.

line and Lucy and future generations, not the respect that a legal trial would represent to a black family during the mid-nineteenth century. Clifton retells the infamous story from her own perspective:

> And Lucy was hanged. Was hanged, the lady whose name they gave me like a gift had her neck pulled up by a rope until the neck broke and I can see Mammy Ca'line standing straight as a soldier in green Virginia apart from the crowd of silent Black folk and white folk watching them and not the wooden frame swinging her child. And their shame making distance between them and her a real thing. And I know she made no sound but her mind closed around the picture like a frame and I know that her child made no sound and I turn in my chair and arch my back and make this sound for my two mothers and for all Dahomey women. (*GW* 245)

Samuel's pride thus gives way to Clifton's grief. The hanged woman's name ironically bestowed on her "like a gift," she recalls an event whose particulars she can only imagine. Even at a remove of many years, she still feels the horror of the scene, and it manifests itself in her like a birth. Arching her back and crying out, she is truly bearing the pain endured by a long line of Dahomey women. Overcome by thoughts of her familial past, Clifton is like Sethe in Morrison's *Beloved*, whose "brain was not interested in the future. Loaded with the past and hungry for more, it left her no room to imagine, let alone plan for, the next day."[8]

Clifton's version of the hanging reverberates with meaning because she endows it with her own narrative elements and symbolism, thereby challenging Samuel's role as family storyteller. We might even see the hanging scene as her feminist revision of the Crucifixion, with Clifton, her great-grandmother Lucy, and her great-great-grandmother Caroline forming a female trinity. The "sound" Clifton makes upon reflecting on her great-grandmother's hanging calls to mind Jesus's agonized cry on the cross: "My God, my God, why hast thou forsaken me?" (Matthew 27:46).

Just as she is coming "out of my mother's life" and "into my own" in her signature poem, "the thirty eighth year" (*GW* 159), so she is coming out of the life of her father—which is to say Samuel's and perhaps also the patriarchal Christian God—and into her own in *Generations*. By devel-

---

8. Toni Morrison, *Beloved* (New York: Plume, 1988), 70.

oping Samuel's stories and responding to them, she honors Samuel while asserting her own viewpoint, her own voice. In relation to this self-assertion, Clifton's visceral identification with Caroline and Lucy—the "two mothers" in a long line of foremothers—complements the strong cross-generational kinship with women evident in her poetry. By making "this sound," a primal scream of grief or the "sound" of the written memoir, Clifton speaks for all women silenced by patriarchal institutions that determine the shape and direction of their lives.

In their different ways, all of Clifton's sources seem to believe that excavating the family history—and, with it, the history of slavery in America—is a subjective process that will uncover more paradoxes than anything else. The venerable Caroline, who embodies the strength and courage of the Dahomey Amazons, seems intent on erasing the horrors she endured. The young Samuel, with a child's boundless curiosity, tries to determine what those horrors were even as he proudly embraces the Dahomey heritage and imagines his place in this line of powerful women. Once grown, Samuel passes on what he knows to his daughter, who transforms the oral narrative into a complex work of literature.

Clifton's husband plays a role here, too. In response to her doubts about the accuracy of the hanging story, Fred Clifton tells her "not to worry, that even the lies are true. In history, even the lies are true" (GW 245). This riddle of a response suggests that African Americans' apocryphal stories are no less valid or important than those of white America. Furthermore, Fred seems to know that stories told and retold accumulate a grandeur and a significance that cannot be denied. Such is the power of myth, literature, and history. Recalling Caroline's admonition to Samuel—"Don't you worry, mister"—Fred's words ease his wife's mind and release the tension in this chapter. Maybe it is recognition of her own role in the grand fabrication of history that enables Clifton to end the chapter on a conciliatory, humorous note: "And there would be days when we young Sayles would be trying to dance and sing in the house and [my brother] Sammy would miss a step and not be able to keep up to the music and he would look over in the corner of the room and holler 'Damn Harvey Nichols.' And we would laugh" (GW 245). Her brother's joke comes as a relief after Clifton's soul-rending pain. Yet like his father and sister, he is talking back to the past, entering into a dialogue with silent ghosts. The life of a story, of all history, depends on just this sort of communication. As the hanged woman's namesake, Clifton feels obligated to get the story right, a process which for her involves knowing the facts that will determine the appropriate moral perspective. While attempting this, however, she seems to realize that there are at least as many "right" ways of framing Lucy's story as there are family members surviving to frame it.

The multiple perspectives presented in the vignette about Lucy, and throughout *Generations,* argue for the vibrant, protean nature of history. History is alive in the minds of listeners and readers, all of whom feel compelled to touch and reshape it before passing it on. We might say the same of Samuel, whose life Clifton contemplates over the course of her memoir. He is the complex hero of *Generations,* a character who demands our attention just as he does Clifton's. But the memoir, for all of its fond recollections of Samuel the man and the storyteller, also exposes his imperfections. In the last chapter, titled "thelma," Clifton finally turns to her mother, the woman who lived her short, seemingly unexceptional life in Samuel's shadow. But because Thelma, who died young, spent her entire adult life married to Samuel, he remains an important presence here. It is in "thelma" that Clifton removes him from the pedestal she has placed him on:

> He hurt us all a lot and we hurt him a lot, the way people who love each other do, you know. I probably am better off than any of us, better off in my mind, you know, and I credit Fred for that. Punkin she has a hard time living in the world and so does my brother and Jo has a hard time and gives one too. And a lot of all that is his fault, has something to do with him. (*GW* 273)

In acknowledging the pain he has inflicted on the family, Clifton reinforces the impression of Samuel's patriarchal power. A stubborn, self-centered man, Samuel often disregards other people's interests and desires. With the exception of Caroline, who died long ago, the women in Samuel's life find themselves relegated to supporting roles.

In "thelma," Clifton writes about herself—her name is Thelma Lucille, after all—as much as about her mother; it seems that their stories cannot be rendered separately. She recalls her protective attitude toward her introverted mother, whose epileptic seizures vexed and angered her uncomprehending husband. As a girl, Clifton would go to the movies with her mother and spend New Year's Eve with her, all the while worrying obsessively about Thelma's health and her parents' peculiar marriage: "I wanted to make things right. I always thought I was supposed to. As if there was a right. As if I knew what right was. As if I knew" (GW 275). In retrospect, Clifton recognizes the futility of mothering her own mother, who did not always welcome her daughter's attentions. She also realizes that making things "right" is an endless, exhausting enterprise, equal in difficulty to pursuing and grasping the ever-elusive truth.

Thelma herself is a metaphor for the truth that Clifton seeks to understand and claim. The woman who is "like a dreamwalker in a field" in the 1969 poem "my mama moved among the days" is still elusive in *Generations* seven years later (GW 16). In the midst of discussing her parents, Clifton suddenly declares, "And Mama, Mama's life was—seemed like— the biggest waste in the world to me, but now I don't know, I'm not sure any more" (GW 273). The truth of Thelma, like the truth of everything else, refuses to stay fixed in place. The daughter's uncertainty about the meaning of her mother's life is evident in the sentence's meandering syntax. Clifton is clearly worrying over the puzzle of Thelma throughout this chapter of *Generations,* perhaps because Thelma's life does not contain, or at least does not offer up for public consumption, the history and heroism so essential to Samuel's presentation of himself.

If Clifton measures her mother against the narrative standards that her father has set, then Thelma will inevitably come up short. But without Samuel figuratively standing in the way, then Thelma's life begins to make more sense:

> She married him when she was a young twenty-one and he was the only man she ever knew and he was the only man she ever loved and how she loved him! She adored him. He'd stay out all night and in the morning when he came home he'd be swinging down the street and she would look out the window and she'd say loud "Here come your crazy Daddy." And the relief and joy would make her face shine. (GW 273)

These observations revel in Thelma's unconditional love for her often obtuse husband. Such a description provides Clifton with a means of framing, if not fully understanding, the mystery of her parents' marriage and the mystery and grace of Thelma herself. Thelma's grace is also evident in the warmth and comfort of the household: "Oh she was magic. If there were locks that were locked tight, she could get a little thing and open them. She could take old bent hangers and rags and make curtains and hang drapes. She ironed on chairs and made cakes every week and everybody loved her. Everybody" (*GW* 273). Although as a child Clifton yearned to set things right, Thelma was the one eminently capable of doing so. Like Jesus feeding the crowds with a few loaves and a couple of fish, Thelma was a miracle worker in her daughter's eyes. Her capacity for giving and inspiring love casts a warm light on Clifton's world. Yet Thelma's love—her "magic"—is at one with her ordinariness, her willingness to live the life that fate and a domineering husband have assigned to her. Put another way, love is very much part of Thelma's identity; Clifton must take that into consideration when she contemplates the meaning and value of her mother's life—and goes on with her own life.

While Samuel is a gregarious man, a storyteller who helpfully places his life and family in a narrative context, Thelma, as portrayed in *Generations*, is quite the opposite. She keeps to herself much of the time and allows others to draw their own conclusions about her. Part poet, part poem, Thelma is a woman whose magic cannot be easily quantified. Clifton has said that her mother wrote poems—and burned them. This painful image of Thelma, the mother-poet who destroys her creations, appears in the 1993 poem "fury": "she gives them up. / they burn / jewels into jewels" (*BL* 45). As this excerpt illustrates, the lyrical essence of Thelma, the self-immolating flame of brave black womanhood, finds moving expression in Clifton's poetry. *Generations* is mostly her father's book, as is made clear by the dedication to Samuel Louis Sayles Sr., "who is somewhere, / being a man" (*GW* 223). Her poems, by contrast, frequently pay homage, directly or indirectly, to Thelma. As much as Clifton continues to admire and love her assertive, headstrong father, she seems to identify much more profoundly with her shy, kind-hearted mother, "whose only sin was dying" and "whose only strength was love" ("morning mirror," *N* 43).

That identification no doubt stems in part from Clifton's clairvoyant communications with the deceased Thelma, which provide the basis for poems in *An Ordinary Woman*, the volume preceding *Generations*, and *Two-Headed Woman*, the volume coming after it. Clifton does not allude to those alarming but enlightening conversations in the memoir, however, perhaps because doing so would alter the book's shape and direction. This memoir is very much a group portrait. Exploring Clifton's own mystical spirituality would shift the focus considerably. Interesting as those conversations with Thelma were, furthermore, Clifton may have found that they belonged to the province of poetry more than prose. Thelma's haunting impact on Clifton's life comes through in *Generations*, in any case, even without the dramatic import that a discussion of the supernatural conversations would have provided.

The construction of *Generations* is a collaborative enterprise. Herself an active teller of tales, Clifton joins her father in recounting the family history. Her book contains and frames the stories he told her. It is a tribute to his life and the family line that he helped to perpetuate, but it is also an indirect tribute to her own forbearance and power to forgive. Though Clifton has published poems alluding to her father's sexual molestation of her—most explicitly in "moonchild" in *Blessing the Boats*—she does not go into that experience in *Generations*, probably for the same reason that she remains silent on the subject of her supernatural communications with her mother: these are stories that belong elsewhere. She has a mature appreciation of Samuel's strengths and weaknesses, and his presence as a narrator in *Generations* further illustrates the cooperative spirit that informs so much of her writing.

Generations is also an elaborate response to the white woman in Bedford, whose Sale family history does not take into account the African Americans who share her name. Clifton seems determined to redress the oversight. The slave graves in Bedford may still be unmarked, but the stories of those slaves and their descendants are now on record. This family's story, Clifton assures us from the very first section, is not over yet. Her own sense of history far outstrips the version Miss Sale of Bedford has mailed to her: "I look at my husband and our six children and I feel the Dahomey women gathering in my bones" (*GW* 228). Primary among those Dahomey women is Caroline, who outlived slavery in America and is the first known link in the Sayles family line. Caroline is yet another impetus for this story filled with multigenerational selves.

The strength Clifton derives from the Dahomey women in her bones illustrates a clear alternative to Frederick Douglass's notion of a singular— and secular—masculine self. Clifton is more interested than Douglass is in the collective, sacred self that a spiritually aware family represents, and she is determined to give slave women more of a voice than Douglass does. It is out of her collective, historically layered self that individuals, male and female, emerge: Caroline and Lucy and Gene and Samuel and Thelma and Lucille are all unique, compelling personalities, but their connections to one another form the core of interest in *Generations*. Again we recognize the African emphasis on organic wholeness characteristic of Clifton's poetry. The book's balancing of male and female perspectives also has its analogue in her verse. Although a strong female voice animates the poetry, Clifton makes liberal use of male personas in her biblical poems, and African American men and boys appear frequently in her other poems. In fact, all of Clifton's writing, including her generous, open-hearted books for and about African American children, appears at times to be a balancing act. Seeking to redress the documented silencing of blacks and women in American literature and history, she writes frankly about African American life from a female point of view without discouraging white readership or male identification.

Like Whitman, Clifton is an elegiac poet whose affirming vision of selfhood counterbalances her deep feelings of loss and sorrow. For both poets, the one a white male contemporary of Frederick Douglass's, and the other a contemporary African American woman, the self is an ever-expanding, regenerative entity. Yet Clifton is not exactly echoing Whitman—far from it. Although she clearly values what Whitman has to say, she treats him in much the same way that she treats Samuel. She is both his descendant, poetically speaking, and his equal, and her book absorbs his poem into a larger realm. The epigraphs from "Song of Myself" in *Generations* feel as much like ghostly responses to Clifton as they do an authoritative call to her across the years. This poet-memoirist's equanimity grows out of that very sense of expansive selfhood that *Generations* embraces.

At the end of the book, Clifton alludes to another of her poetic precursors in her refutation of Yeats's dire predictions in "The Second Coming": "Things fall apart; the centre cannot hold; / Mere anarchy is loosed upon the world, / The blood-dimmed tide is loosed, and everywhere / The ceremony of innocence is drowned."[9] In Clifton's writings, her poems as well as her memoir, the blood-dimmed tide—of loss, of slavery, of all

9. W. B. Yeats, *The Poems*, ed. Richard J. Finneran (New York: Macmillan, 1983), 187.

forms of evil—is acknowledged but not allowed to drown out hope and goodness. The ceremonies of innocence are still observed. We see this in the final chapter of *Generations* when she once more invokes the family members who have inspired her throughout her career:

> Things don't fall apart. Things hold. Lines connect in thin ways that last and last and lives become generations made out of pictures and words just kept. "We come out of it better than they did, Lue," my Daddy said, and I watch my six children and know we did. They walk with confidence through the world, free sons and daughters of free folk, for my mama told me that slavery was a temporary thing, mostly we was free and she was right. (*GW* 275)

CHAPTER 9

Lucille Talks about Lucille: An Interview

THIS INTERVIEW TOOK PLACE APRIL 11, 1998, on a brilliant Saturday afternoon at Lucille Clifton's home in Columbia, Maryland. Serving as the William Blackburn Distinguished Visiting Professor at Duke University that spring semester, Clifton was home for the weekend with two of her daughters, Gillian and Alexia. After undergoing a kidney transplant the previous summer (with Alexia as her donor), Clifton had returned to her demanding schedule of writing, teaching, and giving public readings. She was in the midst of writing poems for *Blessing the Boats: New and Selected Poems, 1988–2000.*

HH: *Names seem to hold an intrinsic value in your writing. Your name, Lucille, and the names of your family members often show up in your poetry as well as in your memoir,* Generations. *And in the poem "i'm accused of tending to the past," in* Quilting, *you describe the past as "a monstrous unnamed baby" that the narrator has taken to her breast and named "History" with a capital H. So I was wondering, why are names and the process of naming so important to you?*

LC: Well, it seems to me that—let me see if I've thought about any of this—I was alive during the sixties when African Americans changing their names caused a great stir. And naming is as close as we can outwardly come to identifying ourselves, my me-ness. Now, for me, because "Lucille" means light, I can get a lot of metaphor and baggage and all that sort of thing from *that.* And so . . . I suppose I think that being able to name is somehow being able to place, to identify.

HH: *When did you start working with your own name, Lucille, as a poetic device?*

LC: When I understood, when I thought about what it meant.

HH: *And when was that?*

LC: I was very young. I started writing when I was about ten. Perhaps [I was] a little older than that when [my name] began to take on metaphoric meaning for me.

HH: *And your parents, especially your father, put so much store in telling you the history of your family and your names.*

LC: Sayles was my maiden name. We were taught that that was just the most remarkable name. We were taught, if you go into other cities, look in the phone book and look for Sayles. I'm sixty-one years old, and I do that every place I go. I don't *do* anything, but I do look and see if there are, in fact, Sayleses.

HH: *Have you ever called them?*

LC: No! [laughter] But we were told to call up and see if they were related to Old Man John F. [i.e., John F. Sale, the white slaveholder who owned a number of Clifton's paternal ancestors]. Well, what do I care! But on the other hand, we were very name-proud people. My father was a very name-proud man, and so I guess that passed on to us. And then when I was born, I was going to be named Georgia. My father's mother's name was Georgia; my mother's mother's name was also Georgia. And my father said, so proud, that he named me Thelma after my mother, and my mother didn't like her name, nor do I like the name Thelma. And so she said to name me something else, so "name" was always made significant. What's interesting is—now my father had no idea, I'm sure he had no idea—that Lucille meant light. I'm sure of that. Interestingly, my sister—I have a half-sister—Elaine also means light. It's a variation. I didn't know that until a couple of years ago.

HH: *Now, you said you were around ten when you started writing poetry? Why? What happened to you at ten that caused you to sit down and start writing?*

LC: Well, I loved words always, and my mother used to write poetry, so I saw it as something to do. I think everyone has in his or her self the urge to express, and people do it with what they love, I suppose. Cooks do it with food; there are people who do it with hair, with clothing, fabric. I loved words, always, the sound of words, the feeling of words in my mouth, and so I did it that way.

HH: *Did you show your mother your poetry?*

LC: Sometimes.

HH: *What would she say?*

LC: Generally, if it didn't rhyme, she would say, "Baby, that's not a poem."

[laughter] Because she wrote very traditional iambic pentameter verse.

HH: *Do you remember any poems you wrote as a little girl?*

LC: I have some poems from when I was sixteen or seventeen around somewhere. And what is interesting to me—of course, they're in form—I started writing in form. Very strict form. And the concerns were the same kind of concerns that I have now, I think. Poems that were from the Bible, which was very surprising to me, looking at them at this point in my life. Having a bit of sensuousness, a bit of erotica in them, concerns about the things that I still write something about. And I thought that was interesting; I find that interesting.

HH: *It is interesting. I'm thinking about the memoir,* Generations, *and you make an interesting comment there where you write that, when black people moved up North in the early part of the century, they tended to stay together and form families and extended families. But when white people moved North and settled, they were just people in a town. Why do you think black people have that tendency to form families?*

LC: It could've been self-defense. [laughter] I think that probably one *had* to as a group of people outnumbered, you might say, and going to a place that they didn't know. Immigrants do that now. There are a lot of a certain kind of people in one place, and others coming from their home will come to the same place. One wishes to be with people that you think look something like you. And for people whose families were broken up, family means a great deal.

HH: *I was recently approached about writing an entry on you for a reference book on contemporary southern writers.*

LC: Isn't that interesting? I'm in an anthology also of Catholic writers. [laughter] I said to the woman, "But I'm not Catholic." And she said, "Doesn't matter." I don't think of myself as southern, though people think of my home as Maryland . . . though my home is Buffalo, New York.

HH: *That's what I wanted to ask you about. You write about racial identity, gender identity, and family identity, but I'm wondering about geographical identity. How does that fit into who you see yourself as being?*

LC: I don't think that I particularly feel a geographical identity. Why would that be? . . . It may well be somewhat related to something I read about Robert Penn Warren sometime back. The article said that when he graduated from college, he bought an old car and he traveled across the country. And he wanted to see the landscape; he wanted to look at this country. And I was understanding then that that's why, maybe, I know something about the people in this country, but I'm not a landscape person. I don't see landscape. I don't identify that much with landscape.

HH: *Why do you think that is?*

LC: Because it was not available to me. There's no way a person of my age, who looks like me, could have got a car and gone across this country safely. It's not possible. We're talking about the fifties and sixties, it would've been. And so what I did know was the people— and the "I" there I'm using as a broad "I." Having studied them for some time, having had to, and that may be related. I don't know how many African American poets are like Mary Oliver, who knows the landscape so well. It has not been available to us to know.

HH: *But you've had to know the people.*

LC: Had to know the people.

HH: *And that's partly what you were saying a moment ago about maybe it's a little bit a matter of self-defense, just having a sense of the social environment that you're in.*

LC: Of being in a place where you were safe and you knew it.

HH: *Now you've written, of course, all those books for children, and you're one of many African American writers who've done that. I'm thinking of Ann Petry. She wrote for children as well as adults, and you do, and Nikki Giovanni comes to mind as well.*

LC: Well, Eloise Greenfield, Sharon Belmont. There are many.

HH: *You could certainly do nothing but write poetry, if you wanted. But why the commitment to writing children's literature?*

LC: Well, it wasn't a particular commitment at first. I think that I probably have as many, if not more, children than most of the poets or the people writing, especially women. I don't know a lot of women, who have six children, who are writers. Men are something different entirely, as always. [laughter]

When I first started writing, when *Good Times* was first accepted by Random House, someone knew I had children and wanted to know if I had ever tried writing for children. I had not. But I did tell my kids stories. And so I started thinking about what could I do in the field, and I came up with the first book of Everett Anderson, *Some of the Days of Everett Anderson*. I found that I was able to write for children. It seems very easy, but it's not necessarily so. And so I thought, "Well, here's two different things." And, to me, they are absolutely two different things, two different careers entirely. They impact on each other, of course. But they are two different careers. People who know me as a children's author tend to not know me as a poet.

HH: *What do they think when they get to know your poetry?*

LC: Well, I have had children's librarians come up and say, "When did you start this?" Both of the first books came out in November of '69, but [readers of the two different genres] tend to just not know. I then began to think about children's literature, especially picture books, which is what I write, and understand that there has been traditionally in this country an absence of . . . well, I have a little talk that I give sometimes about windows and mirrors, that children—and humans, everybody—all need both windows and mirrors in their lives: mirrors through which you can see yourself and windows through which you can see the world. And minority children have not had mirrors.

That has placed them at a disadvantage. If you want to call white children majority children—[they] have had *only* mirrors. That has placed them at a disadvantage also. And so it became important to me to have, for my own children and others, [characters] like them and others *not* like them—books dealing with family and love and support and all of that.

HH: *Why do you say the white children would be disadvantaged because they had only mirrors?*

LC: Because they live on a planet that is more window than mirror. And they have tended to believe that the planet is a planet like them or people who wish to be like them. And it's not necessarily so. It's a mistake to believe oneself one's only valid participator in life, that that is the standard, the standard for human is white. I tell children the standard for flowers is many-colored; the standard for all kinds of things is many-colored. That is also the standard for humans, though they have not been taught that.

So I began to think that writing for children was important. I have two children's books coming out in the next year. But when people talk to me about children's literature, [they sometimes ask] if I had to stop [writing for children or adults], which would I stop? What they tend to want me to say—because it's very romantic—they want me to say that I must write for children. That is not so. I could stop writing children's books tomorrow, I could. I could *not* stop writing poetry. Poetry is where my heart is. That's something I must do. Children's books—I choose to do that; I respect and value it, but I don't have to do it. Poetry I *have* to do.

HH: *Critics often talk about your affirming spirit and the celebratory qualities in your verse, and I certainly see those, too. But there's also a lot of anger and sorrow and uncertainty in your writing, and it seems like the hopeful essence really has to struggle against those other forces.*

LC: It does! [laughter] That's because I'm human. I'm doing a "new and selected" now, and a couple of friends have seen some of the poems, and they say this is going to be a *dark* book.

HH: *Is it?*

LC: Well, I don't think it's dark. I think it's just . . . you know, I have a poem about dialysis, for instance. I was on dialysis. And it ends, something about "i am alive and furious," and then it ends with a question, "blessed be even this?" [Some critics] would expect of me, "blessed be even this." Well, I'm not sure about that. You know, dialysis is not fun. Kidney failure is not fun.

HH: *It seems that, maybe more than most poetry, people can see what they want to see in your verse.*

LC: I think so.

HH: *If they want affirmation, it's there.*

LC: There is affirmation there. And that makes people comfortable. And I understand that. I say sometimes at readings something I heard an old preacher say a long time ago: "I come to comfort the afflicted and to afflict the comfortable." Of course, I would be nuts if I didn't see the negativity and despair in the world, if I didn't sometimes feel it myself. I am always hopeful because that's the kind of personality I have. But it does not mean that I do not see what there is to be seen and do not feel what any other human being would feel.

HH: *Last night I watched the tape of your reading in Los Angeles, the Lannan Series of 1988. It was very interesting to me. And I heard you read in Chapel Hill when I was a grad student, long before I had any idea that I would someday be writing a book about you. It seems you're very accessible in your readings, and you're kind of giving yourself over to the audience. But it also strikes me that each of your readings is a very artfully arranged process, that it's even an artful exercise in consciousness-raising that you're leading your audience through.*

LC: I like to connect with people. I like people. Now, I am, on the other hand—nobody ever believes that—I'm shy. I *am* shy.

HH: *I believe you.*

LC: Do you? Thank you so much, because nobody ever believes me, and I'm *very* shy. But on the other hand, I think that one can teach without preaching, you know what I mean? And I know that there are some things that it would be helpful if people understood, and I want to say the truth. I want to tell the truth, you know?

I don't care about facts—I've said that lots of times. But I care tremendously about the truth; I care tremendously about justice. . . . When I first went to St. Mary's College, I didn't know southern Maryland. I know it was a great Confederate [stronghold]. It's my second home. But on the other hand, I wanted to know, where would I live? I didn't know where to look for places to live. And the president at that time said to me, "Well, you could live anywhere; you're Lucille Clifton." I said, "Where would my *sister* live?" She's *not* Lucille Clifton. And it's important to think about that, too. Because that's just, and I do believe in justice. I'm a great believer in justice.

HH: *Well, how did you decide on settling in Columbia, a comparatively young and consciously planned community? It seems to me a very interesting choice for a poet so preoccupied with history.*

LC: Well, I knew the founder of Columbia; I know the people who are the administration people in Columbia. It's a very mixed community, and it started out that way. People in Columbia were interested in everybody living together, and I think they were interested in possibility.

HH: *And that's a real theme in your writing—possibility.*

LC: I have a poem that says something like, "the future is possible." I do believe that. I believe that people, if we face up to our responsibility and the possibility of evil in us, we then will understand that we have to be vigilant about the good. But if we all think that it all happens to somebody else, somewhere else, over there, then we don't have to take responsibility for what we do.

HH: *Is this interest in the possibility of evil what leads you, in part, to write about Lucifer so much?*

LC: I've said that I know there's Lucifer in Lucille, because I know me—I can be so petty, it's amazing! And there is therefore a possibility of Lucille in Lucifer. Lucifer was doing what he was supposed to do, too, you know? It's too easy to see Lucifer as all bad. Suppose he were merely being human. That's why the Bible people—it's too easy to think of them all as mythological, saintly folk. It is much more interesting to me that these were humans—caught up in a divine plan, but human. That seems to me the miracle.

HH: *You really do humanize those biblical characters in your poems, consistently, by taking on their personas and by having "eve thinking," "adam thinking" [titles of poems in* Quilting]. *And, as for Lucifer, it seems to me that you really kind of like him.*

LC: Well, it's kind of cool. [laughter] Well, suppose he was obeying orders. Wouldn't that be interesting. I mean, what does that mean then? Exploration of possibilities, that's all.

HH: *If he were sitting here, what would you want to ask him?*

LC: "Do you regret? What are your regrets?"

HH: *What do you think he'd want to ask you?*

LC: "Why are you doing this?" [laughter] But as I said to somebody whose class I talked to, "If Milton can do it, so can I." Why not?

HH: *Let's go back to what you were saying about being shy and how nobody believes that. You majored in drama. That might be one reason people don't believe it.*

LC: I hate people to think that, though, because I'm not acting. I *rarely* am acting. What I think I do is, I know how to appear not shy. If I'm being "Lucille Clifton," whoever that is, I know how to do that. If I'm just walking down the street, being "big lady walking down the street," it's not my best thing.

HH: *Has "Lucille Clifton" become a persona in your mind, because you've written about her?*

LC: In a way, in a way. A little bit. Only in that there seem to be expectations of Lucille Clifton and thoughts about what she's like, and I know what *this* person is *really* like. For instance, I have these fox poems [in *The Terrible Stories*]. Well, these are fairly accurate poems. I mean, it became metaphor for me.

HH: *Was the fox coming here?*

LC: No, it was in St. Mary's County. I have an apartment there when I'm teaching in southern Maryland. I'm here only some weekends and summertime. And I know I'm supposed to think, "What a wonderful thing, a fox, my totem"—all that. I was petrified! I was afraid of the fox! [laughter] My students get so upset when I say that. Lucille Clifton isn't supposed to [be afraid]; she's supposed to [love] all living creatures. Sometimes even the creatures seem to think so. Because creatures come to me all the time. However, I'm afraid of them.

HH: *What happened to that fox?*

LC: I don't know. I finally moved, since I could not *bear* this fox! My friend was moving, my dear friend who's just had her first book published; she had been a student of mine. Her name is Anne Caston. She's a wonderful poet, an amazing poet. Anyway, she was moving, too. So we decided to move to this new apartment complex in St. Mary's County. And she moved so that her apartment backed up to mine. But at the last moment, I said, "Well, Anne, I've got a fireplace in mine, and you don't have one." She has children, so I thought the fireplace would be nicer for a family with kids. And so we changed apartments; we exchanged.

Well! The first night we were there, the fox comes to her apartment! A fox. Who knows if . . . I choose to believe it was the same fox. And Anne—this is why I love this woman—she came out of the door and said, "She moved around there!" And the fox got up and trotted around to my apartment and spent the night there and then left and was never seen again.

HH: *Well, another visitation.*

LC: Indeed, indeed. And I recognize the honor. You know, I feel humbled by the compliment. But I was glad I didn't see it anymore. Except I do wonder, you know, what I was to understand.

HH: *Now, you say you're shy, but are you also a "people person"? And if so, is that a contradiction?*

LC: I'm friendly.

HH: *Or are you a "person person"? Do you like individual connections?*

LC: I like to watch people. I understand people, I think. I think I understand "human." I like to be with people sometimes. [But] there are days when I don't want to see anybody. I tend to not mind being solitary at all. It's necessary for me.

[Clifton's daughter Gillian walked into the house.]

LC: Gillian, *she* thinks I'm shy! My children don't think I'm shy.

GILLIAN: No, you're shy; you're about the shyest person I know.

LC: Yes, I am.

HH: *I think you're very layered, just like your poetry is layered.*

LC: Thank you! Yes, my poetry is.

GILLIAN: Oh, that's true. I would agree with that.

LC: I think my poetry *is* layered. Thank you for saying so.

HH: *And what I was getting to was connected with that. There are critics who say that you're "deceptively simple." And I just think that's a little wide of the mark. I don't think you're deceptive.*

LC: Well, I've been called that so much.

HH: *But you're not deceptive in your poetry. It's very clear. It's multilayered.*

LC: Thank you. I prefer "clear" to "simple," because simple has negative connotations, and I try to write clearly. And I do it on purpose. Often people seem to feel that I use the language I use because I don't know any other words! Well, I do!

HH: *I think that the other part of that, the "deceptive" part, is also off base. To say that you're "deceptively simple" implies that you're trying to trick readers in some way, and to me, you're not. You're trying to connect.*

LC: I'm trying to be very clear and to make it so that people of all sorts can get some feel for what I'm trying to do.

HH: *I would say that rather than "deceptively simple," it's "clearly complex."*

LC: Oh, that's nice! May I borrow that?

HH: *You certainly may. I'm reminded of what you said in the Lannan interview when the interviewer asks you, "What do you try to avoid as a poet?" and you said you try to avoid being clever. Can you elaborate on that? Why would that be a problem?*

LC: In school, I was a good English student. Cleverness gets in the way of creativity. Cleverness is often the easy way, the expected in your work, and I try very hard not to take the easy way out. I think about Rilke's "Ode to the Difficult." And I try very hard not to do the easy, expected, smart thing.

Poetry for me is not an intellectual exercise. I really think that—to understand my poetry—I don't think approaching it simply intellectually will help. It has to be a balance, I think, between intellect and intuition. For me, there is a kind of intuitive feeling for the language, for what wishes to be said—you know what I mean? I never had classes in this, I never took courses in this business, so I had to learn, I had to feel my way into the language. And you can have a visceral response to these things coming together, if you have enough authenticity behind them, enough power.

HH: *When you read your poems publicly, do you feel the emotions that originally inspired them?*

LC: Sometimes. . . . I have a reading at Duke on Wednesday, and I'm thinking about what I'd like to hear, and there are some poems I haven't heard in a while, so I think I'll read them. But I don't have a set pattern. I rarely—once in a while I do—have a set pattern of what I'm going to read, because I try to feel the audience. I try to feel, what does it seem that they need? What does it seem that they want? You know what I mean? And I try to feel that out. And so I read; as it's going, I try to make it a flow that fills the need and desire I feel in the room. It uses a lot of energy, I want you to know, so I'm really exhausted at the end.

HH: *The sequence of poems you have called "in white america" seems to be about going on a reading tour. Where was that?*

LC: I think it was Wells College in upstate New York. Wells is a woman's school. I've been there many times, and I'm going again in the fall. It might've been Ithaca College, one of those upstate New York colleges, in the hinterlands.

HH: *You talk in that series about what it's like to give readings to white people.*

LC: I've read in every state. I'm reading in London in May, and I've read in Jerusalem.

HH: *How many readings do you think you've given?*

LC: Oh lord, when I was younger I used to read every week almost.

HH: *Hundreds?*

LC: Hundreds.

HH: *Five hundred?*

LC: Oh, let's see, I've been reading for twenty-something years. I'd say in that time I've read over five hundred times.

HH: *And how many times at mostly black venues?*

LC: Less than a dozen, if that. There have been a few black people in a lot of readings, mostly all white. Often I'm the only black person.

HH: *Well, in that series, "in white america," it seems you're wrestling with that, wrestling with the fact that, in a way, it's compromising, but in a way you really want to do it.*

LC: Well, I do. I've had a couple of students interviewing me in the last two or three days, and they want to know who I think my audience is. That is not something that I know. And I have learned that I can't put boundaries around it. I don't know who my audience is. I'm constantly surprised. I've had two letters from soldiers in Albania. I think they were on opposite sides. The poems were printed in an Albanian newspaper, and I guess in Albanian, it must've been, because they struggled with the language in writing to me. And that's amazing to me. I would never have supposed that people there would read them.

HH: *So you just got these stray letters. Were they fan letters?*

LC: Yes, they were, very much so. And in trying to do the English, I think it's so interesting: It was like, "Most wondrous and wise poet." [laughter] Whoa! Also, a woman in Italy is doing a dissertation on me. One would think, how would that happen? I don't *know* who my audience is.

HH: *It doesn't bother you that they're all over the place?*

LC: No. I would like African American people to be proud of me and to like what I do. Women, I would like them to be proud of me and like what I do. But I write for the poem. That's what I'm trying to do: serve the poem. And who is to receive it, will. Who can receive it, will. Who doesn't—I have a moment of thinking, "How can they think I'm not nice?"—nice as I am! [laughter] But I understand that. People say, "Well, I never heard of you." Well, half the world hasn't heard of me, more than half.

HH: *In the 1988 Lannan Series reading, you start off with "homage to my hips" and then you do "wishes for sons." And everybody's laughing, everybody's having a good time. By the end of the reading you're doing the "shape-shifter poems," which is a completely different mood, and you've brought the audience along to that point. Is that a typical movement for you?*

LC: It is. I try to vary it. Right now I have a Lorena Bobbitt poem ["lorena" in *The Terrible Stories*], and I try to do that [during a reading].

HH: *Where does that poem come in?*

LC: That's after some poems that might be a little difficult, as a rule. Or, I might start with it. It depends. The danger of starting with it is that everybody thinks that everything you do is funny after that. That has happened on occasion, and that bothers me. And I will say, "Well, now what was funny about that?" I will say that, because it's too easy for people to think that "well, she's just full of joy and laughing."

HH: *And merriment.*

LC: And merriment, yes. And I'm not, particularly, any more than anybody else is, you know? I want to do the whole thing, so it can all be accepted in some way. I was reading some children's books to kids one time, and the children asked me wonderful things, which is among the reasons I love them. And one little boy asked me—and these were all white kids—"Why are all the people in your books so poor?"

Well, these kids happened to be poor kids, and I knew it, you know, but they didn't think they were. And what I said was, "Well, they're poor, but they just don't have any money. They're not poor in spirit. Are you poor in spirit?" No, they're not. And then one child asked me why were they all brown? And I said, "Well, look at me. Suppose I didn't write about anybody brown." And he looked at me for a while, and then he said, "That would be weird." [laughter] And I said, "Wouldn't it be weird?" It would be very weird. Kids understand these things.

HH: *You seem to view words as physical objects in a way, as very interesting physical objects. You take "everywhere" and split it into two parts, and you do the same thing with "everybody" and "somewhere."*

LC: When I feel that's what it wants, yes. I like when I hear somebody saying a word and pronouncing it in a way I have not heard. I like to repeat it. Galway Kinnell has a poem about frogs. He says, "frahg." He's a friend; I've heard him do it a thousand times. And I always think, "How does that feel in your mouth?" I know what "frog" sounds like, feels like, in my mouth. How does that "frahg" feel in his mouth?

HH: *It seems to me that, when I was saying that you view words as physical objects, you could say that of William Carlos Williams and Gertrude Stein.*

And I'm wondering if you have any particular interest in either one of those.

LC: Actually, no. [laughter] That's interesting, because I'm not a particular fan of either of them. When I was very young, the writers that I liked very much to read were Edna St. Vincent Millay for poetry and Thomas Wolfe for prose. Now, I write like neither of them, you know?

HH: *What did you like about them?*

LC: I loved Wolfe's wonderful spate of words. "Oh lost, and by the wind green ghosts, come back as first I knew you in the timeless valley!" Oh, I thought that was great stuff!

HH: *He's a southern white man.*

LC: Indeed! He probably wouldn't have liked me at all! But when I was younger, that's what I thought of. For a while, I would write standing up—I read he did.

HH: *You use a lot of questions in your poetry, especially at the ends of your poems. How conscious are you of that?*

LC: I was not particularly conscious of using a lot of them. But I do think that poetry is about questions.

HH: *Why do you say that?*

LC: Well, because I don't write out of what I know; I write out of what I wonder. I think most artists create art in order to explore, not to give the answers. Poetry and art are not about answers to me; they are about questions.

HH: *Do you consider Yeats . . .*

LC: I like Yeats.

HH: *Do you like him or do you love him?*

LC: I probably just like him a whole lot. [laughter]

HH: *Who do you love?*

LC: I love—well, do we have to have writers?

HH: *Yes. Then we can move on to others.*

LC: Adrienne [Rich]! We lived in the same town for a while. She's a fabulous person. We each had a child who had cancer at the same time at one point in our lives. We used to talk about that and commiserate quite a lot. I think we exchanged a poem at that time, something about "our children are bald," because they were both having chemotherapy.

HH: *Which of your children?*

LC: My second daughter [Fredrica]. [Gillian] is my third daughter.

HH: *Gillian is the third. And Alexia is the other daughter who lives here?*

LC: She's the one who donated a kidney to me.

HH: *Any other poets who come to mind as just a passion for you? Old or contemporary?*

LC: I don't know about loving.

HH: *Or admiring?*

LC: I admire Derek Walcott. I admire cummings. Though that's not why I don't capitalize, okay? I admire Whitman, I admire Yeats, I admire Gwen Brooks.

HH: *What about Plath and Sexton?*

LC: I begin to respect Plath more now. When I was younger, I wasn't as into her. Sexton I do, and I knew her a little bit. She was a friend of Maxine Kumin, whom I've known for a very long time. As I get older, for some reason, I admire Plath more.

HH: *I wonder why that is.*

LC: I don't have the faintest clue! She was so young, too. It seems to me odd that I do.

HH: *Well, you were contemporaries, and then she died so young, and you kept going, and so it's interesting to compare your work.*

LC: Sharon [Olds] I like very much. I think Sonia Sanchez is an underrated poet. Oh, there are so many! Joy Harjo. There's a poet in Arizona, Richard Shelton, a remarkable poet. He has a wonderful line: "We will be known as the ones who murdered the earth."

HH: *You're very interested in environmental issues in your poetry. It comes up in almost every book. How did that get started?*

LC: It isn't as if I sat down and thought about it. I've always been a person who, if I was interested in something, I wanted to know as much about it as I can. Because I'm a learning kind of person. I've always been a learner, I try to learn about things. The environment, which includes humans, seems to me in danger. I belong to a group which is very concerned with the biodiversity of the planet, and I was a bit put out that, in thinking about that, and the preservation of this biodiversity, they were not particularly concerned about humans! I found that appalling.

HH: *Do you read a lot of newspapers?*

LC: I do. How could you tell that?

HH: *It's evident in your poetry, because there's a real strain of topicality. There's the universal level, but there's also that topicality where you're dealing with the Civil Rights movement for obvious reasons, the women's movement . . .*

LC: I love history. On Sunday, we get the *Baltimore Sun,* the *Washington Post,* and the *New York Times.* One of the [good] things about [living in] Durham is that my student helper, every Sunday morning, she puts the *New York Times* and the *Washington Post* in my doorway.

HH: *Did you grow up reading newspapers?*

LC: Yes. My parents were great newspaper readers, my father particularly. And my father, as I said, couldn't write. My mother could write. Couldn't spell! As her daughter can't exactly, either. But they both had great interest in what was going on in the world. They were people who were curious about things, learners as well, I think.

HH: *Which magazines do you read?*

LC: Well, I try to read as many as I can. Let's see, what do I read? I don't subscribe to them, but I read the *New Yorker,* I try to read *Lingua Franca;* I read all kinds of things like that. I also read *People,* I read *Jet,* I read *Essence,* I read *Ebony. Mode* is for big women. [laughter] I like to tell my students, "I'm very eclectic—deal with it!" I *am* eclectic. I love Bach. . . . I also love the Four Tops. And now I'm into Kenny Burrell and jazz. I like opera very much. I don't know if I love it or not; I like it very much.

HH: *What else do you love?*

LC: I like to laugh. I can tell you better what I can't stand. I can't stand injustice. I can't stand seeing people being unfair to each other. I can't stand cruelty, indifference. I don't like that a lot. Oysters! [laughter]

HH: *You make an important distinction between being a woman and being a girl. But is there still a little girl lurking within you? Sort of rolling around and having some fun? Like your poem "there is a girl inside" [in* Good Woman*]?*

LC: I think so, because I like fun, I like adventure. My idea of a good time is going to Universal Studios and Disney World. My oldest daughter lives in L.A., and the kids say, if we go, you've got to promise not to go to Universal Studios, because they're very bored with it. They've been there too many times already.

HH: *Can you take the grandchildren as a way to get back in?*

LC: Well, I go anyway. They don't tell me what to do. Since my daughters aren't here, I can say that.

HH: *If you were going to have a dinner party for three people from history, famous people, whom would you want to have?*

LC: David of Israel. Oh, these are two people I love. Crazy Horse of Dakota Nation.

HH: *You can have one more person.*

LC: It has to be a woman. Hmmm. Mary, the mother of Christ.

HH: *Why didn't you invite Lucifer? Are you done with him?*

LC: Yes! [laughter] No, I don't think he's done with me! But those are three that I would very much like to talk to.

HH: *And what would you want to ask them?*

LC: Well, they all are people with contradictions in their lives. They all were people who were faced with something larger than themselves and tried to meet it with grace, I think. And I would ask them how that felt, what were they feeling, maybe a little bit about what they were thinking, but what were they feeling?

   With Mary, is that *really* what happened? With David, who did you really love? Because he didn't know how to love women, I don't think. He wanted them, he lusted after them, but I don't think he loved them. Crazy Horse—his life was a series of strangenesses, even for him, [and] he was a mystical guy. I'm always interested in people who are a bit mystical, and those three I think all were. I'd like to know, "How was it for you? How was it for you?"

HH: *You've been interested in Crazy Horse for a long time. Did you read Dee Brown's* Bury My Heart at Wounded Knee *and get interested in him then or were you interested in him before?*

LC: I think I was always a bit interested. I don't remember what I read first. Mari Sandoz has a book called *Crazy Horse, the Strange Man of the Oglalas.* I think what really bound me to him was, with Crazy Horse, it was always the second thing that came to fruition for him. His birth mother died, and he was raised by his stepmother. . . . Black Shawl was the name of his wife. But he was in love with Black Buffalo Woman.

HH: *I've wondered if you connect Crazy Horse with your father.*

LC: Oh, it never occurred to me.

HH: *Because of being married to one woman and having relationships with other women.*

LC: Not at all! That never would occur to me. I think Crazy Horse was much nicer than my father. [laughter] Oh, he was much truer, and everything—oh my goodness!

HH: *Can you see why I would have made that connection?*

LC: I suppose so. But with Crazy Horse, he loved Black Buffalo Woman first.

HH: *Well, why didn't he marry her?*

LC: Because he went away somewhere on some expedition, and when he came back, her father had married her to someone else. And he ran away with her at one point, and that's when she conceived the daughter that when he came back, he didn't stay with her, because he had visions, and he knew this was not the right thing to do. So he came back with her and she had a daughter called They Are Afraid of Her, and I think that daughter died young. He had another daughter with Black Shawl, who also died young. So people who are saying they're descendants—there are no direct descendants of Crazy Horse, but they're people who were his cousins and all that.

HH: *In* Two-Headed Woman, *some of the poems suggest to me that you have had visions. True or false?*

LC: I have had experiences which could be called that. I have had spiritual kinds of experiences. I have.

HH: *What are they like?*

LC: Well, what are they like? I don't know what you could say, if you could compare them to . . . I would say this, if people had had dreams and visions, they would know the difference. But if you've only had dreams, you wouldn't. I can understand why somebody would say, "Well, it was just a dream." But if you've had them both, then you know the difference.

HH: *You've written about both. You've written about dreams.*

LC: Mm-hmm. And I know the difference! And I sometimes can read palms, for instance. That is to say, it's not reading palms like people read palms. Sometimes when I touch things, I can hear something, and it has to do with the thing I'm touching. And sometimes I can't and sometimes I can.

HH: *Are there others in your family who've talked about a similar sensation?*

LC: No. Not really. My kids, especially my two youngest daughters, can feel things sometimes.

HH: *I see you as a visionary poet. And I put you in the same continuum as Blake.*

LC: I like Blake. I have a poem about Blake [in *The Terrible Stories*].

HH: *Blake and Whitman and Yeats and Clifton—what do you say to that continuum?*

LC: I like those people! [laughter] Yeats I think is wonderful. People never talk about his mysticism.

HH: *It's all over the place, and it's all over your poetry, too.*

LC: It probably is.

HH: *Are you a mystic?*

LC: I don't know what a mystic is. My husband, if you'd asked him, would've said yes. He thought he was a mystic.

HH: *Did he think you were?*

LC: I don't know, I doubt it.

HH: *What made him one?*

LC: Well, he was a yogi, and he was a very interesting, mystical kind of person. He had a whole different way of being than I do.

HH: *Was your mother a mystical sort of person?*

LC: I don't think so, but she may have been. I don't have to have known it for it to have been true. She was born with twelve fingers also. And I always just decide this is it, this is why we're strange, because we have all these fingers. My oldest daughter was [born with twelve fingers], though I doubt if she would think of herself as mystical.

HH: *You said in the Lannan video that you wished you had been able to keep your extra fingers.*

LC: That would have been interesting.

HH: *Well, you had the chance with your daughter, to let her keep hers.*

LC: I know. Well, with her, with my first child, I had ether. I saw the rest of them born, she was the only one I didn't see born. And they had hers off by the time I came to. Isn't that awful?

HH: *And then the others didn't have them.*

LC: I like to think that it's the first daughter, or it's a woman thing, excepting that my brother—my brother's now dead—but he had a son, his oldest son was born with twelve fingers. But he and his wife divorced, and he hadn't seen that son, and I'm pretty sure they were off, too—as an abnormality.

HH: *Were they whole fingers, or were they little flipper-like things?*

LC: This is the only reminder I have. [indicating scar on little finger]

HH: *Is there one on the other hand?*

LC: No, no. They [took] them off. When I was born, they tied thread very tightly around and stopped the blood circulation. And so after a certain point, they dried up and then fell off. So I assume there was no bone.

HH: *I've been thinking about Langston Hughes and his essay, "The Negro Artist and the Racial Mountain." He writes, in response to a young poet who said he wanted to be a poet, not a Negro poet, "[T]his is the mountain standing in the way of any true Negro art in America—this urge within the race toward whiteness, the desire to pour racial individuality into the mold of American standardization, and to be as little Negro and as much American as possible."*

It seems to me that you've acknowledged and climbed that mountain a long time ago, that your blackness is very much part of who you are in your poetry.

LC: Exactly, exactly. And what the young man was probably talking about was not what he was, but what people saw him as. And I'm seen as that quite often. There's the poets and there's the subgenre and Lucille is in there. Because people see it that way, that does not make it so. And I am not an either/or person. I'm not either American or black. I am an American poet, and that's what American poetry is: me, Li-Young Lee, Joy Harjo, David Mura, you know what I mean?

HH: *Yes.*

LC: That *is* American poetry. I aspire to be the poet that Marianne Moore was, that Langston [Hughes] was, that Richard Wilbur is. I aspire to be as much poet as Auden—whom I like, by the way—Lowell, whom I like. I aspire to be all of that. But that's what American poetry is. Now, whether or not critics think so—they're wrong, that's all. I don't mind. I don't have a problem with that. . . . I am not an American poet who happens to be black. I did not *happen* to be black. My mother was black, and my father was black. And so there I was. I was gonna be black! It didn't just zap me. And that's okay, that is all right, that is not a subgenre of anything. I am an American poet; this is what American poetry is.

Bibliography

WORKS BY LUCILLE CLIFTON

Poetry

Good Times: Poems. New York: Random House, 1969.
Good News about the Earth: New Poems. New York: Random House, 1972.
An Ordinary Woman. New York: Random House, 1974.
Two-Headed Woman. Amherst: University of Massachusetts Press, 1980.
Good Woman: Poems and a Memoir, 1969–1980. (Compilation of first four volumes
    of poetry and *Generations.*) Brockport, N.Y.: BOA Editions, 1987.
Next: New Poems. Brockport, N.Y.: BOA Editions, 1987.
Ten Oxherding Pictures. Santa Cruz, Calif.: Moving Parts, 1988.
Quilting: Poems, 1987–1990. Brockport, N.Y.: BOA Editions, 1991.
The Book of Light. Port Townsend, Wash.: Copper Canyon, 1993.
The Terrible Stories. Brockport, N.Y.: BOA Editions, 1996.
Blessing the Boats: New and Selected Poems, 1988–2000. Rochester, N.Y.: BOA Edi-
    tions, 2000.

Memoir

Generations: A Memoir. New York: Random House, 1976.

Books for Children

Some of the Days of Everett Anderson. New York: Holt, Rinehart and Winston, 1969.
The Black BC's. New York: Dutton, 1970.
Everett Anderson's Christmas Coming. New York: Holt, Rinehart and Winston, 1971.
All Us Come Cross the Water. New York: Holt, Rinehart and Winston, 1973.
The Boy Who Didn't Believe in Spring. New York: Dutton, 1973.
Don't You Remember? New York: Dutton, 1973.
Good, Says Jerome. New York: Dutton, 1973.
Everett Anderson's Year. New York: Holt, Rinehart and Winston, 1974.
The Times They Used to Be. New York: Holt, Rinehart and Winston, 1974.
My Brother Fine with Me. New York: Holt, Rinehart and Winston, 1975.
Everett Anderson's Friend. New York: Holt, Rinehart and Winston, 1976.
Three Wishes. New York: Viking, 1976.

Amifika. New York: Dutton, 1977.

Everett Anderson's 1 2 3. New York: Holt, Rinehart and Winston, 1977.

Everett Anderson's Nine Months Long. New York: Holt, Rinehart and Winston, 1978.

The Lucky Stone. New York: Delacorte, 1979.

My Friend Jacob. Coauthored by Thomas DiGrazia. New York: Dutton, 1980.

Here Is Another Bone to Pick with You. Minneapolis: Toothpaste, 1981.

Sonora Beautiful. New York: Dutton, 1981.

Everett Anderson's Goodbye. New York: Holt, Rinehart and Winston, 1983.

Dear Creator: A Week of Poems for Young People and Their Teachers. New York: Doubleday, 1997.

One of the Problems of Everett Anderson. New York: Holt, 2001.

Uncollected Prose

"It's All in the Game." *Negro Digest,* August 1966, 18–19.

"The Magic Mama," *Redbook,* November 1969, 88–89.

"Christmas Is Something Else." *House & Garden,* December 1969, 70–71.

"The End of Love Is Death, the End of Death Is Love." *Atlantic,* March 1971, 65–67.

"Stories for Free Children: The Boy Who Didn't." *Ms.,* August 1973, 67.

"We Know This Place: Reaffirm Black's Sense of Being." *Essence,* July 1976, 53.

"If I Don't Know My Last Name, What is the Meaning of My First?: *Roots,* The Saga of an American Family." *Ms.,* February 1977, 45.

"A Simple Language." In Evans, *Black Women Writers,* 137–38.

"Children of Long Ago." Book reviews. *New York Times Book Review,* 17 July 1988, 31.

"Lucille Clifton—Reading." Lannan Foundation Audio Archives, 8 December 1999. www.lannan.org/audio/audioABCD.htm (accessed 22 February 2004).

SELECTED SECONDARY BIBLIOGRAPHY

Works about Lucille Clifton

Chapters in Books

Baughman, Ronald. "Lucille Clifton." In *American Poets since World War II,* edited by Donald J. Greiner, vol. 5 of *Dictionary of Literary Biography,* 132–36. Detroit: Gale Research, 1980.

Holladay, Hilary. "Song of Herself: Lucille Clifton's Poems about Womanhood." In *The Furious Flowering of African American Poetry,* edited by Joanne Gabbin, 281–97. Charlottesville: University Press of Virginia, 1999.

Hull, Akasha (Gloria). "Channeling the Ancestral Muse: Lucille Clifton and Dolores Kendrick." In *Female Subjects in Black and White: Race, Psychoanalysis, Feminism,* edited by Elizabeth Abel, Barbara Christian, and Helen Moglen, 330–48. Berkeley: University of California Press, 1997.

———. "In Her Own Images: Lucille Clifton and the Bible." In *Dwelling in Possibility: Women Poets and Critics on Poetry,* edited by Yopie Prins and Maeera Shreiber, 273–95. Ithaca: Cornell University Press, 1997.

———. *Soul Talk: The New Spirituality of African American Women.* Rochester, Vt.: Inner Traditions, 2001.

Johnson, Dianne. "Perspectives on Unity and the African Diaspora: Examples from the Children's Literature of Lucille Clifton and Rosa Guy." In *Work and Play in Children's Literature: Selected Papers from the 1990 International Conference of the Children's Literature Association,* edited by Susan R. Gannon and Ruth Anne Thompson, 55–59. Pleasantville, N.Y.: Pace University, 1990.

"Lucille Clifton." In *Contemporary Literary Criticism,* vol. 19, edited by Sharon R. Gunton, 108–11. Detroit: Gale Research, 1981.

"Lucille Clifton." In *Contemporary Literary Criticism,* vol. 66, edited by Roger Matuz, 63–88. Detroit: Gale Research, 1991.

Madhubuti, Haki. "Lucille Clifton: Warm Water, Greased Legs, and Dangerous Poetry." In Evans, *Black Women Writers,* 150–60.

McCluskey, Audrey T. "Tell the Good News: A View of the Works of Lucille Clifton." In Evans, *Black Women Writers,* 139–49.

Peppers, Wallace R. "Lucille Clifton." In *Afro-American Poets since 1955,* edited by Trudier Harris and Thadious M. Davis, vol. 41 of *Dictionary of Literary Biography,* 55 60. Detroit: Gale Research, 1985.

Rushing, Andrea Benton. "Lucille Clifton: A Changing Voice for Changing Times." In *Coming to Light: American Women Poets in the Twentieth Century,* edited by Diane Wood Middlebrook and Marilyn Yalom, 214–22. Ann Arbor: University of Michigan Press, 1985.

Worsham, Fabian Clements. "The Poetics of Matrilineage: Mothers and Daughters in the Poetry of African American Women, 1965–1985." In *Women of Color: Mother-Daughter Relationships in 20th-Century Literature,* edited by Elizabeth Brown-Guillory, 117–31. Austin: University of Texas Press, 1997.

Essays in Journals

Anaporte-Easton, Jean. "Healing Our Wounds: The Direction of Difference in the Poetry of Lucille Clifton and Judith Johnson." *Mid-American Review* 14, no. 2 (1994): 78–87.

———. " 'She Has Made Herself Again': The Maternal Impulse as Poetry." *13th Moon: A Feminist Literary Magazine* 9, nos. 1–2 (1991): 116–35.

Holladay, Hilary. "Black Names in White Space: Lucille Clifton's South." *Southern Literary Journal* 34, no. 2 (Spring 2002): 120–33.

———. "'I Am Not Grown Away from You': Lucille Clifton's Elegies for Her Mother." *CLA Journal* 42, no. 4 (June 1999): 430–44.

———. "'Our Lives Are Our Line and We Go On': Concentric Circles of History in Lucille Clifton's *Generations*." *Xavier Review* 19, no. 2 (1999): 18–29.

———."'Splendid in Your Red Dress': Menstrual Imagery in Lucille Clifton's Poetry." *Abafazi* (2000): 30–34.

Johnson, Dianne. "The Chronicling of an African-American Life and Consciousness: Lucille Clifton's Everett Anderson Series." *Children's Literature Association Quarterly* 14, no. 3 (1989): 174–78.

Johnson, Joyce. "The Theme of Celebration in Lucille Clifton's Poetry." *Pacific Coast Philology* 18, nos. 1–2 (1983): 70–76.

Lazer, Hank. "Blackness Blessed: The Writings of Lucille Clifton." *Southern Review* 25, no. 3 (1989): 760–70.

Ostriker, Alicia. "Kin and Kin: The Poetry of Lucille Clifton." *American Poetry Review* 22, no. 6 (1993): 41–48.

Wall, Cheryl. "Sifting Legacies in Lucille Clifton's *Generations*." *Contemporary Literature* 40, no. 4 (Winter 1999): 552–74.

Waniek, Marilyn Nelson. "Black Silences, Black Songs." *Callaloo* 6, no. 1 (1983): 156–65.

White, Mark Bernard. "Sharing the Living Light: Rhetorical, Poetic, and Social Identity in Lucille Clifton." *CLA Journal* 40, no. 3 (March 1997): 288–304.

Whitley, Edward. "'A Long Missing Part of Itself': Bringing Lucille Clifton's *Generations* into American Literature." *MELUS* 26, no. 2 (Summer 2001): 47–64.

Ph.D. Dissertations

Davenport, Doris. "Four Contemporary Black Women Poets: Lucille Clifton, June Jordan, Audre Lorde, and Sherley Anne Williams (A Feminist Study of a Culturally Derived Poetics)." University of Southern California, 1985.

Musher, Andrea Susan. "Vital Connections: The Poetics of Maternal Affiliation in Sylvia Plath, Anne Sexton, Adrienne Rich, Lucille Clifton, and Judy Grahn." University of Wisconsin–Madison, 1989.

Interviews

Glaser, Michael S. "'I'd Like Not to Be a Stranger in the World': A Conversation/ Interview with Lucille Clifton." *Antioch Review* 58, no. 3 (Summer 2000): 310–28.

Holladay, Hilary. "No Ordinary Woman: An Interview with Lucille Clifton." "Poetry in America," special issue of *Poets & Writers Magazine*, April 1999, 30–35.

Jordan, Shirley M. "Lucille Clifton." In *Broken Silences: Interviews with Black and White Women Writers*. New Brunswick, N.J.: Rutgers University Press, 1993. 38–49.

Laing, E. K. "Making Each Word Count." *Christian Science Monitor*, 5 February 1988, B3.

Moyers, Bill. "Lucille Clifton." In *Language of Life: A Festival of Poets*, 81–95. Garden City, N.Y.: Doubleday, 1995.

Rowell, Charles. "An Interview with Lucille Clifton." *Callaloo* 22.1 (1999): 56–72.

Somers-Willet, Susan B. A. " 'A Music in Language': A Conversation with Lucille Clifton." *American Voice* 49 (Summer 1999): 73–92.

Articles in Magazines and Newspapers

Ammerman, Adrienne. "The Varied Voices of Politics." *Off Our Backs*, July 2001, 11.

Gray, Steven. "A Quiet Poet Gains the Spotlight; National Book Award Recognizes Work of St. Mary's College Professor." *Washington Post* (Southern Maryland Extra), 23 November 2000, M-3.

Prelutsky, Jack. "Lucille Clifton Loves *Star Trek!*" *Instructor*, February 1994, 70.

Scarupa, Harriet Jackson. "Lucille Clifton: Making the World 'Poem-Up.' " *Ms.*, October 1976, 118ff.

Smith, Dinitia. "Sontag Is among Winners of National Book Awards." *New York Times*, 17 November 2000, B47.

"Some States Are Not Ad-Verse to Poets Laureate." *People Weekly*, 2 July 1984, 36.

Selected Book Reviews

Balbo, Ned. Review of *Blessing the Boats*. *Antioch Review* 59, no. 3 (Summer 2001): 637.

Barresi, Dorothy. Review of *The Terrible Stories*. *Gettysburg Review* 10, no. 1 (Spring 1997): 148–66.

Bedient, Calvin. "Short Reviews." Review of *The Book of Light*. *Poetry* 163, no. 6 (March 1994): 344–49.

Bennett, Bruce. "Preservation Poets." Review of *Quilting*. *New York Times Book Review*, 1 March 1992, 22.

Clarence, Judy. Review of *The Terrible Stories*. *Library Journal* 121, no. 12 (July 1996): 120.

Cornish, Sam. Review of *Quilting*. *Ploughshares* 17, no. 4 (Winter 1991): 258.

Garrison, Joseph. Review of *Two-Headed Woman*. *Library Journal* 105 (August 1980): 1639.

Gotera, Vince. Review of *Blessing the Boats*. *North American Review*, May–August 2001, 74.

Hacker, Marilyn. "A Pocketful of Poets." Review of *Next*. *Women's Review of Books* 5, no. 10–11 (1988): 23–24.

Hoffert, Barbara. Review of *Blessing the Boats*. *Library Journal*, 15 April 2001, 102.

Jackson, Angela. "Poetry: *Good News about the Earth*." Review of *Good News about the Earth*. *Black World* 22, no. 4 (1973): 77–78.

Jenkins, Paul. Review of *Next*. *Massachusetts Review* 29, no. 1 (1988): 97–135.

Jong, Erica. "Three Sisters." Review of *Good News about the Earth*. *Parnassus: Poetry in Review* 1, no. 1 (1972): 77–88.

Kirby, David. Review of *The Book of Light*. *New York Times Book Review*, 18 April 1993, 15.

Kuzma, Greg. "Women Hoping for Rain." Review of *Next*. *Georgia Review* 42, no. 3 (Fall 1988): 628–30.

Laing, E. K. "The Voice of a Visionary, Not a Victim." Review of *Good Woman* and *Next*. *Christian Science Monitor*, 5 February 1988, B3.

McKee, Louis. Review of *Blessing the Boats*. *Publishers Weekly*, 17 April 2000, 71.

Mills, Ralph J., Jr. "Six Poets." Review of *Good News about the Earth*. *Poetry* 122, no. 2 (May 1973): 105–10.

Muske, Carol. "Ourselves as History." Review of *An Ordinary Woman*. *Parnassus: Poetry in Review* 4, no. 2 (Spring–Summer 1976): 111–21.

Newson-Horst, Adele S. Review of *Blessing the Boats*. *World Literature Today* 74, no. 4 (Autumn 2000): 817.

Phenner, Lee. "Clifton Notes." Review of *The Terrible Stories*. *George Jr. Internet Monthly*, June 1997, http://www.georgejr.com/jun97/phenner.html (accessed 8 August 1999).

Plant, Deborah. Review of *Good Woman*. *Prairie Schooner* 63, no. 1 (1989): 115–17.

Price, Reynolds. Review of *Generations: A Memoir*. *New York Times Book Review*, 14 March 1976, 7–8.

Review of *Blessing the Boats*. *Publishers Weekly*, 17 April 2000, 71.

Review of *The Book of Light*. *Publishers Weekly*, 1 February 1993, 87.

Review of *Generations*. *New Yorker*, 5 April 1976, 138–39.

Review of *Quilting*. *Publishers Weekly*, 31 May 1991, 68.

Review of *The Terrible Stories*. *Publishers Weekly*, 22 July 1996, 236.

Rosenberg, Liz. "Simply American and Mostly Free." Review of *Good Woman* and *Next*. *New York Times Book Review*, 19 February 1989, 24.

Rosten, Norman. "*SR* Reviews Books: *Good News about Earth*." *Saturday Review* 55, no. 33 (12 August 1972): 58.

Seaman, Donna. Review of *Blessing the Boats*. *Booklist*, 15 March 2000, 1316.

Stenstrom, Christine. Review of *The Book of Light*. *Library Journal*, 15 February 1993, 167.

Townsend, Alison. Review of *The Terrible Stories*. *Women's Review of Books* 14, no. 6 (March 1997): 12ff.

Ullman, Leslie. "Book Reviews." Review of *Quilting*. *Kenyon Review* 14, no. 3 (1992): 174–88.

Vendler, Helen. "A Quartet of Poetry." Review of *An Ordinary Woman*. *New York Times Book Review*, 6 April 1975, 4–5ff.

Weeks, Ramona. "A Gathering of Poets." Review of *Good Times*. *Western Humanities Review* 24, no. 3 (1970): 295–301.

White, Bethany. Review of *Blessing the Boats*. *Black Issues Book Review* 3, no. 1 (January 2001): 29.

Videotapes

The Language of Life: A Festival of Poets. Narrated by Bill Moyers. Produced by David Grubin Productions and Public Affairs Television. Newbridge Communications, 1995.

Lucille Clifton. Produced and directed by Lewis MacAdams and John Dorr. Lannan Literary Series, no. 4. Los Angeles: The Foundation, 1989.

Lucille Clifton. Directed by Dan Griggs. Lannan Literary Series, no. 53. Los Angeles: The Foundation, 1996.

Lucille Clifton. Santa Fe, N.Mex.: Lannan Foundation, 1999.

The Writing Life: Roland Flint Hosts Lucille Clifton. Columbia, Md.: Howard County Poetry and Literature Society, 1991.

Other Works Cited in *Wild Blessings*

Baraka, Amiri, and Amina Baraka, eds. *Confirmation: An Anthology of African American Women*. New York: Quill, 1983.

Bloomfield, Morton W. "The Elegy and the Elegiac Mode: Praise and Alienation." In *Renaissance Genres: Essays on Theory, History, and Interpretation*, edited by Barbara Kiefer Lewalski, 147–57. Cambridge: Harvard University Press, 1986.

Brooks, Gwendolyn. *A Capsule Course in Black Poetry Writing*. Detroit: Broadside Press, 1975.

———. "the mother." In *Selected Poems*, 4–5. New York: HarperPerennial, 1999.

Brown, Dee. *Bury My Heart at Wounded Knee: An Indian History of the American West*. New York: Holt, Rinehart and Winston, 1971.

Collier, Eugenia. "Message to the Generations: The Mythic Hero in Sterling Brown's Poetry." In *The Furious Flowering of African American Poetry*, edited by Joanne V. Gabbin, 25–37. Charlottesville: University Press of Virginia, 1999.

Cone, James H. *For My People: Black Theology and the Black Church*. Maryknoll, N.Y.: Orbis Books, 1984.

Cullen, Countee. "Yet Do I Marvel." In Gates and McKay, *Norton Anthology of African American Literature*, 1305.

Davis, Angela Y. *Blues Legacies and Black Feminism: Gertrude "Ma" Rainey, Bessie Smith, and Billie Holiday.* New York: Vintage, 1998.

Delaney, Janice, Mary Jane Lupton, and Emily Toth. *The Curse: A Cultural History of Menstruation.* Revised ed. Urbana: University of Illinois Press, 1988.

Dunbar, Paul Laurence. "We Wear the Mask." In Gates and McKay, *Norton Anthology of African American Literature*, 896.

Edwards, Jonathan. *Selected Writings of Jonathan Edwards.* Edited by Harold P. Simonson. New York: Continuum, 1990.

Emerson, Ralph Waldo. *Selected Essays, Lectures, and Poems of Ralph Waldo Emerson.* Edited by R. E. Spiller. New York: Washington Square, 1965.

Evans, Mari, ed. *Black Women Writers (1950–1980): A Critical Evaluation.* Garden City, N.Y.: Anchor Press/Doubleday, 1984.

Forché, Carolyn. "The Angel of History." In *The Angel of History*, 3–21. New York: HarperCollins, 1994.

Funk and Wagnalls Standard Dictionary of Folklore, Mythology and Legend. New York: Funk and Wagnalls, 1950.

Gates, Henry Louis, Jr., and Nellie Y. McKay, eds. *The Norton Anthology of African American Literature.* New York: Norton, 1996.

Gilmore, G. S., and James H. Cone. *Black Theology: A Documentary History.* Maryknoll, N.Y.: Orbis Books, 1979.

Graves, Robert. *The White Goddess: A Historical Grammar of Poetic Myth.* 1st American, amended and enlarged ed. New York: Farrar, Strauss and Giroux, 1966.

Greene, J. Lee. *Blacks in Eden: The African American Novel's First Century.* Charlottesville: University Press of Virginia, 1996.

Henderson, Stephen. *Understanding the New Black Poetry: Black Speech and Black Music as Poetic References.* New York: Morrow, 1973.

Herron, Carolivia. "Milton and Afro-American Literature." In *Re-membering Milton*, edited by Mary Nyquist and Margaret W. Ferguson, 278–300. New York: Methuen, 1987.

Herskovits, Melville J. *The Myth of the Negro Past.* 1941. Reprint, Boston: Beacon, 1958.

Holloway, Karla F. C. "Cultural Narratives Passed On: African American Mourning Stories." In Napier, *African American Literary Theory*, 653–59.

Holquist, Eric. *Dialogism: Bakhtin and His World.* New York: Routledge, 1990.

Hubbard, Dolan. *The Sermon and the African American Literary Imagination.* Columbia: University of Missouri Press, 1994.

Hughes, Langston. "The Negro Artist and the Racial Mountain." In Gates and McKay, *Norton Anthology of African American Literature*, 1267–1270.

Hurston, Zora Neale. *Mules and Men.* 1935. Reprint, New York: Perennial Library, 1990.

Jackson, Blyden. *A History of Afro-American Literature.* Vol. 1, *The Long Beginning, 1746–1895.* Baton Rouge: Louisiana State University Press, 1989.

Jones, Major J. *The Color of God: The Concept of God in Afro-American Thought.* Macon, Ga.: Mercer University Press, 1987.

Karenga, Maulana. "Black Art: Mute Matter Given Force and Function." In Gates and McKay, *Norton Anthology of African American Literature,* 1973–1977.

Kroll, Judith. *Chapters in a Mythology: The Poetry of Sylvia Plath.* New York: Harper and Row, 1976.

Lant, Kathleen Margaret. "'The Big Strip Tease': Female Bodies and Male Power in the Poetry of Sylvia Plath." *Contemporary Literature* 34, no. 4 (Winter 1993): 620–69.

May, Herbert G., and Bruce M. Metzger. "Characteristics of Hebrew Poetry." In *The New Oxford Annotated Bible with the Apocrypha,* edited by Herbert G. May and Bruce M. Metzger, 1523–1529. New York: Oxford University Press, 1977.

———. "How to Read the Bible with Understanding." In *The New Oxford Annotated Bible with the Apocrypha,* edited by Herbert G. May and Bruce M. Metzger. 1515–1518. New York: Oxford University Press, 1977.

Milton, John. *Complete Poems and Major Prose.* Edited by Merritt Y. Hughes. 1957. Reprint, Indianapolis: Odyssey, 1980.

Morrison, Toni. Beloved. New York: Plume, 1988.

———. *Playing in the Dark: Whiteness and the Literary Imagination.* Cambridge: Harvard University Press, 1992.

Mullen, Harryette. "African Signs and Spirit Writing." In Napier, *African American Literary Theory,* 623–42.

Napier, Winston, ed. *African American Literary Theory: A Reader.* New York: New York University Press, 2000.

Neal, Larry. "The Black Arts Movement." In Gates and McKay, *Norton Anthology of African American Literature,* 1960–1972.

Ostriker, Alicia Suskin. *Feminist Revision and the Bible.* Cambridge: Blackwell, 1993.

Palmer, R. Roderick. "The Poetry of Three Revolutionists: Don L. Lee, Sonia Sanchez, and Nikki Giovanni." In *Modern Black Poets: A Collection of Critical Essays,* edited by Donald B. Gibson, 135–46. Englewood Cliffs, N.J.: Prentice-Hall, 1973.

Plath, Sylvia. *The Collected Poems.* Edited by Ted Hughes. New York: Harper and Row, 1981.

———. *The Journals of Sylvia Plath.* Edited by Ted Hughes, consulting editor, and Frances McCullough. New York: Dial, 1982.

Ramazani, Jahan. *Poetry of Mourning: The Modern Elegy from Hardy to Heaney.* Chicago: University of Chicago Press, 1994.

Reich, David. "'As Poets, As Activists': An Interview with Sonia Sanchez." *World: The Magazine of the Unitarian Universalist Association,* May/June 1999, http://www.uua.org/world/0599feat1.html (accessed 16 July 2002).

Rich, Adrienne. "Diving into the Wreck." In *The Fact of a Doorframe: Poems Selected and New, 1950–1984,* 164. New York: Norton, 1984.

———. *Of Woman Born: Motherhood as Experience and Institution.* New York: Bantam, 1977.

Sacks, Peter M. *The English Elegy: Studies in the Genre from Spenser to Yeats.* Baltimore: Johns Hopkins University Press, 1985.

Sexton, Anne. *The Complete Poems.* Boston: Houghton Mifflin, 1989.

Smith, Eric. *By Mourning Tongues: Studies in English Elegy.* Totowa, N.J.: Rowan and Littlefield, 1977.

Spencer, Jon Michael. *Blues and Evil.* Knoxville: University of Tennessee Press, 1993.

Stepto, Robert B. "Narration, Authentication, and Authorial Control in Frederick Douglass's *Narrative* of 1845." In *African-American Autobiography,* edited by William L. Andrews, 26–35. Englewood Cliffs, N.J.: Prentice Hall, 1993.

Stevenson, Anne. *Bitter Fame: A Life of Sylvia Plath.* Boston: Houghton Mifflin, 1989.

Van Dyne, Susan. *Revising Life: Sylvia Plath's Ariel Poems.* Chapel Hill: University of North Carolina Press, 1993.

Vendler, Helen. *The Given and the Made: Strategies of Poetic Redefinition.* Cambridge: Harvard University Press, 1995.

Wagner-Martin, Linda. *Telling Women's Lives: The New Biography.* New Brunswick, N.J.: Rutgers University Press, 1994.

Walker, Barbara G. *The Crone: Woman of Age, Wisdom, and Power.* New York: Harper and Row, 1985.

———. *The Woman's Encyclopedia of Myths and Secrets.* San Francisco: Harper and Row, 1983.

Whitman, Walt. "Crossing Brooklyn Ferry." In *Leaves of Grass,* edited by Sculley Bradley and Harold W. Blodgett, 162. New York: Norton, 1973.

Williams, William Carlos. "Danse Ruse." In *The Collected Poems of William Carlos Williams,* vol. 1, *1909–1939,* edited by Walton Litz and Christopher MacGowan, 86. New York: New Directions, 1986.

Willis, Susan. *Specifying: Black Women Writing the American Experience.* London: Routledge, 1990.

Wordsworth, William. "Ode: Intimations of Immortality." In *English Romantic*

Writers, edited by David Perkins, 279–82. New York: Harcourt Brace Jova-
novich, 1967.

Wright, Richard. "Blueprint for Negro Writing." In Napier, *African American Liter-
ary Theory,* 45–53.

Yeats, William Butler. *The Poems.* Edited by Richard J. Finneran. New York: Mac-
millan, 1983.

Zahan, Dominique. "Some Reflections on African Spirituality." In *African Spiritu-
ality: Forms, Meanings, and Expressions,* edited by Jacob K. Olupona, 3–25.
New York: Crossroad, 2000.

Index